Actes du XIVème Congrès UISPP, Université de Liège,
Belgique, 2-8 septembre 2001

Acts of the XIVth UISPP Congress, University of Liège,
Belgium, 2-8 September 2001

SECTION 10 : ÂGE DU CUIVRE AU PROCHE ORIENT ET EN EUROPE /
COPPER AGE IN THE NEAR EAST AND EUROPE

Colloque / Symposium C 10.2

Chalcolithic and Early Bronze Age Hydrostrategies

Edited by

Dragos Gheorghiu

BAR International Series 1123
2003

Published in 2016 by
BAR Publishing, Oxford

BAR International Series 1123

Acts of the XIVth UISPP Congress, University of Liège, Belgium, 2-8 September 2001
Colloque / Symposium C10.2

Chalcolithic and Early Bronze Age Hydrostrategies

ISBN 978 1 84171 499 8

© The editor and contributors severally and the Publisher 2003

Typesetting and layout: Darko Jerko

The authors' moral rights under the 1988 UK Copyright,
Designs and Patents Act are hereby expressly asserted.

All rights reserved. No part of this work may be copied, reproduced, stored,
sold, distributed, scanned, saved in any form of digital format or transmitted
in any form digitally, without the written permission of the Publisher.

BAR Publishing is the trading name of British Archaeological Reports (Oxford) Ltd.
British Archaeological Reports was first incorporated in 1974 to publish the BAR
Series, International and British. In 1992 Hadrian Books Ltd became part of the BAR
group. This volume was originally published by Archaeopress in conjunction with
British Archaeological Reports (Oxford) Ltd / Hadrian Books Ltd, the Series principal
publisher, in 2003. This present volume is published by BAR Publishing, 2016.

Printed in England

BAR titles are available from:

        BAR Publishing
        122 Banbury Rd, Oxford, OX2 7BP, UK
EMAIL   info@barpublishing.com
PHONE +44 (0)1865 310431
  FAX   +44 (0)1865 316916
        www.barpublishing.com

Contents

Acknowledgements ii

Contributors iii

Introduction iv

BASIC PSYCHOLOGICAL AND PHYSIOLOGICAL HYDROSTRATEGIES
IN HUMANS
John D. Wagner 1

THE LITTORAL FOUNDATIONS OF THE URUK STATE: USING
SATELLITE PHOTOGRAPHY TOWARD A NEW UNDERSTANDING
OF 5TH/4TH MILLENIUM BCE LANDSCAPES IN THE WARKA SURVEY
AREA, IRAQ
Jennifer R. Pournelle 5

BY LAND OR BY SEA: CHALCOLITHIC AND EARLY BRONZE AGE
SETTLEMENTS IN SOUTHERN GREECE AND THE AEGEAN SEA
Daniel J. Pullen 25

DOMESTIC WATER MATTERS
(FINAL NEOLITHIC - EARLY BRONZE AGE GREECE)
Christina Marangou 31

WATERS, TELLS AND TEXTURES: A MULTI-SCALAR APPROACH
TO GUMELNITA HYDROSTRATEGIES
Dragos Gheorghiu 39

THE CHALCOLITHIC AND EARLY BRONZE AGE HYDROSTRATEGY
IN THE BLACK SEA STEPPE AREA
Yuri Rassamakin 57

HYDROSTRATEGIES IN SOUTHERN LUXEMBOURG
Ralph M. Rowlett 79

Acknowledgements

Many thanks to Professor Marcel Otte for all the help provided during the organization of the session and to Professor Ralph Rowlett for helping with the paper on the anthropology of water.

Many thanks also to all contributors for the long patience during the sluggish elaboration of this book.

As always my gratitude to Dr. David Davison for his tolerance and for the help with the improving the English of many papers.

My deeply appreciation to Corina Sarbu and Cornelia Catuna for the wonderful help provided as drawings, editing and support of the expeditions to the Danubian tells.

D. G.

Contributors

Dr. Dragos Gheorghiu
Department of Design
National University of Arts
19, Budisteanu, Bucharest
Romania
dgheorghiu@digi.ro

Dr. Christina Marangou
6, Neophytou Douca
Kolonaki 138
10674 Athens
Greece
Marangou@phl.uoc.gr

Dr. Jennifer R. Pournelle
Department of Anthropology
University of California
San Diego
9500 Gilman Drive
LA Jolla, CA 92093-0532
USA
jpournelle@ucsd.edu

Professor David J. Pullen
Department of Classics
The Florida State University
Tallahassee, Florida 32306-1510
USA
dpullen@mailer.fsu.edu

Professor Ralph M. Rowlett
Department of Anthropology
University of Missouri-Columbia
Columbia, MO 65211
USA
rowlettr@missouri.edu

Dr. John D. Wagner
Department of Anthropology
University of New Mexico
Albuquerque, NM 87131
(505) 277-0454
USA
wagner@unm.edu

INTRODUCTION

The present book is the result of a session organised at the XIVth UISPP Congress in Liège and its purpose is to define water, generally insufficiently present in the archaeological literature, as a fundamental category for the study of prehistoric societies.

Compared to Neolithic, the Chalcolithic and Early Bronze Age were epochs with a better control of wetlands, characterized by an anthropogenic colonization of river valleys and littorals. Starting with Neolithic in Mesopotamia, and with Chalcolithic in the Balkans, a developed management of water could be identified in the design of settlements, houses and objects, as a means of improved protection and communication. Overlapping settlements grew, in time, in strategic places, with a high degree of protection and visibility in relation to water, improving systems for collecting, transporting and storage of water.

In the Near East, systems of irrigation as dams and dikes were used to control flooding, and in the temperate zones agriculture based on ploughing with traction animals suggests an improvement in the rainfall-dependent cultivation of cereals. A new type of complex economy emerged combining 'dry harvest' with 'wet harvest', in a process of intensification of water resources exploitation. An analogous model of complementary economy seems to have been applied by North-Pontic steppe populations.

The Neolithic water trade routes from Southern Mesopotamia to the Persian Gulf, or from Greece to the Balkans were maintained, and new routes and cultural networks generating long-distance systems of communication emerged. As navigation developed, trade gradually turned to the sea in Southern Mesopotamia, as well as in Early Bronze Age Greece.

A new attitude towards water that involved a ritual connotation in collecting, transporting and utilization, could be detected also from figurines, offerings in temples, the shape of some objects, the (materialization of) rites of passage, and the relationship between the sources of water (springs or wells), settlements and objects. All these infer the image of a religion whose symbolism depended on the fertility of water, from the Near East to the Eastern Carpathians. In the Balkans, the frequent relationship between ceramic containers and the female body, as well as the exuberant decoration of ceramic vases, could be assigned to a fertility cult of water, visualised under the anthropomorphic image of the female body. Since water made possible the life of plants, animals, and humans, it was restrictive to depict only the fertility of humans under the shape of female figurines; therefore I suggest that the "Goddess" model be replaced with a "Water Goddess" one.

One main objective of the book is to propose an archaeology of the study of strategies to exploit water, from macro-scale policies at a geographical level, to micro-scale designs of objects and material textures, and in such a way offering a multifaceted image of the physical and cultural implications of the phenomenon. Starting from the Near East to Western Europe a large geographical area is examined, including a diversity of Chalcolithic and Early Bronze Age cultures.

In the introductory paper, John D. Wagner advocates an anthropology of water, discussing the essentiality of this element for human existence. The basic hydrostrategies in humans, biological, physiological and psychological to alimentary, are examined; the role of this paper being to present water as a fundamental anthropological perspective to study past societies, to familiarize the researcher with the complexity of the phenomenon.

Jennifer R. Pournelle discusses the paleogeography of the Mesopotamian alluvium, suggesting the role of *littoral ecotones* as essential in forming the social structures that led to the emergence of urbanization of Southern Mesopotamia. Pournelle's paper is a geomorphological analysis of satellite photographs, allowing an interpretation, in light of surface and excavation discoveries, of the dependence of local populations between Neolithic and Early Bronze Age on littoral resources.

A study of the resources and (social) engineering reveals an increase of human management on environment from the design of the technologies of flood control to administration.

Compared to Early Bronze Age, the Chalcolithic/Final Neolithic in Southern Greece and the Aegean Sea is poorly documented and understood. By using data from some coastal and inland surface surveys, as well as geomorphological data, Daniel J. Pullen examines the Final Neolithic/Chalcolithic and Early Bronze Age/Early Helladic I strategies, as island colonisation and settlement relationship with water.

If in the Late Neolithic settlement patterns follow the rule of proximity to coast and to well-watered large plains, with a little occupation of inland or poorly watered areas, Final Neolithic/Chalcolithic settlements are found in well-watered lands and uplands. In Early Helladic I the number of coastal settlements increase at the expense of inland settlements, some of them dominating the neighbouring areas.

Christine Marangou examines the continuities and transformations in the practices related to domestic water between Final Neolithic and Early Bronze Age in a number of sites from continental and island Greece, illustrating the methods of drawing water, like simple wells or with balance pole, and the architectural techniques to control atmospheric water, like platforms, paved streets, canals for drainage, unroofed spaces, pithoi, and bothroi.

By employing historical and ethnographic models, Marangou tries to define gender role in water procurement for domestic purposes. Special attention is devoted to the relationship between shape and distance to water sources.

An holistic approach, from a geographic level to the micro-level of objects and their textures, is taken by Dragos Gheorghiu, who investigates Gumelnita Chalcolithic culture in the Danube and Pontic areas. Making use of experimental archaeology (perceived as a complex made of ethnographic data, object reconstruction, and 3D evocations), as a complementary instrument to the archaeological record, Gheorghiu tries to identify the strategies of water abduction, and protection against water in a network of Gumelnita settlements, as well as to understand Chalcolithic religion in relation to the identified hydrostrategies.

According to Yuri Rassamakin, hydrostrategies are the most important pointers to the general economic strategy of the steppe populations. His approach to water strategies from the river system as communication networks, to ritual functions in social life, extends from Neolithic to Early Bronze Age steppe and forest-steppe zones of the North Pontic area. Steppe population developed an economy based on river resources, alongside agriculture, cattle breeding and hunting. In the North Pontic Chalcolithic, river valleys received a sustained anthropogenic pressure.

Beginning with Early Bronze Age one might detect in Yamnaya culture the emergence of a network of land communications, due to the development of pulled vehicles, as water transportation lost its importance.

Ralph M. Rowlett investigates the hydrostrategies of the Rollange Group from Southern Luxembourg, focussing on the Titelberg settlement. Riverine adaptation and use of water for cultural interaction, resulting from the position of settlements along the Meuse river and its tributaries, as well as the cultural similarities along the Meuse, the presence of some far-away raw materials, as well as the existence of logboats, infer that this river was a water way.

Rowlett concludes that Rollange Group hydrostrategies were structured especially outwards, with the intention of facilitating contacts with other communities along the hydrographic network, and to have access to the sources of supply.

As one can see from the panorama of the hydrostrategies presented, at the macro-level, many Chalcolithic traditions can be characterized by the interface networks of settlements along water shorelines, away from seasonal flooding.

At a micro-level, there are analogies features between cultures practising agriculture. Unfortunately, the archaeological record does not preserve the countless objects used to satisfy the thirst of humans and animals, or the systems for drying, storage, covering, and many other functions. These are evoked only through examples from traditional societies, revealing the complexity of the relationship with water in the past.

Dragos Gheorghiu

BASIC PSYCHOLOGICAL AND PHYSIOLOGICAL HYDROSTRATEGIES IN HUMANS

John D. WAGNER

Abstract : Humans are strongly tied to water and our bodies show a number of hydrostrategic attributes—both psychological and physiological—for interacting and dealing with water. We value living near water, derive pleasure and even health benefits from viewing water scenes, and seek out water areas for recreation. Compared to other terrestrial mammals, humans are exceptionally thirsty and have physiological mechanisms useful for interacting with water such as subcutaneous adiposity and the diving reflex. Intriguingly, our health is critically dependent on dietary sources of essential fatty acids, which are predominantly found in water environments.

Resumé : Les êtres humains sont fortement lies à l'eau et notre corps démontre un grand nombre d'attributs hydrostratégiques – en même temps psychologiques et physiologiques- pour l'interaction avec l'eau.
Nous apprécions vivre près de l'eau, nous éprouvons du plaisir et des avantages en ce qui concerne la santé en regardant des scènes aquatiques et nous cherchons des zones avec de l'eau pour nous récréer.
En comparaison avec d'autres mammifères terrestres, les humains sont des êtres avec une soif avide et possédant des mécanismes physiologiques pour l'interaction avec l'eau, comme l'adiposité et le réflexe de plongé. Notre santé est dépendante des sources d'acides gras, qui sont prédominants dans les milieux aquatiques.

This chapter considers human hydrostrategies in terms of our psychologies and physiologies. It is undeniable that humans have a special connection to water. Eleven of the world's 15 largest cities are located on seacoasts or estuaries (Cohen and Small, 1998) and a majority of the world's population live close to major rivers or coasts (Small and Cohen, 2001). We also seek out recreation sites that are situated close to lakes, rivers or oceans and associated activities such as swimming, skiing, diving, snorkeling, boating, and fishing. Folklore, myths, and rituals are also deeply rooted in and replete with references to water (Roede 1991). As inveterate users of water - whether drinking, cooking, or washing - our connection to water is nearly visceral.

Perhaps then, not surprisingly, humans have [evolved] psychological preferences for interacting with water. U.S. real estate markets consistently show that housing prices increase as the distance to water decreases (Benson et al. 1998; Brown and Pollakowski 1977). Houses with scenic views of water are also worth more (Benson et al. 1998). Watching videos of water scenes has been found to inspire feelings of tranquility (Herzog and Bosley 1992), linked to lowered stress levels (Ulrich et al. 1991), and improves convalescence (Ulrich 1984). Studies of landscape preferences reliably converge on water being the feature that is most desired (Yang and Brown 1992), with a bias towards preferring large and calm bodies of water with mountain backdrops (Herzog 1985).

On a more fundamental level however, water is not only preferred by humans, it is essential. Compared to other terrestrial mammals, humans are by far the most dependent on water. It has been suggested that this strong reliance on water may be related to a number of unique physiological characteristics found in humans but not other primates

Fig. 1 The hamlet of Proieni on the Olt River, Southern Romania

(Morgan 1990). Consider our exceptional thirst. Whereas a typical terrestrial mammal can withstand dehydration of up to 20%, humans typically succumb around 10% (Schmidt-Nielsen 1979). Moreover, when it comes to thermoregulation we are profligate sweaters, capable of secreting 15 liters per day in hot environments (Newman 1970). This amount must be replaced by drinking but even so, when humans take on excess water, instead of conserving, we rapidly excrete water through our kidneys (Schmidt-Nielsen 1979). Clearly, humans have come to rely on abundant and permanent sources of water.

Humans are also considerably fatter than other primates and contain roughly ten times the number of fat cells as would be expected for a mammal of similar size (Pond 1987). This fat is also distributed differently than it is in other terrestrial mammals and primates. Instead of being largely confined to internal body cavities, our fat has migrated out to become attached to our skin, forming a continuous fat layer. This fat distribution pattern is also found in aquatic mammals such as dolphins, dugongs, whales, and seals. Alistair Hardy, a marine biologist, first pointed out this similarity when he noted that the skin of flensed sea mammals bore a striking resemblance to the skin layer in humans (Hardy 1960). A subcutaneous fat layer is generally held to be an effective insulator against heat loss in water and also aids flotation.

A fat layer would be useful for diving and humans are very adept for a primate at doing this. The famed Ama divers of Korea and Japan forage ocean bottoms for shellfish and edible seaweed and will exceed depths of 25 meters, while holding their breath for up to two minutes. Although male pearl divers in the South Pacific reach depths of 40 meters, women are generally more effective divers because they have higher body fat than men (Hong and Rahn 1967).

A useful mechanism for diving is the "diving response", which is a general mammalian defense against asphyxia involving a decrease in heart rate along with a redistribution of blood through so that oxygen is diverted to the brain and heart (Andersen 1966) and other necessary muscle groups (Butler and Woakes 1987). The diving response is most developed in diving mammals and birds and can be triggered by apnea but more strongly by submerging the face or head in water. Cold water causes a more pronounced response although the critical factor is the difference between the ambient air and water temperatures (Schagatay and Holm 1996). Training greatly improves the response and trained humans have been found to have diving responses in the range of semi-aquatic mammals like the beaver and the otter (Schagatay 1996). Developing an improved diving response through practice is useful for exploiting underwater food resources.

A final hydrostrategy in humans concerns our diet and is doubly worth mentioning here because of the ramifications for our current health. Humans have a dietary requirement for essential fatty acids (EFA) and obtaining these acids is critical for developing optimal mental and visual functioning. Further, there are two types of EFA: omega-3 and omega-6 and obtaining these in equal amounts is considered optimal for health. However, much higher levels of omega-6 fatty acids are now common in Western diets mainly through the increased use of vegetable oils. Modern diets can also be very low in omega-3 intake overall and low levels have been linked to a litany of adverse health outcomes including heart disease, stroke, Type II diabetes, arthritis, depression, breast and prostate cancer, hypertension, and several autoimmune disorders (Simopoulos 1999). Omega-3 supplementation during and after pregnancy has also been found to increase gestation periods, birth weight, and cognitive development in some groups (McGregor et al. 2001).

Omega-3 fatty acids are most plentiful in marine-based food chains. Shellfish and fish in general are typically good sources of omega-3 fatty acids with coldwater species such as mackerel and herring providing relatively more. Lesser amounts (and in a somewhat less useful form) can be had

Fig. 2 Collective fishing on the Crusovu Lake, near the Danube, summer 2001. Children are chasing the fish to the adults' nets, while they are collecting shellfish and playing.

from seeds, nuts, and leafy plants. Terrestrial plants and animals tend to have low levels of omega-3 fatty acids except for animal brains, which are a very rich source. A hydrostrategy for exploiting marine-based resources may have had beneficial health effects on those living near water.

Taken together, hydrostrategies in humans appear to run deep, influencing both our mental and physiological selves. Compared to most other terrestrial mammals, humans' physiology and psychology literally impel us to seek adaptively close hydrostrategies.

Bibliography

ANDERSEN, H. T., 1966, Physiological adaptations in diving vertebrates. *Physiological Reviews* 46: 212-43.

BENSON, E. D., HANSEN, J. L., SCHWARTZ, A. L. JR., and SMERSH, G. T., 1998, Pricing residential amenities: The value of a view. *Journal of Real Estate Finance and Economics* 16: 55-73.

BENSON, E. D., HANSEN, J. L., SCHWARTZ, A. L. JR., and SMERSH, G. T., 1999, Canadian/U.S. exchange rates and nonresident investors: their influence on residential property values. *Journal of Real Estate Research* 18: 433-61.

BROWN, G. M. JR., and POLLAKOWSKI, H. O., 1977, Economic value of shoreline. *Review of Economics and Statistics* 59: 272-78.

BUTLER, P. J., and WOAKES, A. J., 1987, Heart rate in humans during underwater swimming with and without breath-hold. *Respiration Physiology* 69: 387-99.

COHEN, J. E. and SMALL, C., 1998, Hypsographic demography: The distribution of the human population by altitude. *Proceedings of the National Academy of Sciences* 95: 14009-14014.

HARDY, A., 1960, Was man more aquatic in the past? *The New Scientist*; pp. 642-5

HERZOG, T. R., 1985, A cognitive analysis of preference for waterscapes. *Journal of Environmental Psychology* 5: 225-41.

HERZOG, T. R., and BOSLEY, P. J., 1992, Tranquility and preference as affective qualities of natural environments. *Journal of Environmental Psychology* 12: 115-127.

HONG, S. K., and RAHN, H., 1967, The diving women of Korea and Japan. *Scientific American* 216: 34-43.

MCGREGOR, J. A., ALLEN, K. G. D. HARRIS, M. A., REECE, M., WHEELER, M. FRENCH, J. I. and MORRISON, J., 2001, The omega-3 story: Nutritional prevention of preterm birth and other adverse pregnancy outcomes. *Obstetrical and gynecological survey* 56: 1-13.

MORGAN, E., 1990, *The Scars of Evolution: What our bodies tell us about human origins*. London: Souvenir Press, Ltd.

NEWMAN, R. W., 1970, Why man is such a sweaty and thirsty animal: a speculative review. *Human Biology* 42: 12-27.

POND, C., 1987, Fat and figures, *New Scientist*; pp. 62-66

ROEDE, M., 1991, Aquatic man. In: Vernon Reynolds (ed.), *The Aquatic Ape: Fact of Fiction?*; pp. 306-328. London: Souvenir Press

SCHAGATAY, E., 1996, *The Human Diving Response: Effects of temperature and training*. Lund: University of Lund Press

SCHAGATAY, E., and HOLM, B., 1996, Effects of water and ambient air temperatures on human diving bradycardia. *European Journal of Applied Physiology* 72: 1-6.

SCHMIDT-NIELSEN, K., 1979, *Desert Animals*. New York: Dover Publications.

SIMOPOULOS, A. P., 1999, Essential fatty acids in health and chronic disease. *American Journal of Clinical Nutrition* 70: 560S-569S.

SMALL, C., and COHEN, J. E., 2001, Continental physiography, climate and the global distribution of human population. *International Symposium on Digital Earth.*

ULRICH, R. S., 1984, View through a window may influence recovery from surgery. *Science* 224: 420-1.

ULRICH, R. S., SIMONS, R. F., LOSITO, B. D., FIORITO, E., MILES, M. A. and ZELSON, M., 1991, Stress recovering during exposure to natural and urban environments. *Journal of Environmental Psychology* 11: 201-30.

YANG, B.-E., and BROWN, T. J., 1992, A cross-cultural comparison of preferences for landscape styles and landscape elements. *Environment and Behavior* 24: 471-507.

THE LITTORAL FOUNDATIONS OF THE URUK STATE: USING SATELLITE PHOTOGRAPHY TOWARD A NEW UNDERSTANDING OF 5TH/4TH MILLENIUM BCE LANDSCAPES IN THE WARKA SURVEY AREA, IRAQ

Jennifer R. POURNELLE

INTRODUCTION

In examining the precursors of social complexity, in the Near and Middle East, consideration of riparian, lacustrine, estuarine, and riparian (referred to collectively hereinafter as "littoral") resource exploitation for the most part has been subordinated to close examination of agro-pastoral economic components characterized by grain cultivation and ungulate husbandry (Pollack 1992; Kouchoukos 1998; Zarins 1989).[1] Naomi Miller has succinctly summarized this overarching view: "By about 6000 BC, domesticated animals, notably sheep, goat, and cattle, had joined the familiar crop complex of Near Eastern cereals and pulses, forming the economic basis of later Neolithic society and the first civilizations" (Miller 1991:144–145).

Underlying prevailing models of the Mesopotamian path to complexity (e.g. Wittfogel 1959, Adams 1981, Park 1992) is the primary assumption that extension of sedentary agriculture made possible the hydrologic engineering used to intensively exploit arid settings wherein, as compared to equal hectarage in rain-fed agro-pastoral economies, exponential agronomic return was possible per unit labor input. Following Frankfort (Frankfort 1932: 18) and Perkins (Perkins 1949: 73), the southern Mesopotamian wetlands, recognized as a locus of presumptive colonization from elsewhere, were tacitly viewed as an impediment to expanded agropastoral production and hence expanded settlement until the region became sufficiently "dry" during the late-4th millennium BCE Uruk period (Nissen 1988).

These views have largely persisted, despite Murdock's noting as early as 1969 the high correlation between specialized *fishing* economies and early sedentism, even in non-maritime contexts (Murdock 1969); mounting evidence from the New World and Far East of pisco-molluscan exploitation as a basis for early sedentism and territorial consolidation in those regions (Aikens 1981; Moseley 1975; Akazawa 1981; Pearson and Underhill 1987); and the obvious riparian situation of the Old World's oldest known civilizations.

That the role of estuarine exploitation in early Near Eastern sedentism and social evolution has received insufficient attention is unsurprising, particularly given the timeframe of the bulk of regional excavation, concluded decades before the invention and introduction of systematic fine-mesh screening, floatation, and deflocculation for small and organic find recovery. However, during the past decade mounting evidence suggests that systematic examination of geomorphologic, archaeological, glyptic, and epigraphic data from fifth–fourth millenium BCE Mesopotamia will add a third necessary pillar to the agropastoral dyad so vigorously examined during the twentieth century.[2]

In this paper I review recent research conducted at the University of California, San Diego Mesopotamian Alluvium Project laboratory that reconstructs with far greater precision than that available to mid-twentieth century theorists the paleogeography of the Mesopotamian alluvium during the formative Chalcolithic. I offer an interpretive methodology especially appropriate to viewing regional scale interactive spheres inaccessible through single-site excavation, and establish a hypothesis emphasizing the essential nature, not merely of *water*, but of *littoral ecotones*, in supporting and shaping complex social institutions that underlay urbanization in southern Mesopotamia.

I use recent geomorphologic investigations that relate mid-Holocene Nile delta paleogeology to fifth millenium BCE site locations (Butzer 20001; van den Brink 1993; van den Brink 1989) as a model for interpreting recently declassified

---

[1] I am especially greatful to Guillermo Algaze, Robert McC. Adams, Tony Wilkinson, McGuire Gibson, Jennifer Hyundal, Nicholas Kouchoukos, Robert Englund, and Elizabeth Carter for substantive comments. Errors and omissions naturally remain my own.

[2] Regarding the greater Egyptian heartland, until the latter quarter of the 20th century similar arguments posited "a swampy Nile delta hostile to all settlement" (Rizkana and Seeher 1987: 21). Challenging this view are careful faunal analyses at deltaic (Maadi, Buto, and. Merimde) and lacustrine sites (Eiwanger 1984; Boessneck, von den Dreish, and Ziegler 1989). During the sixth and fourth millenium BCE, pluvial, mesic conditions prevailed, and the Fayum Depression/Lake (Birket) Qarun was connected to and received flood overflow from the Nile. Lake levels rose some 60m above present levels. At that time, fresh waters were surrounded by thickly vegetated shallows interspersed with thick reed beds, and tree-lined shores. Nile catfish (*Clarias* sp.) were the most common animal represented in both Fayum B (6170–5670 BC) and Fayum A (4341–3020 BC) faunal remains. At Fayum B these also included significant proportions of migratory waterfowl (Brewer 1989: 28). The faunal remains of the Nile Neolithic/Predynastic transition can be broadly characterized by an accumulation of fishing technologies, from seasonal opportunistic clubbing of catfish stranded in recessional pools, to shore netting of *Tilapia*, to deep-water angling/harpooning of Nile perch, especially in Upper Egypt. In the delta, while the latter Fayum A (late fifth/early fourth millennium BC) saw the introduction of ovicaprids at some sites, in only one case did this constitute a significant proportion of remains—and then only *after* a full complement of fishing technologies had been developed elsewhere.

Corona KH4B photography of the southern Mesopotamian alluvium, This exercise is especially useful in that the region so considered will remain closed to systematic coring operations for the foreseeable future. I conclude that south of the 32d parallel, during the Neolithic Ubaid 0–3 periods (6500–4900 BCE), archaeologically visible early villages were concentrated on river levees at locations bordering swamps and marshes. However, during Chalcolithic Ubaid 4 (4900-4350 BCE), as in the Nile delta, all but one new site, constituting half the extant sites in the survey area, were founded on exposed surfaces of Pleistocene 'turtlebacks'[3] that once overlooked anastomosing distributaries subject to seasonal flooding.

As in the Egyptian delta, the Mesopotamian inter-gezira depressions are probably buried under meters of alluvial accumulation, and we cannot know what sites are buried with them. Nonetheless, larger sites situated on the once-elevated turtlebacks are accepted as (proto-)typical. These presaged an explosion of new sites founded during the Early Uruk period, when virtually all identifiable turtlebacks became inhabited. I therefore argue that a significant component of the resource basis for precocious, large deltaic towns (such as Eridu) was probably derived from surrounding marshland; and conclude that only following Chalcolithic specialization and integration of, not two, but three specialized productive economies: horticultural, husbanding, and "littoral," could and did Mesopotamian urban civilization flourish.

THE MESOPOTAMIAN HEARTLAND REVISITED

Four factors are important to assessing the extent and character of surface water and vegetation in the archaic Mesopotamian southern alluvium (figure 1). The first is the timing, rate, and volume of Tigris and Euphrates water discharge, determined primarily by the quantity and seasonality of precipitation (and melting of the snowpack) in at their Zagros/Taurus headwaters—in turn affected by climatic oscillation of the Mediterranean storm track. Second is the amount, extent, and seasonality of rainfall on and east of the alluvium, primarily affected by northwest–southeast displacements of the summer Indian Monsoon. The third is the extent of saline penetration and tidal flushing, determined by the location and timing of marine transgressions and regressions at the head of the Persian Gulf. The fourth is the location of major Tigris and Euphrates distributaries, and their associated permanent marshlands. In this paper, while taking into account recent paleoclimatological and sedimentological work regarding the first three factors,[4] I introduce new evidence, derived from satellite photographic interpretation, regarding the fourth.

In brief, the alluvium is flat, and even small changes in precipitation and sea level markedly affect the degree and extent of inundation as well as local soil and water salinity. These are of course considerations exceptionally relevant to the location of specific communities; nonetheless, conclusions to date regarding "habitability" of the southern alluvium based on such geologic events have been driven largely by the imbedded notion that the earliest large, permanent settlements were a result of "colonization" under conditions newly, uniquely, or primarily favorable to agropastoral production—a position which, in light of findings of the last two decades, becomes increasingly untenable (Potts 1997: 47–55). Joan Oates' early views regarding the attractions of a rich hunting and fishing potential in southernmost Mesopotamia (Oates 1960) would seem over recent decades to have been born out in a number of Middle Eastern locales, where even well outside the alluvium, close association of large, sedentary sites to littoral settings has been noted.[5] Paleobotanical evidence suggests that, in general, the early-mid Holocene (7th-4th millenium BC) was a good deal wetter than at present, and that especially during the late 5th millenium the alluvium may even have experienced summer rains (el-Moslimany 1994; Hole 1998b; Miller 1998; Zarins 1990: 49–50).

Seeking to understand the origins and development of civilizations in the alluvial lowlands of the Tigris and Euphrates rivers, over two decades Robert McCormick Adams, Hans-Jeorg Nissen, Henry T. Wright, and MacGuire Gibson conducted broad scale regional settlement surveys that located, recorded, and dated thousands of archaeological sites, using these to date the relict water courses that intricately lace the region (Adams 1981; Adams 1965; Adams and Nissen 1972; Wright 1981; Gibson 1972). Adams was thereby able to document aspects of long-term settlement patterns and demographic changes in the Mesopotamian lowlands from the beginnings of settled towns to the present day. His work clarified how the natural environment of the area affected human life; what changing strategies Mesopotamian societies used throughout history to adapt to that environment; how successive Mesopotamian societies transformed that environment; and what selective environmental pressures existed in the region that favored the development of the world's earliest urban societies (Adams 1981).

---

[3] Often conflated with the Arabic *gezira*, meaning sand island, which is misleading for two reasons. Firstly, *gezira* (with many transliteration variants) is broadly used to designate any island, plateau, or upland, including vast tracts of upper Mesopotamia. Secondly, turtlebacks are not necessarily sand, nor are they islands. Turtlebacks, in the sense used herein, are formed during pluvial periods, when meandering rivers downcut through (relatively) uniform alluvial surfaces, leaving former surfaces exposed above the newly formed floodplain. The channels between these exposures infill during subsequent conditions of alluvial aggradation, leaving weathered humps of the older surface protruding slightly above the newer alluvial plain—like a floating turtle's back, protruding above calm water.

[4] Potts and Kouchoukos provide critical summaries of relevant geomorphologic and paleoclimatic analyses, based upon Sanlaville 1989 and 1992, and el-Moslimany 1994. (Potts 1997: 31–42, 47–55; Kouchoukos 1998: 216–231). More recent work by Sanlaville (1996) and Aqrawi (1997, 2001) tends to reinforce these.

[5] The walls of precocious Jericho may have served primarily for flood control within a marshy alluvial fan (Bar-Joseph 1986). Sixth millenium BCE Umm Dabghiyah in the north Mesopotamian *Jezirah* was situated near marshland (Oates and Oates 1977: 116–117). Sedges (*Scirpus*) apparently comprised a significant dietary element at marshy Çatal Höyük (Hodder et al. 2001: http://catal.arch.cam.ac.uk/catal/Archive_rep01/content01.html). Fifth millenium BCE hunter-gatherer-herders processed grasses and cereals near playa lakes in the Rub al-Khali. Faunal remains at 4,340–4,040 BCE site K160 on the lower Khabur included burned clam shells and crab claw, indicating a permanent freshwater Khabur tributary at that time (Hole 1998a: 45).

Prior to Adams' studies, it had been generally thought that heavy alluvial deposits over the lower Mesopotamian alluvium would have made it impossible to determine the origins of deeply buried cities. However, the surface surveys conducted by Adams, Adams and Nissen, Gibson, and Wright have shown that this was not necessarily the case. Wind erosion periodically re-exposes long-buried artifacts that, when systematically collected, dated, mapped, and plotted with reference to ancient canal traces, reveal a distinct pattern of urbanization and extension of irrigation technology over a period of five millennia. Thus, the corpus of archaeological survey over Mesopotamia, although incomplete, has already proved to be an invaluable resource, adding a corrective rural and non-literate dimension to the predominantly urban, literate, elite focus of historical texts—which texts themselves lend invaluable interpretive dimension to the archaeological data.

A significant conclusion of Adams' work was that the present-day courses of the Tigris and Euphrates rivers are, geologically speaking, of recent and anthropogenic origin. Adams argued that the late mid-Holocene courses of these rivers ran nearly coincidently down a narrow corridor through what is now the lower Mesopotamian alluvium, which corridor is demarcated by ancient cities, strung like pearls along relict water courses. Adams was able to document thousands of now-deserted canals in association with these sites, and hypothesized linear connections between them. The accumulation, argued Adams, of silt carried and deposited by these irrigation activities gradually aggraded the central steppe through which the progressively canalized rivers and canal offtakes ran, ultimately forcing the "wild" rivers respectively westward and eastward (Adams 1981).

Fortunately, although the original air photos are no longer available, declassification of late 1960s–early 1970s-era 2-meter resolution Corona KH4B satellite photographs, available to the public through the Unites States Geological Survey (USGS) Earth Resources Observation Systems (EROS) Data Center (USGS 1997), have allowed Adams and Pournelle to expand on Adams' original work. In 1998 I began an attempt to map comprehensively 5th-4th millennium BCE courses of the Tigris and Euphrates, from Samara to ancient Ur, reasoning that establishing an entire, connected system associated with period sites would clarify channel dating and subsequent anthropogenic geomorphology in a way impossible by localized analysis—particularly since the region is unlikely to open to systematic coring for the foreseeable future.

A Synthetic Protocol

South and east of a line between Shurrupak (vic. WS 020)[6] and Jidr (WS 004), an area where watercourses are from the earliest historical times epigraphically well-attested, much of the ground was covered by standing water, drifting dunes,

---

[6] WS: Warka Survey (Adams and Nissen 1972); NS: Nippur Survey (Adams 1981); ES: Eridu Survey (Wright 1981); KS: Kish Survey (Gibson 1972).

and the accumulated alluvial silt. Recent understanding of the mid-Holocene marine transgression make clear the need to account for marsh, estuary, and deltal conditions now obtaining along, south, and east of the modern Shatt al-Gharraf, the lower Tigris and Euphrates, the Shatt al-Arab, and the deltal mouth on the Persian Gulf (Sanlaville 1996; Geyer and Sanlaville 1996; Kouchoukos 1998).

The joint Tigris-Euphrates delta, constrained in its outflow by the Wadi Batin fluvial cone west of Bubiyan Island, and by the Karkheh–Karun deltas emanating from the Susa plateau, is characterized by a littoral zone transitioning from fresh water marshes at the Tigris-Euphrates confluence at Qurna, through brackish channels south of Basrah and the Kurun confluence at Mhuhammera, to permanent salt marshes at the Persian Gulf head. Sanlaville, using soils classification, and Kouchoukos, using multispectral imagery vegetation classification, have clearly depicted the resultant, prevailing domain of permanent and semi-permanent marshes north of Basra, where annual floodwaters mingle, spread, and slow as they meet the strong action of tidal flushing.

The mid-Holocene marine transgression, pushing northward through the deltal cones during the 6th–4th millennium BCE and subsequently receding, would have pushed the estuary inland, so that conditions obtaining in 20th-century Tigris-Euphrates marshlands would have been extended northward and west of the Shatt al-Gharraf, into the Warka and Eridu survey areas (Sanlaville 1996: 96; Aqrawi 2001). Declassified Corona satellite photographs, imaged in 1968, before massive irrigation, drainage, and water diversion projects brought and end to millennia-old marsh formation processes, allow us to compare the geomorphology of "active" delta, marsh, and alluvium formation to that of the now-desert Chalcolithic urban heartland.

Relics of analogous features are attested in the archaeological record of the Warka and Eridu Survey areas, where the more comprehensive photographic record may be tested against the archaeological. Ground evidence includes artifacts from surface survey, faunal remains, stratigraphic profiles, and limited geomorphologic data. Relict landscapes are photographically revealed especially clearly following the May Euphrates floods that saturate soils, replenish groundwater, and temporarily cover tracts of what is now desert with sheets of water that ultimately drain through a series of seasonal swamps into Lake Hammar. Two zones of geomorphologic action are here examined: the lower delta, where sediment loads are dumped into the sea, and above it, the alluvial plain, a flood-prone region of channel and marsh formation.

Meanders: the Upper Alluvium

River meanders leave fossil traces up to several kilometers in width, characterized by concentric, bending stripes on their crests (Gasche and Tanret 1998: 5–7). Their contours can be preserved for millennia, due in part to their durable function in shaping subsequent agricultural systems, wherein they delineate systems of irrigation dikes and levees that hold recessional silt and demarcate field and crop boundaries (see figure 6A). The breadth and periodicity of relict meanders is determined by volume and flow rate of water discharge (Adams 1981: 16–17). A relict channel succession north and east of Nippur that Adams had identified from air photographs (Adams 1981: 62, fig. 11) is comparable in size and periodicity to the modern Tigris channel downstream from the al-Kut barrage, which diverts considerable flow to the Shatt al-Gharraf and its interconnected irrigation system (figure 6B).

My earlier work focused on tracing river meanders down the entirety of the Mesopotamian alluvium. The conglomeration of these revealed relatively narrow belts within which riverbeds once meandered (Pournelle 1999). The entire (Samara—Adab) charted meander system corresponds generally to interconnecting watercourses posited by Adams among hundreds of Late Uruk sites, and to earlier posited riparian connections between Ubaid and Early Uruk towns such as Ras Al Amiya and 'Uqair (Stronach 1961; Adams 1981; Adams and Nissen 1972; Wilkinson 1990). Accepting Adams dating of these meander relics, by association of numerous sites along their bends, to the fourth millennium BCE leads me to assign a *terminus post quem* for the entire system to that period.[7]

Geomorphologic reconstruction of major fluvial systems from Samara south to Eridu (Northedge, Wilkinson, and Falkner 1989; Gasche and Tanret 1998; Wilkinson 1990; Adams 1981; Stone 2002) paint a revolutionary picture of the Tigris's overall contribution to alluvial settlement and irrigation during the subsequent third and second millennia BCE.[8] As the headwaters of the earlier system, while intermingled with anastomosing channels from the Anatolian Taurus, are primarily located in the Iranian Zagros, in present-day terms I too would refer to its major distributaries to the south and east as "Tigris" waters (Pournelle 2002, 2001a; 2001b, 1999). Of course, this Tigris/Euphrates admixture could have existed in substantially the same bed for centuries—even millennia–prior to the fourth millennium, but it was during this period that it appears to have last meandered in its fully wild state. Thereafter, more or less continuous human intervention profoundly affected the hydrologic evolution of lower Mesopotamia. However, south of Adab, few relict meanders are visible, leading me to turn to other indicators of geomorphology.

Turtlebacks

During the end-late Pleistocene Wurm marine regression, river distributaries scoured channels of up to forty meters depth, leaving terraces at former plain-level protruding above the water surface and dumping scoured sediments at deltal mouths, in a formative process seen today at Bubiyan Island at the modern head of the Persian Gulf. As the Pleistocene river channels meandered or anastomosed into new courses, valleys between these terraces infilled with subsequent alluviation and colluvial silts, leaving the impression of a uniform surface. However, during mid-Holocene flood seasons, the tops of these relict terraces, called "turtlebacks," being of slightly higher elevation, would remain dry while the surrounding plain became inundated by sheets of floodwater. In the Nile delta, Neolithic and early Chalcolithic sites, instead of being aligned along archaic watercourses discharging into the Mediterranean; followed chains of these Pleistocene "turtlebacks" extending *across* the alluvium, suggesting wet-season boat traffic (Van den Brinck 1983; Butzer 2001).

Active turtlebacks photographed from space with high resolution cameras show micro-drainage and differential dampening at their bases, making their slight relief above plain level detectable without detailed elevation data (Coleman, Roberts, and Huh 1986). This is also the case for many relict turtlebacks imaged during the spring spate, when floodwaters saturate lower-lying ground. This can be readily seen in a 1968 image of Telloh (ancient Girsu), where archaic city walls encompass one-third of a turtleback land area (figure 3A). within the Warka survey area, situated on a pronounced turtleback, the linear array of site WS 230 along internal canals, no doubt maintained to allow untrammeled boat access to surrounding marshes, is visible even to the untrained eye (figure 3B). Site WS 298, a low mound located *c.* 10 km northeast of Uruk, is similarly situated on turtleback facing a levee back slope.

Excavations at Tell Oueili (WS 460) confirm this photographic interpretation, and the underlying geomorphology analogous to similar sites in the Nile delta. At Oueili, Pleistocene buttes punctuate a Holocene surface incised to several meters depth by the Shatt al Kar east of the site. Oueili is situated atop one of these earlier surfaces, revealed by excavation as a buried turtleback, where it was most likely located for protection from seasonal flooding. A deep sounding showed 4 meters of alluvial deposition surrounding and eventually burying the channels that would have carried waters past its Ubaid 0 foundations (Porada, Hansen, Sunham, and Babcock 1992: 86; Geyer and Sanlaville 1996; Plaziat and Sanlaville 1991).

Discharge Splays, Levees, and "Bird's Feet"

Three relict features help to chart and date a relict fluvial system in its entirety. Easily detectable in that they leave indelible scars, are flood-season discharge splays preceding from levee ruptures (compare figures 7 and 8). These splays can become the source of new or diverted main channel flows, although, just as often, the sudden fanning drops sufficient alluvial silt that, as floodwaters recede, the natural levees may reestablish. We would expect no permanent sites on top of such features (although there may well be sites predating such extreme events *under* them), since active dramatic

---

[7] Tony Wilkinson cautions that, due to its large amplitude, we cannot rule out an earlier (Pleistocene) dating for this channel succession, which would later have become exposed by aeolian deflation, leaving subsequent Holocene sites pedestalled on its surface. (Wilkinson, pers. com., 2002). I will take up this discussion in detail in a subsequent paper.

[8] These are in braod agreement with conclusions based on study of toponyms in third- and second-millennium BCE cuneiform texts recording shipping and travel itineraries along stretches of the major watercourses (Nissen 1985; Steinkeller 2001). Stone 2002 critiques details of Steinkeller 2001, but agrees that the "Eastern Euphrates" attested in third millenium BCE texts was in fact a distributary branch of the Tigris.

annual flooding would make permanent habitation exceedingly hazardous and unlikely. We may thus take any site located on top of such fans as a *terminus post quem* for active inundation from the breach at their heads, which aids in dating the system of which they form a part.

Flood deposits along riparian distributaries over time build massive levees, as at present along the Tigris south of Amara (figure 4A). There, the agricultural zone extends east and west of the main water channel along the five km.-wide levee system. Excess water drains through light-colored tails of smaller canal levees into seasonal back swamps visible as silty, dark bodies. In otherwise arid zones, during the wet season relict levees appear on black-and-white photographs as brighter in color than surrounding soils. Their slightly higher elevation and greater degree of compaction means that they retain less moisture and dry faster than background terrain, and therefore reflect more light.

Careful examination of the putative Chalcolithic alluvial zone in the now-arid Warka Survey area revealed a five-kilometer-wide levee system, extending south-southeast from meander traces recorded by Adams vic. site WS 175, to a series of distributaries dissipating into relict marshland from site WS 427 to WS 447 (figure 2). The eroded natural levees approach five kilometers in width, indicating a past discharge capacity equivalent to that of the modern-day Tigris system. Particularly clear is a section between sites WS 375–WS 400, showing relict back swamps and offtakes for near-levee cultivation. The thin, black line of the Shatt al-Kar is all that remains to indicate that a once-mighty watercourse flowed here. A historical canal running atop the levee, the Shatt al-Kar could not possibly have transported sufficient silt to build the massive geologic structure depicted at figure 4B.

Active sediment deposition as great rivers abruptly slow on encountering slack water results in the multiple, bifurcating channels of a classic "bird's foot delta," as that of the present-day Mississippi river. The radial pattern of distributaries surrounding Warka speaks to its early situation in an active, alluvial environment. Home of the fourth millennium BCE Uruk urban expansion, the satellite photos reveal the city's placement not so much on the river as in it: the city's walls are clearly surrounded by a relict bird's foot delta extending into spring 1968 Euphrates floodwaters (figures 4, 12). This location would have conferred significant transportational advantage, as the irresistible logic of the riparian dictates that heavy, bulky goods may be moved more easily downstream than up, tending to favor import of raw materials and export of manufactures (Algaze 2001).

A Mesopotamian Littoral Economy

A gross explanation of the close fit of surveyed sites to relict Tigris/Euphrates meander systems down the center of the upper Mesopotamian alluvium could be that large Chalcolithic sites in this region were situated within (or on the levees of) river meanders at locations propitious for primitive irrigation, using what Wilkinson has described as human-assisted, semi-managed avulsion (Wilkinson 2002).

But close examination of the paleogeology of the lower alluvium suggests that a larger role must be given to littoral ecotones as a "third pillar" of the formative Mesopotamian economy. I will now turn to interpretation of the satellite photographs in light of surface and excavation finds. This exercise suggests a settlement progression beginning in the Neolithic Ubaid with dependence on littoral biomass, and ending in the Early Bronze Age Late Uruk/Jemdet Nasr, with intensive usage of what by then had become agricultural zones.[9] For the earlier Neolithic (Ubaid 0–3) periods, as sea levels slowly rose from 15 meters below to within several meters of their current levels (Sanlaville 1989), mid-Holocene (6000/5500–3500 BCE) monsoon variations brought increased rainfall to the lower alluvium (el-Moslimany 1994; see Potts 1997 Chapter 1 and 52 *passim*). Because freshwater outflow to the Gulf is constrained by the twin cones of the Wadi Batin and Karun-Karkeh drainages, even absent the effects of tidal forcing concomitant with later progradation of the Gulf head, these comparatively pluvial conditions would have increased the likelihood of seasonal flooding and marsh formation.[10]

Neolithic Precursors

Available excavation evidence indicates a long period of Neolithic Ubaid adaptation to littoral conditions. No surface finds can be dated to Ubaid 0 (6516–5955 BC),[11] but the deep sounding at Tell Oueili (WS460), characterized even at this early date by extensive mud-brick construction, showed five meters of Ubaid 0 material remaining above the water table (figure 2, near E). Botanical finds included edible sedge tubers (Cyperus rotundus) and giant reed (Phragmites australis) (Neef 1989), both suggesting that water pooled near the site, which was situated on a Pleistocene turtleback surrounded by infilled channels (Huot 1989, 1991, 1996; Forest 1996) (figure 2).

Within the Warka survey area, two Ubaid 1 ("Eridu Phase," 5916–5236 BC)[12] sites—WS 267, and Haji Mohammed, which would undergo a flourit as the Ubaid 2 type site—were aligned north-to-south along a Tigris distributary that rejoins the Euphrates system after dissipating into marshlands (figure 2 line AC). A third site–the early foundations of the great 3d millenium BCE city of Larsa, bordered the marshes fed by the great Tigris distributary east of Uruk (figure 2, line BD). South of the Euphrates, type-site Eridu itself

---

[9] For the following discussion (Figures 13–15), I follow Nissen's ceramic seriation (Adams and Nissen 1972), and the Porada et al. 1992 as amended by SAR 1998 chronologies for Mesopotamia (Rothman 2001). I understand that reseriation based on Oueili finds revises the Nissen ceramic chronology; but such adjustments, while refining, will not alter the substantive conclusions made here.

[10] Flooding and marsh recharge is primarily related to melting of the Tigris and Euphrates headwaters snow packs, but increase in either early Fall (October-November) or late spring (March–May) precipitation even south of the 34th parallel reinforces and lengthens the regular flood seasons. Flooding and marsh formation associated with peak lower alluvium precipitation years occurred in 1870, 1894, and 1918–19. (McFayden 1938; Roux 1960: 30–31).

[11] All dates calibrated C14. Oueili: shell; Sawwan, Choga Mami: tree charcoal.

[12] Calibrated C14, tree charcoal. (Valladas, Evin, and Arnold 1996: 383)

straddled a Euphrates levee backslope bordering a marsh rim. Beneath later sacred areas were pedestalled mud structures, showing signs of burning, presaging a succession of temples with burnt offerings of fish (Safar, Mustafa, and Lloyd 1981; Porada, Hansen, Sunham, and Babcock 1992). "Eridu period peoples...had on hand copious marsh resources. A canoe model and numbers of perforated clay ovoids, perhaps net weights (Lloyd and Safar: 118, pl. III), from Eridu period levels suggest that the marshes were already being used in a sophisticated manner." (Wright 1981: 323).

By Ubaid 2 ("Haji Muhammad Phase," 5236—[5064?] BC) two more sites were added to the back slopes of the Uruk distributary levee AC, continuing a line northward. The more southerly (WS247) overlooked an (undated) marsh rim,[13] while at the juncture of this levee with an anastomosing distributary continuing southeastward to join the Tigris system (figure 2, line AB), the first (WS42) of what would become a complex of sites characterized by surface finds of spools and net weights also appears on its back slope. In 20th century marsh districts near al-Hiba (Lagash), characterized by a mixed agropastoral-fishing-reed manufactures economy, similar spools and weights are employed in spinning yarn for and weighting fishing and fowling nets (Ochsenschlager 1993).

Continuing linearly southeast, two additional sites (WS51, WS178) were situated along the levee/marsh rim AB. Spools were also noted at WS 298, while excavated bitumen toggles at Uruk, and the first appearance of "tortoise jars" at Eridu, were assigned to this period (Adams 1981; Porada, Hansen, Sunham, and Babcock 1992: 86). Ceramic evidence that the emphasis on levee colonization was directly tied to mastery and reliance on water travel as far away as the Persian Gulf is tantalizing. While most common at Uruk and Ur (Porada, Hansen, Sunham, and Babcock 1992: 86), founded during Ubaid 2 on a levee/marsh rim, "the Haji Muhammad style...is the first to occur in sites along and behind the Saudi Arabian shoreline, more than 600 km southeast of Eridu...[Chemical analyses indicate that the painted pottery there was of southern Mesopotamian manufacture, implying periodic visits by fishermen from settlements along the Tigris-Euphrates delta with craft sufficiently well-developed for them to master deep-sea travel." (Adams 1981: 58, citing Oates 1976: 22; Oates, Davidson, Kamilli, and McKerrel 1977). Near Ur, type site al-Ubaid, was founded on a low sand knoll (Hall 1930, Hall and Woolley 1927).

Ubaid 3 ([5064?]—4893 BC) surface finds are noted at one new site (WS4/Jidr) on the Tigris levee BD; one (WS275) on a turtleback at the back slope of the Uruk levee AC; and although Oueili (WS460) itself appears to have undergone an occupation hiatus, a new site (WS459) appears adjacent to Tell Oueili on the marsh rim E. At Eridu "tortoise jars" abound, temple platforms are raised, and clear evidence of mud brick directly associated with adjacent reed domestic construction is exposed (Safar 1950: 28) even as a flourit of Mesopotamian-manufactured (imported) pottery appears at Gulf coast sites.

Thus, throughout the latter Neolithic, archaeological evidence from the southern alluvium is consistent with our reconstruction of a riparian distributary system and concomitant marshy zone, shading from seasonal inundation to permanent lakes. At Ubaid-period Uruk, Hajji Mohamed, al-Ubaid, Ur, and Eridu, in addition to mud brick the deepest soundings all revealed remains of reed platforms, traces of reed structures, plastered reed walls, and reed matting plastered with dung, earth, or bitumen (summarized in Moorey 1994: 361). Inhabitants of the southern alluvium were apparently dependent upon liberal access to littoral biomass for food, construction material, and fodder (fish, fowl, pig, reed); water supplies and transport; and riparian (cattle) browse.

The Chalcolithic Transition

Ubaid 4 (4893—4357 BC) marks a more visible settlement trend. Thus far, the oldest period reached beneath the tens of meters of overburden at Uruk itself dates to this period. Surface finds show five new sites (WS137, WS160, WS218, WS260, and WS411) on turtlebacks, of which three abut levee back slopes. One (Raidu Sharqi) is added to a levee distributary at the marsh rim southwest of Uruk. Surface finds at site WS 218 included spools. At Oueili, added to the earlier botanical constellation of dates, tubers, and reeds are water-loving poplar (*Populus euphratica*) and sea club-rush (*Scirpus maritimus*), with a continuing faunal emphasis on cattle and pig (Neef 1989) (figure 8).

Eridu, 12 hectares in extent, sported a temple on a raised terrace and, for some individuals, substantial brick tombs. Boat models indicate that sailing craft had been developed; and quantities of marine fish were recovered in the temple precinct and from the alter, presumably laid as offerings. Botanical remains included dates. (Safar 1950, Safar et al. 1981; Wright 1981). Similarly, Ur and al-Ubaid had grown to about 10 ha. size (Hall 1931, Safar et al. 1981). Clay sickle distribution indicates extensive harvesting along back slopes (Wright 1981). Wear pattern and phytolithic analyses of similar sickles make intensive reed-harvesting for fodder and construction material likely (Anderson-Gerfaud 1983:177–91; Benco 1992:119–34).

By the Early Uruk period (4000–3500 BCE), as rising sea levels reached (3800 BCE) and then exceeded by one–two meters (3500 BCE) those of today, settlement was marked by a continuing colonization of turtlebacks. Progradation of the Gulf head as far north and east as modern Qurna would certainly have resulted in tidal flushing as far northeast as Ur, and perhaps as far as Uruk itself. This would have been accompanied by at least seasonal marsh formation over all but the highest ground of the Warka and Eridu survey areas, as the outlets of the combined Tigris and Euphrates discharge became flooded, slowing drainage to the sea.

---

[13] This area has repeatedly flooded, most recently during the 19th and 20th centuries, and remains unsurveyed, rendering dating of the marsh zone difficult at best without sediment sampling (Potts 1997: 39). However, as the prevailing geosyncline (Buday and Jassim 1987) would have tended to pool floodwaters predominantly west and south of the Uruk distributary–a process apparent along lower Tigris distributaries until the mid 1990s–I consider contemporary marshland formation in this zone exceedingly likely.

Two new sites clustered on the Uruk levee A vicinity fishing site WS42 (WS20, WS22), with two more on its back slope (WS23, WS24) perhaps fed by a minor canal, but net weights (WS26), and spools (WS20, WS24) attest a continuity of purpose with that earlier site. Site WS245 on the levee AC back slope exploits the same locale as Ubaid 2 site WS247. But in a completely new development, their linear arrangement suggests that regularized waterways up to twelve kilometers in length may have extended south from the Tigris tributary levee AB to sites WS107; WS109; and WS178-201-215; aligned toward turtleback sites WS137, WS160, WS218 (respectively) (figure 8). These linear arrangements need not be interpreted as canals extending through arid zones. Equally likely is that they represent permanent boat transport routes with villages along their banks, kept clear of reeds during wet seasons and allowing access to the river during dry. Similar village distributions are visible extending southward from the Euphrates as it wends through the eastern Iraqi marshes, for example vic. Kabaish (el-Chubayish) (Roux 1960; Salim 1962).

These presage a site explosion during the late Uruk (3500—3000 BCE). As sea levels and the Gulf shoreline fell back to approximately their present locations, over one hundred new sites spread fanlike north and east from the emergent city at Warka, south from the levee system tying the Uruk and Tigris channels, and eastward from the Tigris levee. Added to net weights (figure 2),[14] spools,[15] and spindle whorls[16] are a profusion of mace heads,[17] possibly indicators of local conflict (although they seem rather light weight for this purpose)or local office. Late Uruk (Uruk IVA) seals, sealings, and tablets recovered from excavations at Warka depict cattle emerging from reed byres, hunting scenes with pigs stalked among reeds, palms, and frogs, with many tablets showing the clear imprints of the reed mats upon which they lay as they dried (Boehmer 1999: 51–56, 66–67, 71–74, 90–104). Contemporary protoliterate economic texts include dozens of ideographs for reeds and reed products, pigs, waterfowl, fish, dried fish, fish traps, dried and processed fish flour, as well as those for cattle and dairy products (Englund 1998).

The site distribution implies a gradual withdrawal of the seasonal marsh zone southward, and opening up of land area amenable to grain cultivation. However, it could as well be an artifact of site visibility, indicating only the limits of aeolian scouring in exposing buried sites, that no *further* inundation occurred *after* the late Uruk, or both. Intensification of cattle production in riparian and littoral habitat would have simultaneously and steadily degraded browse and the watershed, necessitating intensified fodder gathering and production (Belsky 1999). The profusion of visible Late Uruk small sites could therefore be evidence that, concomitant with intensified agricultural production, reed and other marsh products were becoming intensively harvested to underwrite urbanizing consumption. Notable is a match between the geographic clustering of sites around centers on turtlebacks, with Adams' hypothetical Jemdet Nasr/EDI territories, based on site sizes and nearest neighbor analysis (Adams 1981: 20, fig. 8) (figure 2).

This would suggest that during the Chalcolithic Ubaid and Early Uruk, palm groves, gardens, temples, kilns, and other institutions, long consolidated on turtlebacks and levees away from seasonal inundation by peoples well-preadapted to thorough exploitation of marshland resources, presaged later political and economic organization.

RESOURCES AND (SOCIAL) ENGINEERING

Agricultural colonization of the southern Mesopotamian alluvium was made enduringly possible through exploitation by specialized communities of marsh fowl, fish, bitumen, shell, and reeds; by grazing herds on pastures left by receding flood backwash; and by trading boat cargoes with near river neighbors. Sixth- and fifth millennium settlements initially took localized advantage of productive riparian littoral ecotones. Through time, by practicing local, small scale damming and diking to build up permanently habitable platforms and control the rate and progression of flooding and runoff, they accumulated "hydrologic capital." This served not only toward possession of the most suitable landscapes, but in the invention of technologies for flood control. Construction of regularized dykes and channels accumulated irrigation and drainage technologies and concomitant institutions for labor mobilization.

Complementarity of resources would of course have provided local resiliency; but just as important would have been the replicability of these small, bounded, human-maintained ecosystems at each meander loop; on each turtleback, and at each levee junction, where locally shifting plans brought minimal acreage into well-drained cultivation. Specializations and complementarities, through reciprocal social institutions, could have been maintained on a sub- regional basis, beyond the reach of any locally destructive flood or drought. Communities sustained by marshland biomass and fed by the combination of farming-fishing-husbandry were enabled to produce sufficiently consistent agricultural surpluses and sufficiently robust trade networks to tilt the balance: Consolidation of local management structures that must have preceded the work of straightening and regularizing channels and building new canals that came to characterize and fuel urban growth during the third millenium BCE.

Just as excavation over-focused on massive temple and administrative architecture has skewed attention to and perception of the scope and scale of Mesopotamian domestic settlement, osteologial analysis over-focused on mammalian megafauna has skewed attention to and perception of the littoral component of domestic diet. "For the vast majority of the working population, the primary dietary protein source was dried fish." (Englund 2000, pers. com.) Fish, shellfish, turtle, waterfowl, and pigs; reeds, sedges, tubers, and seasonal

---

[14] WS110, WS219.

[15] WS28, WS48, WS191, WS219, WS282, WS297.

[16] WS137, WS181, WS185, WS219, WS260, WS274, WS407.

[17] WS109, WS129, WS152, WS162, WS219, WS230, WS242, WS260, WS262, WS274, WS276.

grasses sustained human and animal (especially bovid) populations and provided massive quantities of handicraft and construction material. Littoral ecotones constrained habitation; annual floods replenished marshes and recessional gardens; the watery environment provided lines of communication that ensured rapid transmission of technologies, trade goods, and peoples themselves—even as these factors concentrated resources, produce, institutions, and know-how into the hands of the few, setting the stage for hierarchy and heterarchy.

East of the Warka survey area, we can see clearly a relict levee, cut by modern canals, extending into a modern seasonal flood zone. Tel al-Hiba (Lagash) surmounts a Pleistocene turtleback appearing as an 'island' to the south (figure 9). Numerous linear sites are visible along the levee, and multiple occupation mounds are visible on the turtleback. During the historical Early Dynastic III period (2600–2350 BCE), sea levels once again rose one meter above present, and thus a similar hydrologic regime to that of the late Chalcolithic probably prevailed. ED III faunal remains included not only seven species of marine mollusk shell (which could merely have been imported for bead manufacture) (Carter 1990; Kenoyer 1990), but two of marine fish, as well as duck, coot, cormorant, flamingo, gull, and spoonbill–the latter particularly preferring open marshes, shallow lagoons, and estuarine mud flats (Mudar 1982: 29–30, 33–34).[18] Analysis of faunal remains from 1970–71 excavations of distinct temple and administrative/residential precincts showed a decided differentiation in their distribution. All fish, fowl, and mollusk (shell) were found in the administrative/residential zone; none in that of the temple. This marked differentiation in consumption was reinforced by mammalian finds. In the temple precinct, ovicaprids comprised a proportionally higher; bos a slightly higher, and sus a significantly lower percentage than finds in the residential/administrative precinct (Mudar 1982). It is tempting to conclude that (elite) mutton and beef had become appropriate; pork less so; and fish inappropriate as temple offerings and priestly food; a marked reversal from the Ubaid precincts at Eridu—and one marking the transition from a time of Neolithic social integration served by fish as everyman's food, to one of Early Bronze Age consolidated social hierarchy marked by fish as poor man's food.

Al-Hiba was hardly unique in its littoral reliance, which continued through the third millenium BCE. Cylinder sealings from the ED III Seal Impression Strata at Ur depict reed structures (333–344), cattle fed in and lead from reed byres (337, 342, 344); personages poled along fish-filled watercourses in high-prowed boats (300), fishing from small watercraft (310), and persons carrying tribute of fish and waterfowl (302, 303). Robert Englund has treated at length regulation and management of late third millenium Ur III fisheries (Englund 1990). Umma texts record quotas for production of reed, bitumen, boats mats, and standardized fish baskets (de Genouillac 1920: 6036). Proto-Elamite lexical lists record 58 terms relating to wild and domestic pigs; 'professions' lists record offices including 'fisheries governor' and 'fisheries accountant' that endure one and one-half millennia to the Old Babylonian period.

This subsequent administration of marshland resources was not a mere addendum to a better-studied agropastoral irrigation economy. Its managerial origins in Chalcolithic hydrostrategies were *a priori* dependent upon a littoral landscape—one that we have here attempted to better reconstruct; one that endured in various forms for seven millennia; and one that during the 20th century AD was finally managed to extinction (GOI 1956; UNEP 2001).

Bibliography

ADAMS, ROBERT M. 1965. *Land Behind Baghdad: A History of Settlement on the Diyala Plains*. Chicago: U. of Chicago Press.

ADAMS, ROBERT M. 1981. *Heartland of Cities: Surveys of Ancient Settlement and Land Use on the Central Floodplain of the Euphrates*. Chicago and London: U. of Chicago Press.

ADAMS, ROBERT M., and HANS J. NISSEN. 1972. *The Uruk Countryside: The Natural Setting of Urban Societies*. Chicago and London: U. of Chicago Press.

AIKENS, C. MELVIN. 1981. The last 10,000 years in Japan and eastern North America: parallels in environment, economic adaptation, growth of social complexity, and the adoption of agriculture. *Senri Ethnological Studies* 9: 261-73.

AKAZAWA, TAKERU. 1981. Maritime adaptation of prehistoric hunter-gatherers and their transition to agriculture in Japan. *Senri Ethnological Studies* 9: 215–258.

ANDERSON-GERFAUD, P. 1983. "L'utilisation de certains objcts en ceramique de Tell el'Oueili (Obeid 4): Rapport preliminaire sur les microtrances.," in *Larsa et Oueili, Travaux de 1978–1981*. Edited by J.-L. Huot, p. 177–91. Paris: Editions Recherche sur les Civilisations.

AQRAWI, A. A. M. 1997. The nature and preservation of organic matter in Holocene lacustrine/deltaic sediments of lower Mesopotamia, SE Iraq. *Journal of Petroleum Geology* 20: 69–90.

AQRAWI, A. A. M. 2001. Stratigraphic signatures of climatic change during the Holocene evolution of the Tigris-Euphrates delta, lower Mesopotamia. *Global and Planetary Change* 28: 267–283.

AURENCHE, O. 1981. *La Maison Orientale: l'architecture do proche orient acien des origines au millieu du quatrième millénaire*. ParisInstitute Français d'Archéologie du Proche Orient.

BAR-YOSEF, OFER. 1986. The walls of Jericho, an alternative interpretation. *Current Anthropology* 27: 157–162.

BELSKY, JOY. 1999. Survey of livestock influences on stream and riparian ecosystems in the western United States. *Journal of Soil and Water Conservation*.

BENCO, N. L. 1992. Manufacture and use of clay sickles from the Uruk mound, Abu Salabikh, Iraq. *Paleorient* 18: 119–34.

BOEHMER, RAINER M. *Uruk: Früheste Siegelabrollungen*. Mainz a. R.: Phillipp von Zabern.

BOESSNECK, JOACHIM, ANGELA VON DEN DRIESCH, and REINHARD ZIEGLER. 1989. "Die Tierreste von Maadi und Wadi Digla," in *Maadi III: The Non-Lithic Small Finds and the Structural Remains of the Predynastic Settlement*. Edited by I.

---

[18] Of note is the lack of Ubaid or Uruk finds, indicating that in Chalcolithic times the Gulf transgression either precluded permanent habitation altogether, or confined it to relatively small areas, not subject to seasonal inundation, now deeply buried beneath subsequent occupation debris. That the earlier periods are represented at nearby Tello (Girsu) and Shurgal (Nina) supports the latter probability.

Rizkana and J. Seeher, Mainz am Rhein: Verlag Philipp von Zabern.

BREWER, DOUGLAS J. 1989. *Fishermen, Hunters, and Herders. Zooarchaeology in the Fayum, Egypt (c. 8200–5000 BP). B.A.R. 478*. Oxford: British Archaeological Research.

BUDAY, TIBOR, and SAAD Z. JASSIM. 1987. *The Regional Geology of Iraq: Tectonism, Magmatism, and Metamorphism*. Baghdad: Gov't of Iraq, Geological Survey and Mineral State Establishment.

BUTZER, KARL W. 2001. "Geoarchaeological implications of recent research in the Nile delta," in *Egypt and the Levant: The 4th-millenium Background*. Edited by E. van den Brinck and T.E. Levy, London: Leicester University.

CARTER, ELIZABETH. 1990. A surface survey of Lagash, al-Hiba, 1984. *Sumer* 46: 60–63.

COLEMAN, JAMES M., HARRY H. ROBERTS, and OSCAR K. HUH. 1986. "Deltaic Landforms," in *Geomorphology from Space: A Global Overview of Regional Landforms*. Edited by N. M. Short and and Robert W. Blair, Washington, D.C.: NASA.

DE GENOUILLAC. 1920. *Texte Cuniform d'Louvre* .

EIWANGER, JOSEF. 1984. *Merimde–Benisâlame I: Die Funde der Urschicht. Archäologische Veröffentlichungen 47* Mainz am Rhein: Verlag Philipp von Zabern.

EL-MOSLIMANY, ANN P. 1994. Evidence of early Holocene summer precipitation in the Middle East. *Radiocarbon* 121–130.

ENGLUND, ROBERT K. 1990. *Organization und Verwaltung der Ur-III Fischerei*. Berlin: Berliner Beitrage zum Vorderen Orient 10.

ENGLUND, ROBERT K. 1998. "Texts from the Late Uruk Period," in *Späturuk-Zeit und Frühdynastische Zeit*. Edited by P. Attinger and Marcus Wäfler, Freiburg//Göttingen: Universitätsverlag// Vandenhoeck and Ruprecht.

FOREST, JEAN-DANIEL. 1996. "Elements de chronologie," in *Oueili: Travaux de 1987 et 1989*. Edited by J.-L. Huot, Paris: Editions Recherche sur les Civilisations.

FRANKFORT, HENRY. 1932. *Archaeology and the Sumerian Problem. Studies in Ancient Oriental Civilization 4*. Chicago.

GASCHE, HERMANN, and M. TANRET. 1998. *Changing Watercourses in Babylonia. Towards a reconstruction of the ancient environment in lower Mesopotamia*. Ghent and Chicago: University of Ghent and Oriental Institute.

GEYER, BERNARD, and PAUL SANLAVILLE. 1996. "Nouvelle Contribution a etude geomorpholgique de la region de Larsa-Oueili (Iraq)," in *Oueili: Travaux de 1987 et 1989*. Edited by J.-L. Huot, p. 392–412. Paris: Editions Recherche sur les Civilisations.

GIBSON, MACGUIRE. 1972. *The City and Area of Kish*. Miami: Field Research Publications.

HALL, H. R. 1930. *A Season's Work at Ur*. London: Methuen & Co.

HALL, H. R., and C.L. WOOLLEY. 1927. *Ur Excavations I. Al-'Ubaid*. Oxford: Oxford University Press.

HOLE, FRANK. 1998a. Comment on Michael Rosenberg's 'Cheating at Musical Chairs: Territoriality and Sedentism in an Evolutionary Context'. *Current Anthropology* 39: 670–671.

HOLE, FRANK. 1998b. Paleoenvironment and human society in the Jezireh of Northern Mesopotamia 20,000–6,000 BP. *Paléorient* 23: 39–49.

HUOT, JEAN-LOUIS. 1989. *Larsa: Travaux de 1985*. Paris: Editions Recherche sur les Civilisations.

HUOT, JEAN-LOUIS. 1991. *'Oueili: Travaux de 1985*. Paris: Editions Recherche sur les Civilisations.

HUOT, JEAN-LOUIS. 1996. *Oueili: Travaux de 1987 et 1989*. Paris: Editions Recherche sur les Civilisations.

IRAQI GEOLOGICAL DEPARTMENT. 1938. "Provisional Geological Map of Iraq, 4 July 1937," in *Water Supplies in Iraq*. Edited by W. A. MacFayden, Baghdad: Gov't of Iraq, Ministry of Economics and Communication, Geological Dep't.

KENOYER, J. M. 1990. Shell artifacts from Lagash, al-Hiba. *Sumer* 46: 64-66.

KOUCHOUKOS, NICHOLAS. 98. "Landscape and Social Change in Late Prehistoric Mesopotamia," in Ann Arbor: UMI.

LLOYD, SETON, and FUAD SAFAR. Eridu: Preliminary communication on the second season's excavations: 1947–1948. *Sumer* 4: 115–127//276–283.

MACFAYDEN, W. A. 1938. *Water Supplies in Iraq*. Baghdad: Gov't of Iraq, Ministry of Economics and Communication, Geological Dep't.

MILLER, NAOMI. 1991. "The Near East," in *Progress in Old World Paleoetnobotany*. Edited by Van Zeist, Wasylikowa, and Behre, p. 133–160. Rotterdam: Balkema.

MILLER, NAOMI. 1998. The macrobotanical evidence for vegetation in the Near East, c. 18,000/16,000 BCE to 4,000 BC. *Paléorient* 23: 197–207.

MOOREY, P. R. S. 1994. *Ancient Mesopotamian Materials and Industries: The Archaeological Evidence*. Oxford: Clarendon.

MOSELEY, MICHAEL. 1975. *The Maritime Foundations of Andean Civilization*. Menlo Park, CA: Cummings.

MUDAR, KAREN. 1982. Early Dynastic III animal utilization in Lagash: a report on the fauna of Tell al-Hiba. *Journal of Near Eastern Studies* 41: 23–63.

MURDOCK, GEORGE P. 1969. "Contributions to anthropology: ecological essays; proceedings of the Conference on Cultural Ecology*. Edited by D. Damas, Ottawa : Queen's Printer.

NEEF, REINDER. 1989. "Plant remains from archaeological sites in lowland Iraq: Tell el'Oueili," in *Larsa: Travaux de 1985*. Edited by J.-L. Huot, Paris.

NISSEN, HANS-JOERG. 1985. Ortsnamen in den archaischen Texten aus Uruk. *Orientalia* 54: 226–233.

NISSEN, HANS-JOERG. 1988. *The Early History of the Ancient Near East 9000–2000 BC*. Chicago and London: U. of Chicago.

NORTHEDGE, ALASTAIR, T. J. WILKINSON, and ROBIN FALKNER. 1989. Survey and excavations at Samarra. *Iraq* 52: 75–84.

OATES, DAVID, and JOAN OATES. 1977. "Early irrigation agriculture in Mesopotamia," in *Problems in Economic and Social Archaeology*. Edited by G. D. G. Sieveking, I. H. Longworth, and K. E. Wilson, p. 109–135. London: Duckworth.

OATES, JOAN. 1960. Ur and Eridu, the prehistory. *Iraq* 22: 32–50.

OCHSENSCHLAGER, E. 1993. Village Weavers: Ethnoarchaeology at al-Hiba. *Bulletin on Sumerian Agriculture* 7: 43–62.

PARK, THOMAS. 1992. Early trends toward class stratification: chaos, common property, and flood recession agriculture. *American Anthropologist* 94: 90–117.

PEARSON, RICHARD, and ANNE UNDERHILL. 1987. The Chinese Neolithic: recent trends in research. *American Anthropologist* 89: 807–821.

PERKINS, A. L. 1949. *The Comparative Archaeology of Early Mesopotamia. SAOC 25*. Chicago: Studies in Ancient Oriental Civilization.

PLAZIAT, JEAN-CLAUDE A. S. P. 1991. "Donnees Recentes sur la sedimentation tardive dans la plaine de Larsa-'Oueili," in

'Ouelli: Travaux de 1985. Edited by J.-L. Huot, p. 342–343. Paris: Editions Recherche sur les Civilizations.

PLAZIAT, JEAN-CLAUDE, and PAUL SANLAVILLE. 1991. "Donnees Recentes sur la sedimentation tardive dans la plaine de Larsa-'Ouelli," in *'Oueilli: Travaux de 1985*. Edited by J.-L. Huot, p. 342–343. Paris: Editions Recherche sur les Civilizations.

POLLACK, SUSAN. 1992. Bureaucrats and Managers, Peasants and Pastoralists, Imperialists and Traders: Research in the Uruk and Jemdet Nasr Periods in Mesopotamia. *Journal of World Prehistory* 5: 297–336.

PORADA, EDITH, DONALD P. HANSEN, SALLY SUNHAM, and SIDNEY H. BABCOCK. 1992. "The Cconology of Mesopotamia, ca. 7000–1600 B.C.," in *Chronologies in Old World Archaeology*. Edited by R. W. Ehrich, p. 77–121. Chicago: University of Chicago Press.

POTTS, D. T. 1997. *Mesopotamian Civilization: The Material Foundations*. Ithaca: Cornell U. Press.

POURNELLE, JENNIFER R. 1999. The Mesopotamian Heartland Revisited: Tentative identification of fourth–third millennium BCE Tigris and Euphrates channels in Sumer and Akkad. *Paper presented to the University of Chicago Oriental Institute Interdisciplinary Archaeology Workshop, March 1999*.

POURNELLE, JENNIFER. 2001a. Founded on sand: The satellite imagery revolution and $5^{th}/4^{th}$ millennium BC southern Mesopotamian societies. *Abstracts of the 100th Annual Meeting of the American Anthropological Association*.

POURNELLE, Jennifer R. 2001b. Figure 1: The ancient Mesopotamian alluvium during the 5th and 4th millennium BCE. In: Initial Social Complexity in Southwest Asia: The Mesopotamian Advantage by Guillermo Algaze. *Current Anthropology* 42, 2 (April 2001): 202.

POURNELLE, JENNIFER. 2002. From KLM to Corona: Using satellite photography toward a new understanding of fifth–fourth millenium BCE landscapes in southern Mesopotamia. *Abstracts of the 103rd Annual Meeting of the Archaeological Institute of America* 25: 58.

RIZKANA, IBRAHIM, and JÜRGEN SEEHER. 1987. *Maadi I: The Pottery of the Predynastic Settlement. Deutsches Archäologisches Institute Archäologische Veröffentlichungen 80*. Mainz am Rhein: Verlag Philipp von Zabern.

ROSS, ANN, and RYAN DUFFY. 2000. Fine mesh screening of midden material and the recovery of fish bone: the development of flotation and deflocculation techniques for an efficient and effective procedure. *Geoarchaeology* 15: 21–41.

ROUX, G. 1960. Recently discovered ancient sites in the Hammar Lake district (southern Iraq). *Sumer* 16: 20–31.

SAFAR, FUAD, MOHAMMAD A. MUSTAFA, and SETON LLOYD. 1981. *Eridu*. Baghdad: Ministry of Culture and Information, State Organization of Antiquities and Heritage.

SAFAR, FUAD. 1950. Excavations at Eridu—third season. *Sumer* 6: 27–38.

SALIM, S. M. 1962. *Marsh Dwellers of the Euphrates Delta. London School of Economics Monographs on Social Anthropology* London: Athlone.

SANLAVILLE, PAUL. 1996. Changements climatiques dans la région Livantine à fin du Pléistocene supérioir et au début de l'Holocène. Leurs relations avec l'évolution des sociétés humaines. *Paléorient* 22: 7–30.

STONE, ELIZABETH. 2002. Whither the Tigris? *Abstracts of the 103rd Annual Meeting of the Archaeological Institute of America* 25: 58.

STRONACH, DAVID. 1961. Excavations at Ras al 'Amiya. *Iraq* 23: 95–137.

U.S. GEOLOGICAL SURVEY. 1997. Corona Declassified Satellite Imagery. *Earth Resources Observation Center Webglis* 1102-2, 39–63: http://edcwww.cr.usgs.gov/Webglis/glisbin/search.pl?DISP (JAN 2001).

UNEP. 2001. *The Mesopotamian Marshlands: Demise of an Ecosystem*, Edited by Partow, H., Nairobi, Kenya: United Nations Environmental Programme, Division of Early Warning and Assessment

VALLADAS, HELENE, JACQUES EVIN, and MAURICE ARNOLD. 1996. "Datation par la Methode du Carbone 14 des couches obeid 0 et 1 de Tel Oueilli (Iraq)," in *Oueili: Travaux de 1987 et 1989*. Edited by J.-L. Huot, p. 381–384. Paris: Editions Recherche sur les Civilisations.

VAN DEN BRINK, EDWIN C. M. 1989. "The Amsterdam University Survey Expedition to the Northeastern Nile Delta (1984–1986)," in *The Archeology of the Nile Delta: Problems and Priorities*. Edited by E. C. M. van den Brink, p. 65–134.

VAN DEN BRINK, EDWIN C. M. 1993. Settlement patterns in the northeastern Nile delta during the fourth-second millennia BC. *Environmental Change and Human Culture in the Nile Basin and Northern Africa Until (sic) the Second Millenium BCE* 279-304.

WILKINSON, T. J. 1990. Early channels and landscape development at Abu Salabikh; a preliminary report. *Iraq* 52: 75–84.

WITTFOGEL, KARL. 1955. Developmental Aspects of Hydraulic Societies," in *The Rise and Fall of Civilizations*. Edited by C. C. Lambert-Karlovsky and J. Sabloff, p. 15–25. Menlo Park: Cummings.

WOOLLEY, C. L. 1934. *Ur Excavations*. London.

WOOLLEY, C. L. 1956. *Ur Excavations IV: The Early Periods*. London and Philadelphia.

WRIGHT, HENRY T. 1981. "The southern margins of Sumer: archaeological survey of the area of Eridu and Ur," in *Heartland of Cities: Surveys of Ancient Settlement and Land Use on the Central Floodplain of the Euphrates*. Edited by R. M. Adams, p. 295–338. Chicago//London: University of Chicago Press.

ZARINS, JURIS. 1989. Jebel Bishri and the Amorite homeland: The PPNB phase, in O. M. C. Haex, H. H. Curvers, and P. M. M. G. Akkermans eds., *To the Euphrates and Beyond*, Archaeological studies in honour of Maurits N. van Loon, Rotterdam 1989, pp. 29-51.

ZARINS, JURIS. 1990. Early pastoral nomadism and the settlement of lower Mesopotamia. *Bulletin of the American Schools of Oriental Research* 280: 31–65.

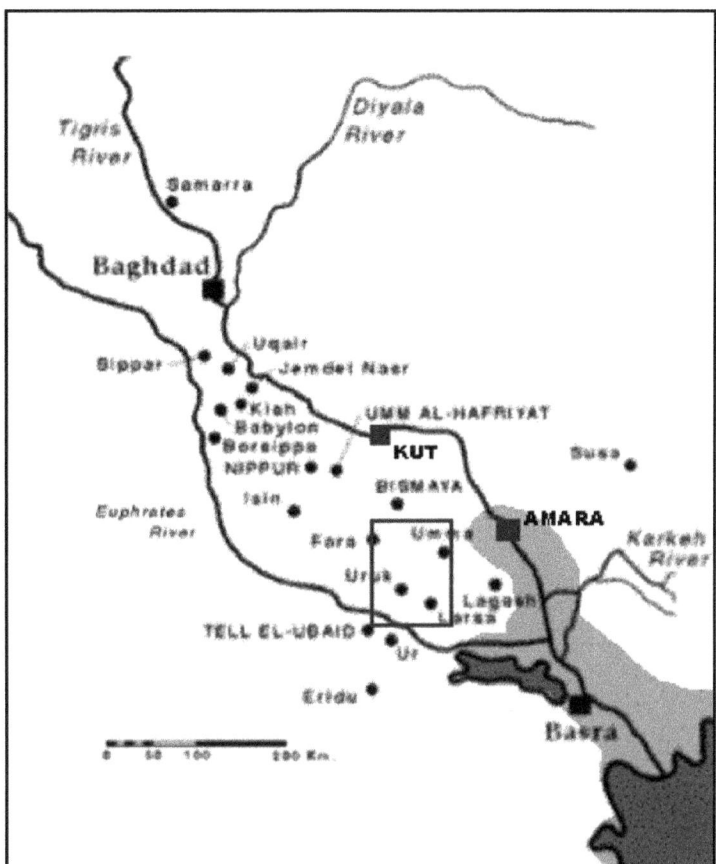

Figure 1: Archaeological sites of alluvial Mesopotamia, showing major settlements and hypothetical extent of the Persian Gulf ca. 3200 BCE. This study focuses on the Warka (Uruk) survey area, red box. After Oriental Institute 1998.

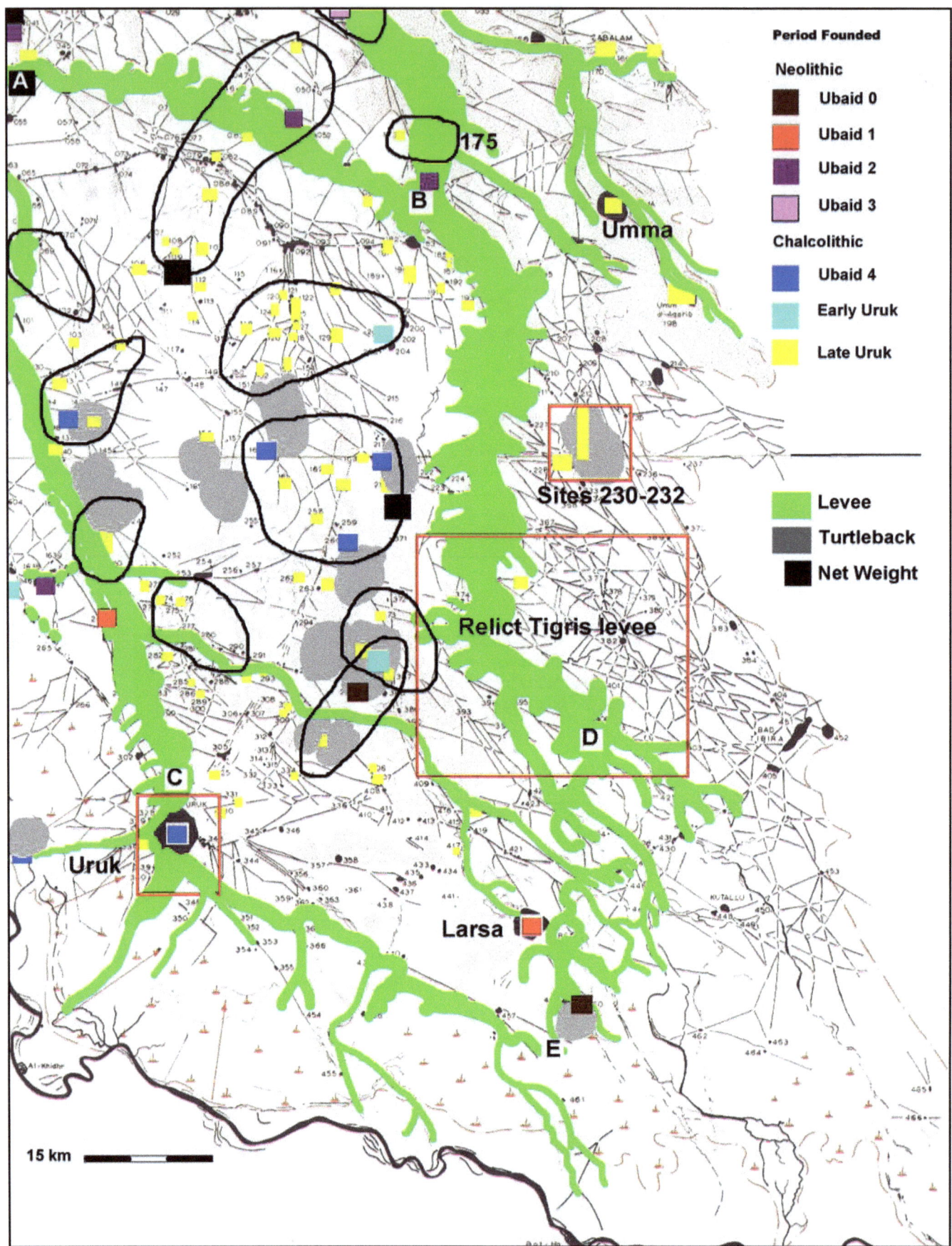

Figure 2: Relict levee systems, Warka survey area. Sites occupied during the Uruk period (4th millenium BCE), with Jemdet Nasr period "nearest neighbor" groupings. Legend (right) indicates earliest settlement period. Boxed insets enlarged in subsequent figures. After Adams 1981.

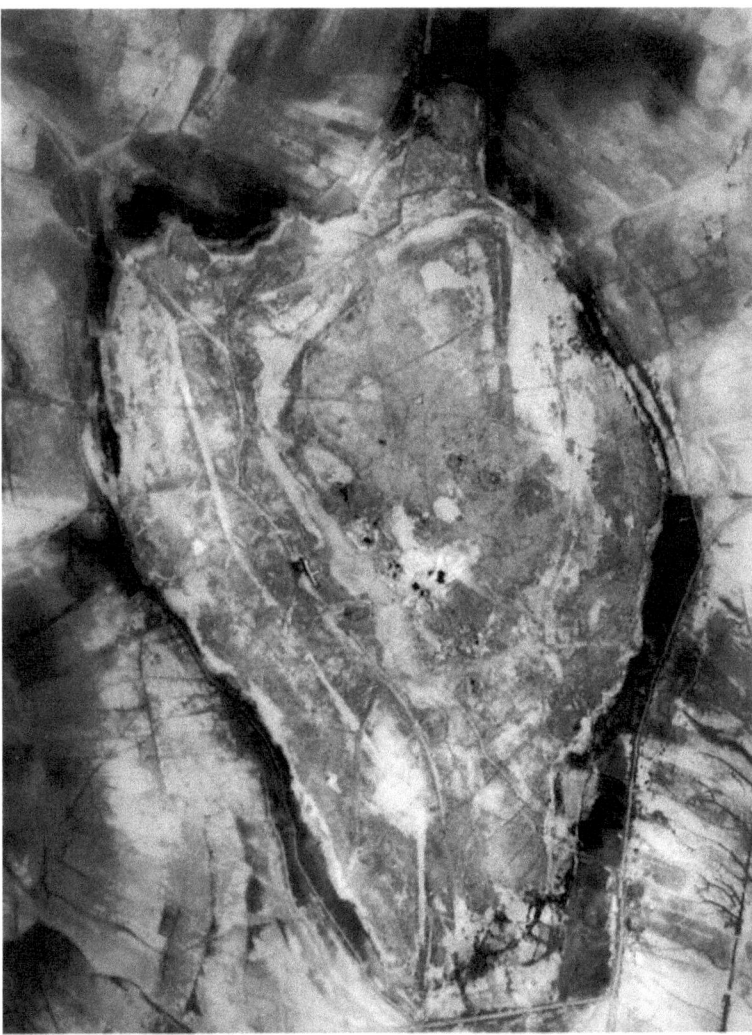

Figure 3A: Telloh (ancient Girsu) appears to float on an island within irrigated croplands. The archaic city walls encompass one-third of the turtleback land area. Source: KH4B_1103-1A-D041-057 (May 1968). 3X enlargement to scale ~1:75,000

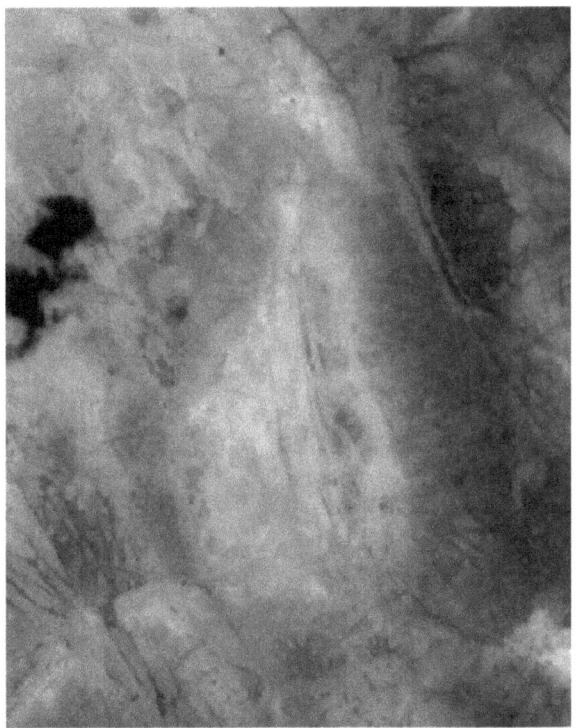

Figure 3B: Sites WS 230–232, arrayed along internal canals within a turtleback. The high water table following spring floods damps dust and reveals fine details of relief invisible at other seasons. Dark body at left is a cloud shadow. Source: KH4B_1103-1A-D041-057 (May 1968). 3X enlargement to scale ~1:75,000.

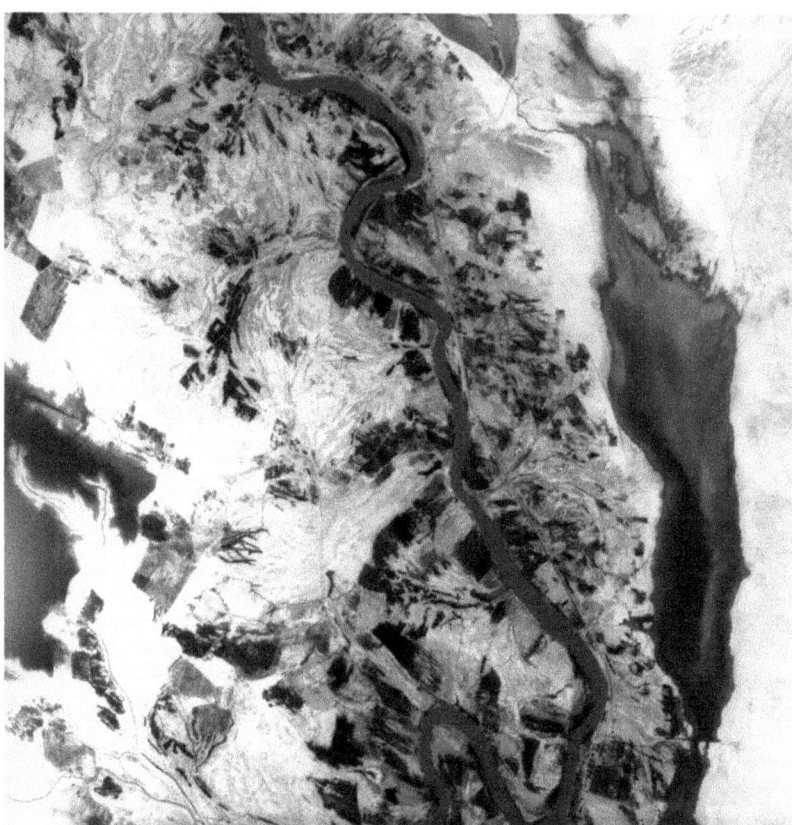

Figure 4A: Tigris south of Amara vic. Qalat Salih. The cultivated agricultural zone extends east and west of the water channel along the c. 5 km.-wide levee system. Excess water drains through light-colored tails of smaller canal levees into seasonal backswamps visible as silty, dark grey bodies. Only two centuries ago these fields were year-round marshlands. Source: KH4B_1103-1A-D041-055 (May 1968).
2X enlargement to scale ~1:75,000.

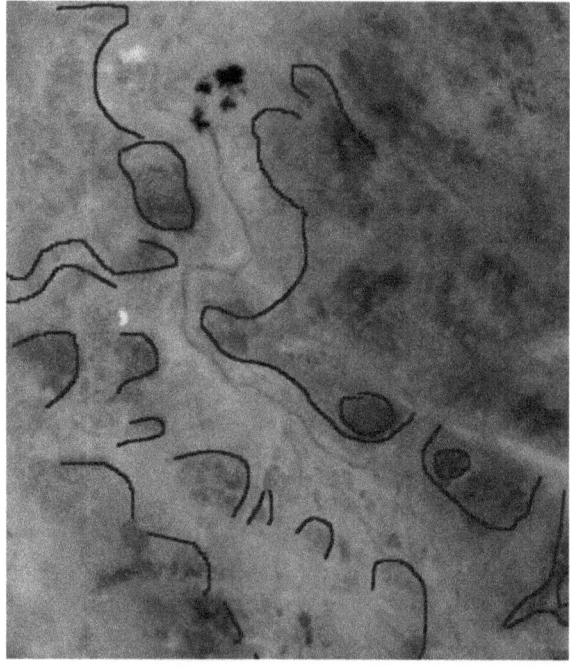

Figure 4B: Relict levee between sites WS 375–WS 400. Better-consolidated levee soils are less water-permeable, and hence appear lighter in color. Source: KH4B_1103-1A-D041-058 (May 1968).
2X enlargement to scale ~1:75,000.

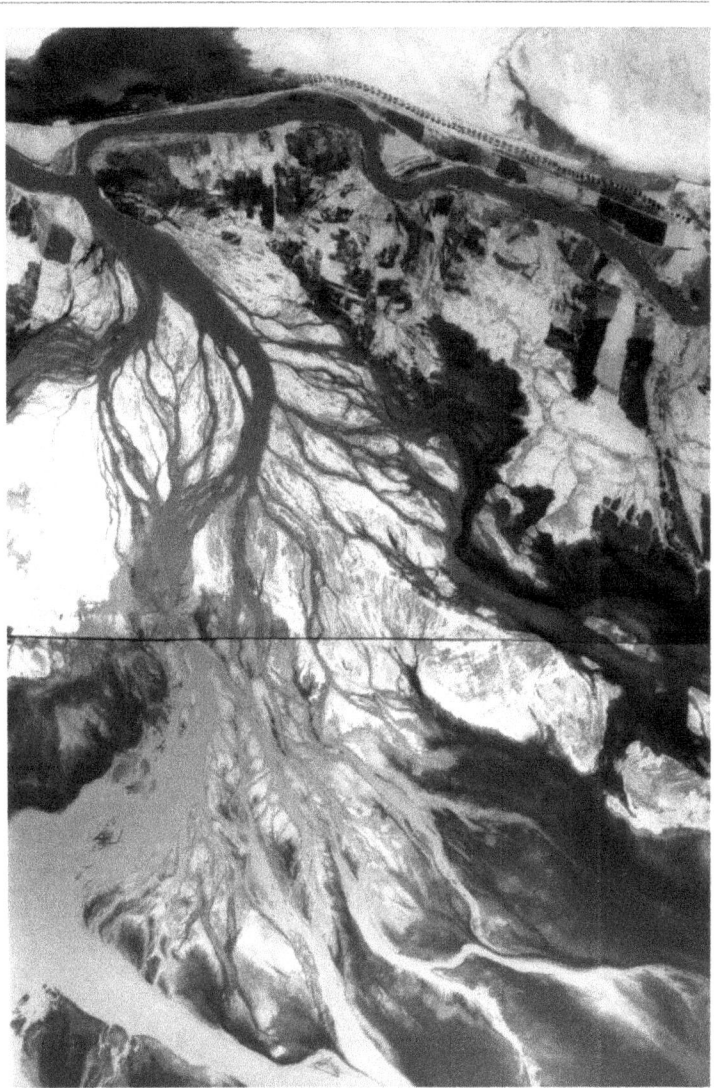

Figure 5A: The Kut barrage on the Tigris between Sheikh Sa'ad and Ali al Carbi drains excess flood discharge into Lake as Sa'adiya. The barrage maintains and augments a natural flood splay.
Source: KH4B_1103-1A-D041-056 (May 1968).
2X enlargement to scale ~1:75,000.

Figure 5B: Relict discharge splay vic. NS 1420.
Source: KH4B_1103-1A-D041-056 (May 1968).
2X enlargement to scale ~1:75,000.

Figure 6A: Modern Tigris east of al Kut, with relict (9th century AD) course to the south. Source: KH4B_1103-1A-D041-058 (May 1968). 2X enlargement to scale ~1:75,000.

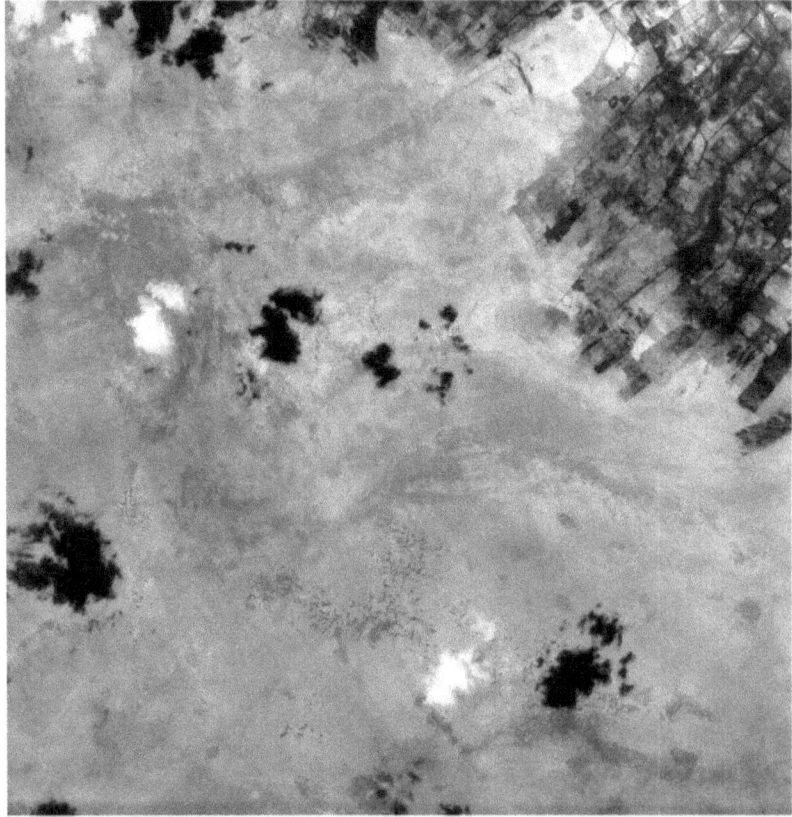

Figure 6B: A relict meander system appears to weave between cloud and shadow northeast of Nippur. While this may represent an underlying Pleistocene fluvial feature, close association of multiple Uruk period sites suggests that it continued to carry water well into the 4th millenium BCE. Source: KH4B_1103-1A-D041-054 (May 1968). 2X enlargement to scale ~1:75,000.

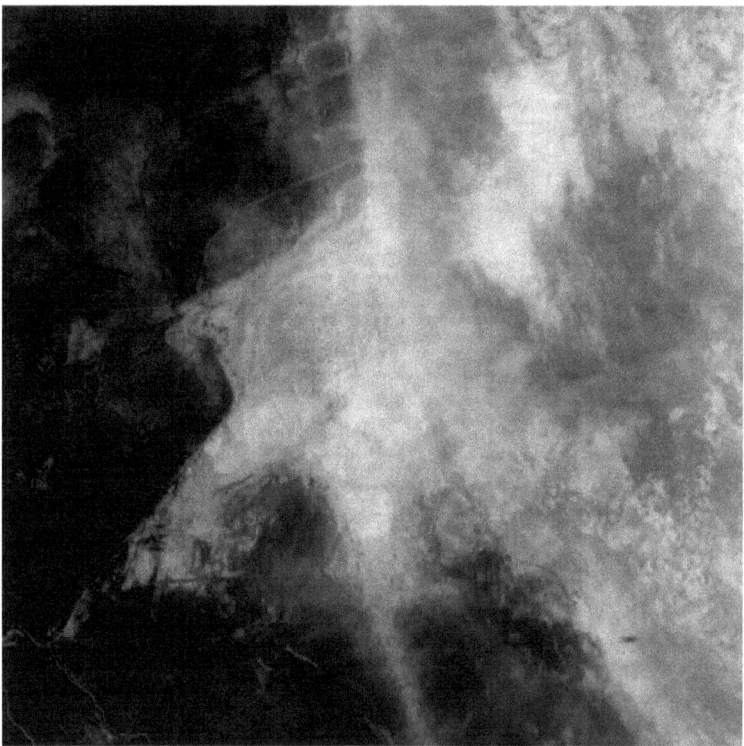

Figure 7A: Warka, surrounded by a relict "bird's foot delta" levee system revealed as late summer dries surrounding marshes and lowers the water table. Darker areas are marginally lower and wetter, lighter areas higher less permiable and dryer. Source: Corona KH4B Mission 1107-1, Frame 139 (August 1969). 4X enlargement to scale ~1:75,000.

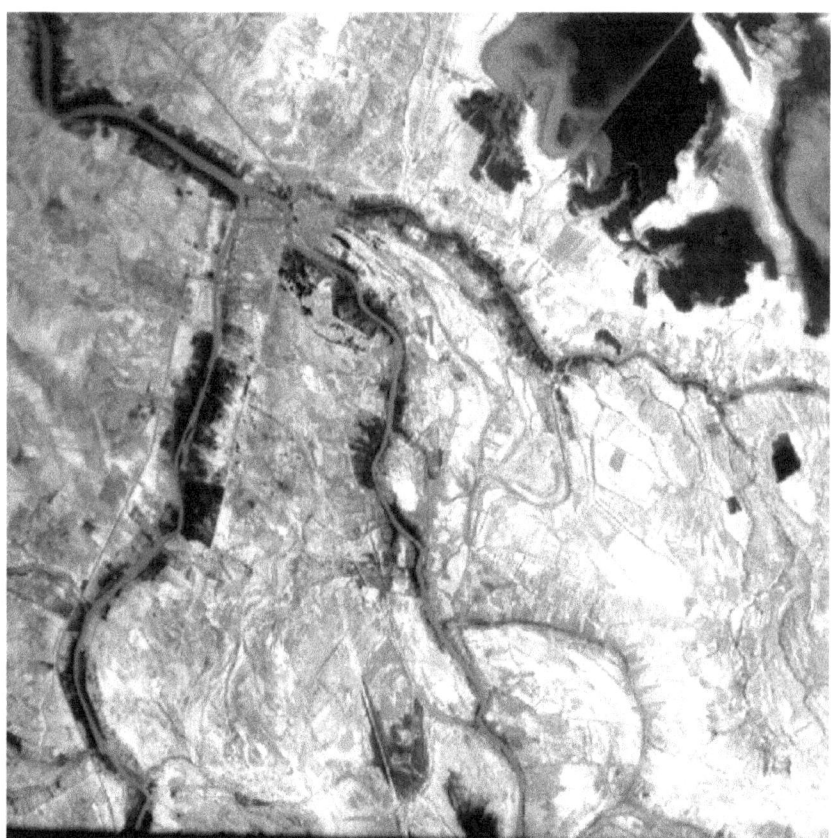

Figure 7B: Amara, straddling Tigris distributaries arrayed in a "bird's foot" delta rapidly built up and extended by riverbank rice cultivation. Source: KH4B_1103-1A-D041-056 (May 1968). 4X enlargement to scale ~1:75,000.

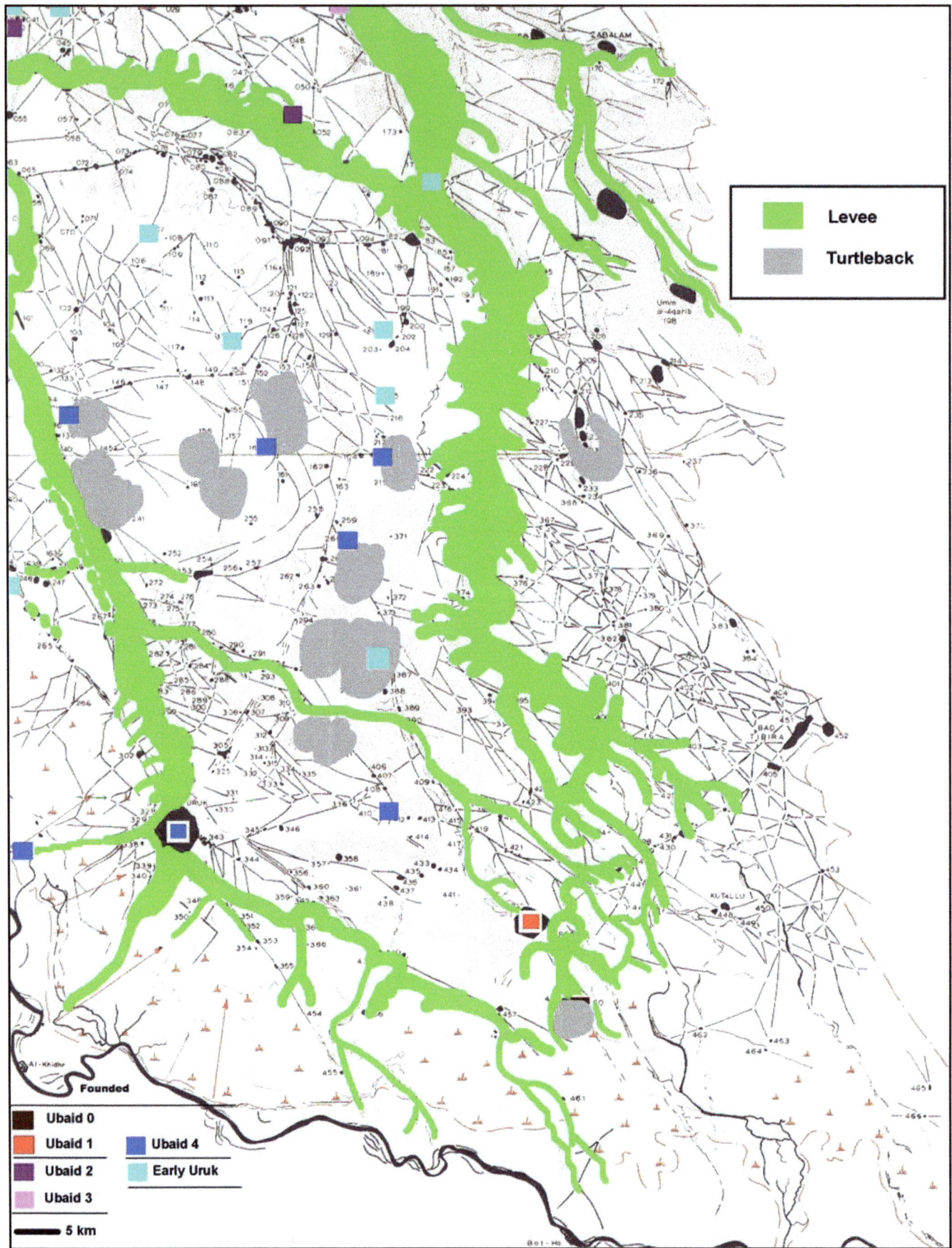

Figure 8: Warka survey area: Sites occupied during the Ubaid 4–Early Uruk periods (late 5th-early 4th millenium BCE). Legend (bottom) indicates earliest settlement period. After Adams 1981.

Figure 9: Relict levee, cut by modern canals, extends northeast-southwest through seasonal flood waters (black). Tel al-Hiba (Lagash) surmounts a Pleistocene turtleback appearing as an island to the south. Note linear sites visible along the levee, and multiple occupation mounds visible on the turtleback.
Source: USGS (Corona KH4) KH4B_1103-1A-D041-058.
2X enlargement to scale ~1:75,000.

BY LAND OR BY SEA: CHALCOLITHIC AND EARLY BRONZE AGE SETTLEMENTS IN SOUTHERN GREECE AND THE AEGEAN SEA

Daniel J. PULLEN

Abstract: The Final Neolithic, or Chalcolithic, period in southern Greece is poorly documented or understood, especially compared to the succeeding Early Bronze Age period. In spite of a paucity of information on the settlement patterns of the FN/Chalcolithic period, the examination of what we do know of these settlement patterns in comparison to those of the EBA raises the question of the relationship between the FN/Chalcolithic period and the EBA. Though there is some overlap in settlement locations between FN/Chalcolithic and EBA, in many regions of southern Greece the EB1 settlement pattern seems to follow a model of island colonization, with emphasis on the sea. This apparent discrepancy between FN/Chalcolithic and EBA also raises the question of whether there was any interest in the sea during the FN/Chalcolithic period. In this paper, what we know of FN/Chalcolithic settlement patterns are compared to those of the EBA. Data from a number of recent surface surveys in southern Greece, some coastal and some inland, are utilized in a broad regional approach to the problem.

Resumé: La période du Néolithique Final, ou Chalcolithique, en Grèce méridionale n'est pas bien connue, particulièrement quand on compare cette période avec la période suivante, le Bronze Ancien. Malgré une manque d'information sur les modèles d'établissement du Néolithique Final/Chalcolithique, l'inspection de l'information que nous avons pour ces modèles, vis-à-vis ceux du Bronze Ancien, souleve la quéstion du rapport entre le Néolithique Final/Chalcolithique et le Bronze Ancien. Malgre la superposition de quelque établissements entre le Néolithique Final/Chalcolithique et le Bronze Ancien dans plusieurs régions de la Grèce méridionale le modèle d'établissement du Bronze Ancien 1 semble à suivre un modèle de colonisation des l'îles, qui a mis l'accent sur la mer. Ce désaccord entre la période Néolithique Final/Chalcolithique et de l'Âge du Bronze ancien enlève aussi la quéstion: y avait-il quelque interêt a l'egard de la mer au Néolithique Final/Chalcolithique. Dans cet article, je compare les modèles d'établissement du Néolithique Final/Chalcolithique avec ceux du Bronze Ancien. Les données qui dérivent de plusieurs projets de prospection en Grèce méridionale, quelquns sur la côte, quelquns sur le continent, sont employés dans une large perspective régionale sur cette question.

The Final Neolithic, or Chalcolithic, period in southern Greece is poorly documented or understood, especially compared to the succeeding Early Bronze Age period. While the Early Bronze Age was seen as the result of a migration of peoples as recently as 40 years ago (e.g., Caskey 1960), more recent work has emphasized the continuity between the Final Neolithic [henceforth FN] and Early Bronze Age [EBA]. In spite of a paucity of information on the settlement patterns of the FN/Chalcolithic period, the examination of what we do know of these settlement patterns in comparison to those of EBA raises the question of the relationship between the FN/Chalcolithic period and the EBA. Though there is some overlap in settlement locations between FN/Chalcolithic and EBA, in many regions of southern Greece the EB1 settlement pattern seems to follow a model of island colonization, with emphasis on the sea. This apparent discrepancy between FN/Chalcolithic and EBA also raises the question of whether there was any interest in the sea during the FN/Chalcolithic period.

In this paper I concentrate on the problem of identifying FN settlement patterns in southern Greece, with an emphasis on two factors: proximity to the coasts and proximity to well-watered agricultural land. I utilize data from both excavations and surveys, supplemented by geomorphological and other geological data. The overall hypothesis that I am testing is whether the model of FN settlement patterns developed here contrasts greatly with the model of EBA settlement patterns in the same regions.

First of all, some terminological discussion is necessary. The term "Chalcolithic" has been employed rarely by archaeologists working in the Aegean. Most scholars working in the southern regions now employ the term "Final Neolithic," first coined by Renfrew (1972), to designate the period of time from roughly 4700/4500 – 3300/3100 B.C. (calibrated). There are, though, a number of scholars, especially Coleman (1992), Lavezzi (1983), Treuil (1983), and Zachos (1987), who employ the term "Late Neolithic II" in order to maintain the traditional tripartite divisions of chronological periods, harking back to Arthur Evans' model of cultural evolution. A few scholars use the term "Aegina-Attica-Kephala culture," but this term has a restricted geographical meaning. Recently, however, arguments have been put forward by Douzougli (1998: 127–131) and Maran (1998: 7) to employ the term "Chalcolithic" in southern Greece in order to recognize the emerging importance of metallurgy in this period as well as changes from the preceding Late Neolithic period. While I am certainly sympathetic to these arguments by Douzougli and Maran for employing the term chalcolithic, I would prefer to use it as a cultural designation, and not employ yet another chronological term where there is still disagreement over terminology and sequences. Thus in this paper I use the term "Final Neolithic" to refer to the period of time, ca.

4700/4500 to 3300/3100 BC (calibrated), in southern Greece. For the Early Bronze Age, I employ the term Early Helladic in keeping with the practice among Aegean archaeologists.

The eastern portion of the Peloponnese is relatively well covered by surface surveys, at least compared to other regions of Greece. Published data are available from intensive surveys in the southern Argolid, Methana, Laconia, and the Berbati Valley (Fig. 1); data in press from the Nemea Valley and the Asea Valley surveys, the directors of which I would like to thank for information utilized in this paper; and the current Eastern Korinthia Archaeological Survey of which I serve as co-director. Extensive surveys have been conducted in several regions including Arcadia, the Argolid, and Laconia. And excavation material of the period is available from several sites including Franchthi Cave, Halieis, Prosymna and Aria in the Argolid, and Kolonna on Aegina, though only at Franchthi do we have a sequence from Late Neolithic to Final Neolithic. Severely lacking, however, is a good stratified sequence covering the Final Neolithic to Early Bronze Age. At Tsoungiza, for example, we have material from both the Final Neolithic and the Early Helladic I periods, but the material derives from a few pits and closed deposits, and does not provide a detail stratigraphic profile. As a consequence our ceramic chronology is not very good. While the quality of data from these various types of archaeological work vary considerably, we do have a broad coverage of a fairly large area.

regions. A small number of LN sherds, ca. 15, from no more than 4 or 5 sites, was reported by me for the southern Argolid (Pullen 1995). Vitelli (1999: 98 and 104 n. 4) in her publication of the Franchthi LN and FN pottery states that of the proposed LN sherds "none is compellingly LN," and suggests that most would not be out of place in the Final Neolithic period. The few vessels found at Franchthi Cave (and unlike the preceding Early and Middle Neolithic, use of Franchthi in the LN period was **only** in the cave and not on the adjoining shore outside) suggest to Vitelli a limited and sporadic usage of the cave. If Vitelli's suggested redating of the southern Argolid survey LN pottery to the Final Neolithic period is accepted, then this reduces LN settlement in that region to just Franchthi Cave. In the ongoing Eastern Korinthia Archaeological survey we have identified one site with Middle and Late Neolithic pottery (among other periods), but no FN, approximately 3 km from Gonia, also known to have Middle and Late Neolithic settlement. In the Argolid Aria, Prosymna, Kephalari, Argos, and several other sites have produced evidence for the Late Neolithic period. (Fig. 2). Thus we seem to have a LN pattern of occupation of well watered, large plains or their margins, such as the Argolid and Corinthian plains, but little to no occupation of interior (Nemea, Berbati, Asea) or poorly watered (southern Argolid) regions. Settlements in the poorly watered regions would have relied on spring-fed agriculture (Jameson et al. 1994: 343), such as suggested for Franchthi.

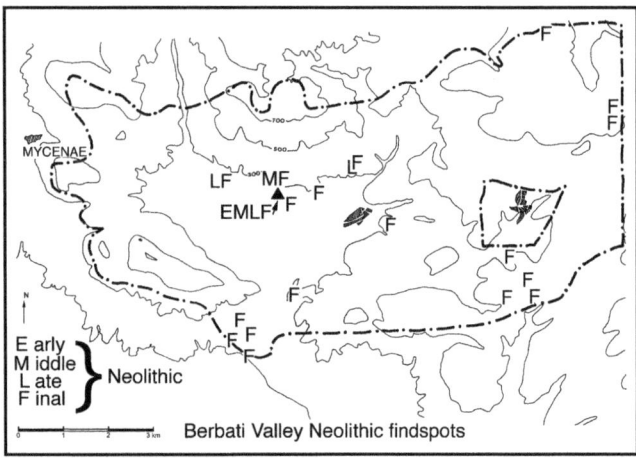

Fig. 1 Berbati Valley Neolithic findspots

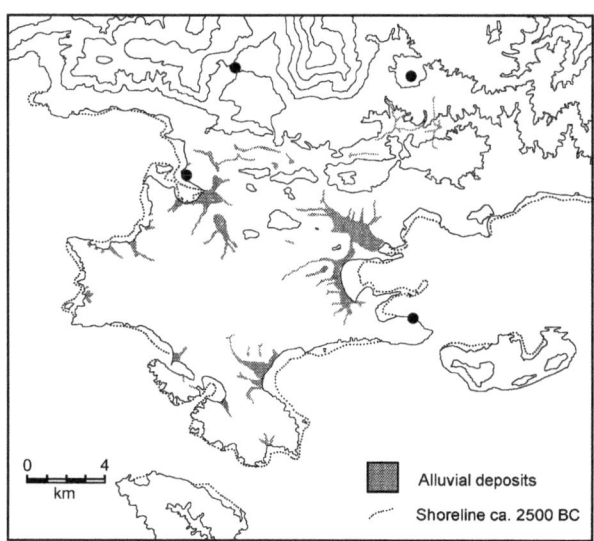

Fig. 2 Southern Argolid. Sites of Late Neolithic period

THE LATE NEOLITHIC PERIOD

Demoule and Perlès (1993) in their masterful review of the Greek Neolithic emphasize the changes in FN settlement patterns from those of the preceding Late Neolithic period in southern Greece. Characteristic of these regional patterns are the increase in the number of usually small sites and a continued, if not increased, use of caves for occupation.

Virtually no "truly diagnostic" (Vitelli 1999: 98) LN sherds are reported from surveys in Berbati (Johnson 1996: 274–5), Nemea (Cherry et al 1988: 174–5), or Asea, though at least one site with LN occupation is attested in each of those

THE FINAL NEOLITHIC

In the Final Neolithic we see a great increase in the number of sites and a variety of locations for these sites in nearly all regions of the eastern Peloponnese. In the southern Argolid 38 findspots have been identified with ceramics of the FN period (Pullen 1995), though 33 of those spots have fewer than 5 sherds dated to the FN. Jameson et al. (1994) include only 8 definite and 6 probable sites of the FN period for a total of 14. Two of the 14 sites have been excavated, Franchthi Cave and the acropolis of Halieis where FN was found in a few cuttings but mostly mixed with later material (Pullen 2000). Several of the FN sites are caves or rock shelters: D3 (Dhidhima), E14 (Mouzaki), G9 (Kotena), Franchthi, but the remaining are open-air. The dispersal of small FN settlements into areas on or near deep brown soils suggests a shift to rain-dependent agriculture (Jameson et al. 1994: 347), while the presence of several sites in high upland areas suggests increased importance of pastoralism. Indeed this period of time is exactly when the Secondary Products Revolution, first expounded by Sherratt (1981), takes off in Greece. (Fig. 3)

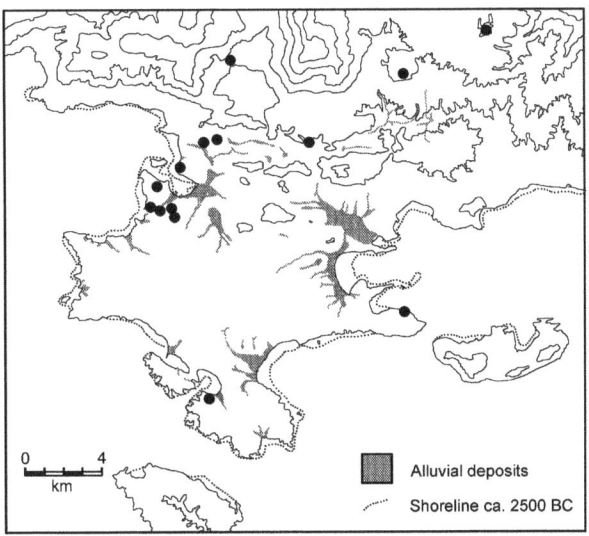

Fig. 3 Southern Argolid. Sites of Final Neolithic period

In the Berbati Valley, a picture similar to that in the southern Argolid obtains (Johnson 1996). From a pattern of one EN site to 2 MN sites, in the FN 19 certain and 4 possible sites are found. These FN sites are found not only in areas of well-watered agricultural land in the valley or along its margins, but also in uplands where agriculture would have been rain-dependent or at even higher elevations where pastoralism would have been practiced.

This pattern of expanded settlement in the FN period derived from surface survey masks the problem of the long duration of the FN period (at least one thousand years), the recognition of several phases within the FN period, and the contemporaneity of the settlements. Phelps (1975) first divided the long FN period into two major ceramic phases, but finer resolutions have not always been possible. Much of the ceramics of the FN period is coarse ware, and those surface treatments which do appear (e.g., crusting, pattern burnish) are often poorly preserved. For this reason a number of survey sites or findspots have been generally dated to the FN period or even to the FN-EH I period, as Early Bronze 1 ceramics from surface surveys often are similar to FN. From the southern Argolid survey, the majority of FN sites were also used in EH I, complicating the picture. And the EH I period is not well understood either, compared to the later EH II period, as few excavations have revealed more than remains in deep soundings. Vitelli's (1999) comparisons of the excavated Franchthi Cave FN ceramics with those from the southern Argolid survey and Halieis points to this problem. She notes few comparisons between Franchthi Cave and the survey or Halieis FN material and concludes that the material from the survey and Halieis is later in the FN period. I too concluded that the Halieis FN material has more connections with the following EH I period than with earlier Neolithic traditions.

If we do then have a large increase in the number of sites represented in the long-lasting FN period, this raises the question of whether we have a settlement pattern of shifting occupation or whether we truly have multiple contemporaneous settlements. Around Franchthi Cave (less than 3 km distance) are found at least 7 of the 14 identified FN sites from the southern Argolid survey. Five of these sites are located within one km or less of another, along the low hills surround the Koiladha Bay opposite Franchthi, suggesting a pattern of shifting occupation over the centuries represented by the FN period. Rutter (1983) suggested that for surveys one apply a correction factor of the number of sites per century represented of the period. If we apply such a correction factor to the southern Argolid and Berbati survey results, we find that the apparent great increase in number of sites is not so great. Still, there is an increase over the preceding LN period in both regions and there is a significant shift to more "marginal" locations

THE EARLY HELLADIC I PERIOD

The EH I period is becoming better understood over the last couple of decades, thanks to work by Douzougli, Weisshaar, Wiencke, and my excavations at Tsoungiza. The so-called Talioti phase, identified throughout the northeast Peloponnese, was originally defined as the end of the EH I period, but Maran (1998: 9) has recently suggested that the Talioti phase is the entire EH I period. This suggestion helps fill the gap between the later Final Neolithic sites such as Halieis and the EH I sites such as Tsoungiza.

In terms of settlement patterns, there is a decided change between those of the FN period and those of the EH I period. While many FN sites continue to see usage in the EH I period, a much larger number of EH I sites is known. And the EH I sites are located in many more environmental settings than the FN sites. Regionally there are differences, however, with settlements in coastal regions increasing at the expense of interior regions.

In the Berbati Valley the absolute number of findspots identified with EH I material decreases to 11 from 19 with FN material (Fig. 4). But when factoring in the site per century correction factor, EH I sites increase slightly (1.9 sites per century vs. 2.75/century). More important is the change in where the sites are located: only 6 FN sites continue with EH I material (though an additional 4 FN sites have EH II, but

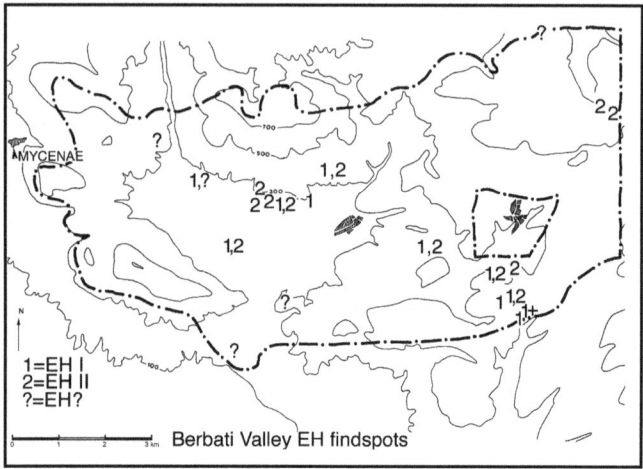

Fig. 4 Berbati Valley EH findspots

EXPLANATIONS: TOWARDS A MODEL OF CHALCOLITHIC SETTLEMENT

So why this change between Late and Final Neolithic and between Final Neolithic and EH I? The Berbati team (Wells and Runnels 1995: 454) believes the expansion co-occurs with a period of erosion, the result of clearing land for agriculture and pasturage on the hillslopes. Intensification of agriculture and the necessity for clearing more land leads to more erosion. The ox-drawn plow was introduced no later than the early part of the EH II period, as seen by our discovery of terracotta models of yoked oxen at Tsoungiza (Pullen 1992), and perhaps earlier if the dating of the erosion in Berbati and northern Argolid is upheld.

not EH I material). Abandoned are the sites high in uplands and hillslopes. Low hills and the lower slopes seem to be the preferred locations for EH I sites.

In the southern Argolid a different picture obtains (Fig. 5). 25 certain and 7 probable sites of EH I have been identified (though a total of 42 sites produced sherds of EH I date). Applying Rutter's correction factor to these numbers we see an increase in 1.4 sites per century to 8/century for sites, 3.8 sites per century to 10.5/century for findspots. Either way there is a substantial increase in numbers. Like in the Berbati Valley, different environmental settings see settlement in the EH I period. Coastal settings, valley bottoms, and low hillslopes are heavily utilized.

We also see in the Early Bronze Age the development of a hierarchy of sites, based on size of scatter and range of artifacts. Whether this perceived hierarchy in EH I has meaning for social or economic organization is unclear, but by EH II there can be no doubt that sites like Lerna and Fournoi dominate their immediate, and perhaps further, regions.

Another suggested explanation has been a switch to external markets, via the sea. Certainly this is plausible for the EH I period when we see settlements placed near the coast and elsewhere. Runnels and van Andel (1987, van Andel and Runnels 1988) have connected the growth in external markets, and hence coastal settlement, with the Secondary Productions Revolution, and hence diversification and intensification in agriculture and pastoralism. Runnels and van Andel suggest that the Secondary Products Revolution as seen in the Argolid or Berbati Valley is the **result** of expansion in seaborne trade. But the settlement patterns do not seem to support this. Coastal settlement sand overseas connections are features **later** than the expansion and diversification of agriculture and pasturage as seen in the Neolithic settlement pattern in Berbati. But I have a suspicion that the poorly defined ceramic chronology for the FN period is obscuring the picture.

At this point I cannot provide an explanation beyond a simple model of wealth intensification, where an increased desire for non-local materials (such as metals) leads to intensification in agriculture, etc., This wealth intensification model builds upon structural changes introduced by innovations lumped together as a monolithic package call the "Secondary Products revolution." Just as V.G. Childe's "Neolithic Revolution" has now been shown to be a complex set of changes over a long period of time, perhaps too the term Secondary Products Revolution should be changed to Evolution.

I see three avenues of research, which may help here.

One is to conduct more survey in coastal regions to look for more LN, FN, and EH I material. This is one of the goals of EKAS. Unfortunately, delays by the Greek Ministry of Culture in issuing permits in 1999 and 2001 has reduced our projected total of 18 weeks of fieldwork over 3 years to a mere 8 weeks. An additional season of fieldwork in 2002 will rectify the situation.

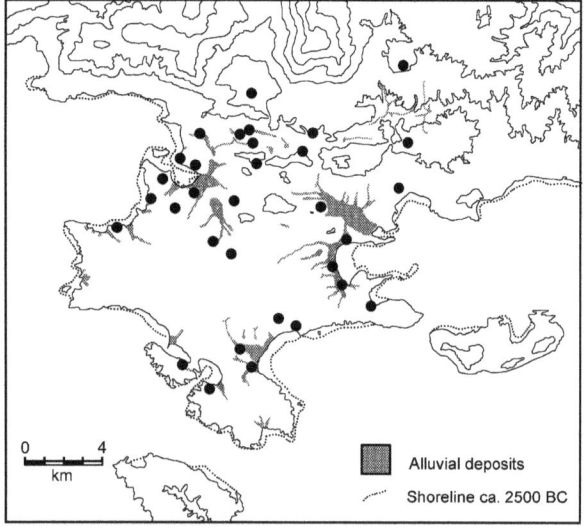

Fig. 5 Southern Argolid. Sites of Early Helladic I period

Related to the first is an increased use of GIS to better explain the environmental settings of individual sites on a regional basis. The EKAS GIS has helped us tremendously in this area, and we hope to test some of our predictions. GIS, however, needs to be applied on a larger scale, integrating coastal and inland regions.

The third avenue is to refine the chronology of the FN period. It is here where the idea of "Chalcolithic" as a cultural term is important. The long FN period, 10 to 16 centuries in length, has been defined in large part by ceramics. Many of us have noted changes occur at the end of the FN period. In the Saronic Gulf regions there is a major contact between the mainland and the Cyclades as seen in ceramics. I propose that we look at not just ceramic styles but also at other cultural patterns. These "Chalcolithic" patterns included abandonment of cave use except for pastoral purposes; beginning of metals, usually markers of wealth or status such as daggers and jewelry, and new rituals that create bonds within the community beyond the family. Thus the common FN "scoop" as found at Tsoungiza would make an appropriate drinking vessel for such a ritual. By EH I, ritual vessels become more elaborate, as seen in the fruitstand.

And also of great importance in the development of the later Bronze Age is the increased emphasis on the sea. The Chalcolithic hydrostrategy of southern Greece, then, is firmly based on the sea.

Bibliography

CASKEY, J.L., 1960, The Early Helladic period in the Argolid. *Hesperia* 29, p. 285–303.

CHERRY, J.F., DAVIS, J.L., DEMITRACK, A., MANTZOURANI, E., STRASSER, T.F., & TALALAY, L.E., 1988, Archaeological survey in an artifact-rich landscape: a Middle Neolithic example from Nemea, Greece. *American Journal of Archaeology* 92, p. 159–176.

COLEMAN, J.E., 1992, Greece, the Aegean, and Cyprus. In *Chronologies in Old World archaeology* (third edition), edited by R.W. Ehrich. Chicago: University of Chicago Press, vol. 1, p. 247–288 and vol. 2, p. 203–230.

DEMOULE, J.P., & PERLES, C., 1993, The Greek Neolithic: a new review. *Journal of World Prehistory* 7, p. 355–416.

ΝΤΟΥΖΟΥΛΗ, Α., 1998, Αρια Αργόλιδος· χειροποιή κεραμική της Νεότερης Νεολιθικής και της Χαλκολιθικής Περιοδου (Αρχαιολογικόν Δελτίον, Δημοσιεύματα 66). Αθήνα· Υπουργειο Πολιτισμου.

JAMESON, M.H., RUNNELS, C., and VAN ANDEL, T., 1994, *A Greek countryside: the Southern Argolid from prehistory to the present day*. Stanford: Stanford University Press.

JOHNSON, M., 1996, The Berbati-Limnes Archaeological Survey: The Neolithic period. In *The Berbati-Limnes archaeological survey 1988-1990*, edited by B. Wells and C. Runnels (*Skrifter utgivna av Svenska Institutet i Athen, 4°*, 44). Stockholm: The Swedish Institute, p. 37–73.

LAVEZZI, J.C., 1978, Prehistoric investigations at Corinth. *Hesperia* 47, p. 402–451.

MARAN, J., 1998, *Kulturwandel auf dem griechischen Festland und den Kykladen im späten 3. Jahrtausend v. Chr.* (*Universitätsforschungen zur prähistorischen Archäologie* 53). Bonn: Verlag R. Hablet.

PHELPS, W.W., 1975, *The Neolithic sequence in southern Greece*. Unpublished Ph.D. thesis, University of London.

PULLEN, D.J., 1992, Ox and plow in the Early Bronze Age Aegean. *American Journal of Archaeology* 96, p. 45–54.

PULLEN, D.J., 1995, Pottery of the Neolithic, Early Helladic I and Early Helladic II periods. In *Artifact and assemblage: Finds from a regional survey of the Southern Argolid, Greece, vol. 1: The prehistoric and Early Iron Age pottery and the lithic artifacts*, by C. Runnels, D.J. Pullen, and S.H. Langdon. Stanford: Stanford University Press, p. 6–42.

PULLEN, D.J., 2000, The prehistoric remains of the Acropolis at Halieis: a Final Report. *Hesperia* 69, p. 133–187.

RENFREW, C., 1972, *The emergence of civilisation*, London: Metheun.

RUNNELS, C.N. and VAN ANDEL, T.H., 1987, The evolution of settlement in the Southern Argolid, Greece: an economic explanation. *Hesperia* 56, p. 303–34.

RUTTER, J.B., 1983, Some thoughts on the analysis of ceramic data generated by site surveys. In *Archaeological Survey in the Mediterranean Area*, edited by D.R. Keller, and D.W. Rupp (*British Archaeological Reports, International Series* 155). Oxford: BAR, p. 137–42.

SHERRATT, A.G., 1981, Plow and pastoralism: aspects of the secondary products revolution. In *Pattern of the past: studies in honour of David Clarke*, edited by I. Hodder, G. Isaac, and N. Hammond. Cambridge, p. 261–305.

TREUIL, R., 1983, *Le Néolithique et le Bronze Ancien égéens. Les problèmes stratigraphiques et chronologiques, les techniques, les hommes* (*Bibliothèque des Écoles françaises d'Athènes et de Rome*, 248). Paris: de Boccard/ Athènes: École française d'Athènes.

VAN ANDEL, T.H., & RUNNELS, C.N., 1988, An essay on the 'emergence' of civilization in the Aegean world. *Antiquity* 62, p. 234–47.

VITELLI, K.D., 1999, *Franchthi Neolithic pottery, vol. 2* (*Excavations at Franchthi Cave, Greece*, fasc. 10). Bloomington: Indiana University Press.

WELLS, B., and RUNNELS, C.N., 1995, *The Berbati-Limnes archaeological survey 1988-1990* (*Skrifter utgivna av Svenska Institutet i Athen, 4°*, 44). Stockholm: The Swedish Institute.

ZACHOS, C., 1987, *Ayios Dhimitrios, a prehistoric settlement in the southwestern Peloponnesos: the Neolithic and Early Helladic periods*. Unpublished Ph.D. dissertation, Boston University.

DOMESTIC WATER MATTERS
(FINAL NEOLITHIC - EARLY BRONZE AGE GREECE)

Christina MARANGOU

Abstract : Water issues were obviously present in the Chalcolithic environment. Human responses to the presence (or absence) of water may be positive or negative. Water and its resources are used or exploited in everyday intra-site routine. Economy and technology, and presumably social life bear its influence. Water procurement or use, even contact with it might be connected to particular gender, or social groups, but relative evidence is scanty. The paper examines various aspects of human reaction to water used in everyday life, illustrating various aquatic influences in technical, economic and symbolic areas of life in the Final Neolithic and Early Bronze Age. Examples come mostly from Greece.

Resumé : Il est évident que la question de l'eau se posait dans l'environnement Chalcolithique. La réponse de l'homme à la présence (ou absence) de l'eau peut être positive ou négative. L'eau et ses ressources sont utilisées ou exploitées dans la routine quotidienne des sites. L'économie et la technologie, et éventuellement la vie sociale portent son influence. L'approvisionnement en eau ou son utilisation, même le contact avec l'eau pourraient être lies à l'un des sexes ou à des groupes sociaux, mais les témoignages relatifs sont maigres. Cet article examine différents aspects de la réaction de l'homme à l'eau utilisée dans la vie quotidienne, illustrant différentes influences aquatiques sur les domaines technique, économique et symbolique de la vie au Néolithique Final et au Bronze Ancien. Les exemples viennent surtout de Grèce

INTRODUCTION

Apart from the fact that settlements were often located in the vicinity of water sources, in particular near springs or along streams, evidence about domestic water supply in the Neolithic is scarce, although it may show surprising technological progress. Wells are attested already at the end of the 9th - beginning of the 8th mill. BC in Cyprus (Peltenburg 2001; Guilaine 2001), in Middle Neolithic Attica (Pantelidou 1991: 104-108) and Thasos (Papadopoulos *et al.* 2002: 28, fig. 2, pl. 4), and in Final Neolithic (FN, Chalcolithic) Attica, Chios and Crete. More substantial evidence comes from Early Bronze Age (EBA) sites in various regions of Greece. The links between the end of the Neolithic and the beginning of the Bronze Age (ca 3000 BC depending on regions) are obscure and diversified (Manning 1995: 41, 43, 168-169). The present paper considers water procurement during this span of time according to available evidence in Greece (ca last half of 4th mill. – 1st half of 3d mill. BC).

EMPORIO (LATE NEOLITHIC (LN)-EBA, ISLAND OF CHIOS, NORTH-EAST AEGEAN)

The earliest occupation deposits at the Emporio hill, on the southeastern coast of Chios, lay below the present water table due to the rise in sea level. The early (phase X, LN) settlement may have only occupied a space of relatively flat ground by the harbour. Water and protection from wind and weather afforded by the steep slope of the hill above it possibly attracted settlers, who may have found a spring on the site of a later well. Although there are no springs now, drinkable water is easily reached by wells (Hood: 1981: 85, 89, 93).

Most of the main excavated area (A) had been occupied in most periods by successive walls, which had surrounded a well and flanked the approach leading down the slope to it from the E. In period IX (LN), two walls might have formed the inner and outer skins of a defensive rampart, 2,50 m. thick. Another wall (width: 1-1,5 m., pres. height 0,85 m.) was the first of a series of massive walls, built descending the slope from E to W to surround the area of the well. X-IX walls could be an extension of the fortification of the settlement in order to protect the inhabitants and ensure the precious for survival water, according to Aslanis (1998: 111). Hood (1981: 93, 97) suggests that the periods IX-VIII walls seem to have been constructed, not for defence, but in order to hold back the accumulating debris of the settlement from invading the spring area. The comparatively low proportion of jugs in relation to vases of other types from levels of X-VIII in contrast to VII-VI and later may be due to the fact that early deposits consisted mostly of occupation debris from houses (Hood: 1981: 273).

Probably during period VIII (Fig. 1) (LN: Alram-Stern 1996: 479; Kum Tepe IA1/2-B1/2: Parzinger 1993: 263) the assumed spring was replaced by a well. Houses were built outside the walls surrounding the site of the well, and their floors were eventually at a higher level than that of the ground inside the walls. These arrangements may have resembled those in the Near East, where, as the occupation debris of the settlement accumulated, an original spring or well protected by retaining walls eventually came to be at the

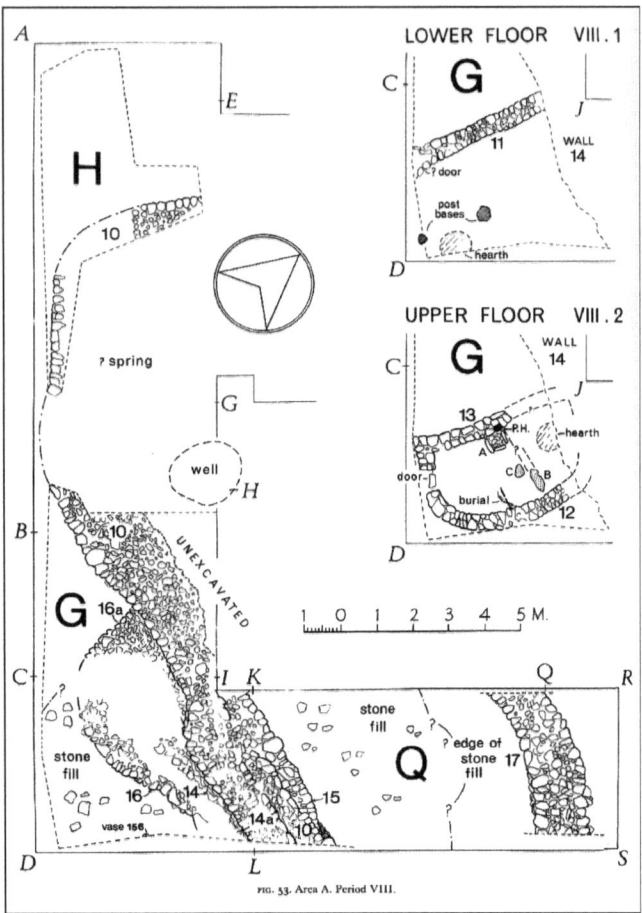

Fig. 1

325). Most are in LBBW, the smaller ones, in FBBW (Hood 1981: 323). Bases of jugs and jars were normally flat or sunk (Hood 1981: 345), thus easier to steady (see further).

In VI (Fig. 2) (VI-V: EBA, Thermi I-III, Poliochni IIa, Troy Ia-c, Kum Tepe 1C: Parzinger 1993: 268; Manning 1995: 75) a massive, defensive-looking wall is constructed on the southern side of the approach leading to the well (width: 1,80-3m; max. height 1,30 m.), while, on the northern side (steep slope towards the harbour) a new parapet was slighter. In connection with the building of the wall the mouth of the well was surrounded with a pavement (diam.: 5,50m.) of large rounded beach stones and it may be now that the well was lined with stones (ellipse diam. 2,30x2,10m; Hood 1981: 106, 109, 134, figs. 58, 59). Ultimately the wall was destroyed, the debris pushed over and the road became level with the top of the slighted wall, perhaps in conjunction with a plan to expand the settlement and build houses round the well. As in VII, VI deposits contained abundant jug fragments (LBBW and FBBW, including with white-painted decoration), mostly from the layers of the VI roadways, but also from rubbish above the wall debris (Hood 1981: 103, 110-111, 114, 350, 352, 354). The high proportion of jug fragments in levels of VII-VI (and later) may mean that jugs had been used in connection with rites of breakage of vessels used for containing water around the spring or well (Hood 1981: 273, 323).

A rectangular post hole (22 x 16 cm) with traces of carbonised wood, found on the edge of the platform round the well and just to the west of it, might have served as the upright for a bottom of a walled pit with steps winding down into it (Hood: 1981: 93, 97). Later, however, the approach was transformed into an extensive raised platform, sloping down steeply from E to W, perhaps in conjunction with the replacement of the spring by a well, and a path or road was made leading down to it (Hood: 1981: 103, 105, fig. 53). Instead of the common in later periods jugs, obviously used in connection with water, vases of other shapes, such as jars of type 41 in various sizes, common in VIII, may have been used (Hood 1981: 241, 258, 273).

In VII (Chalcolithic: Alram-Stern 1996: 479; Kum Tepe IB3-4, Poliochni Black, Agora: Parzinger 1993: 265; Manning 1995: 76), the road (width: 2,20-2,30m.) is a raised causeway, descending the slope, flanked by two walls (width: 0,60-0,90m, max. height: 0,80m). This system remained in use till the end of IV. The well may have been surrounded by a wall. When the area was raised to make a platform for a more massive road, the fill included a large amount of broken pottery, particularly jugs (Hood 1981: 94, fig. 57). Vast numbers of vertical handles of jugs or jars from VII-VI come mostly from light brown burnished ware (LBBW) and fine black burnished ware (FBBW) jug fragments, abundant round the well (Hood 1981: 340-341) among the pebbles of the roadway and the well platform (Hood 1981: 323). The shapes of the jugs, the commonest vase made in LBBW, and their surface colour, might suggest that they were copies of gourds, reproducing the original yellowish colour (Hood 1981: 304). Jugs size ranged from less than 10 cm in height (Hood 1981: 327, fig. 153, no 639) to very large examples (Hood 1981:

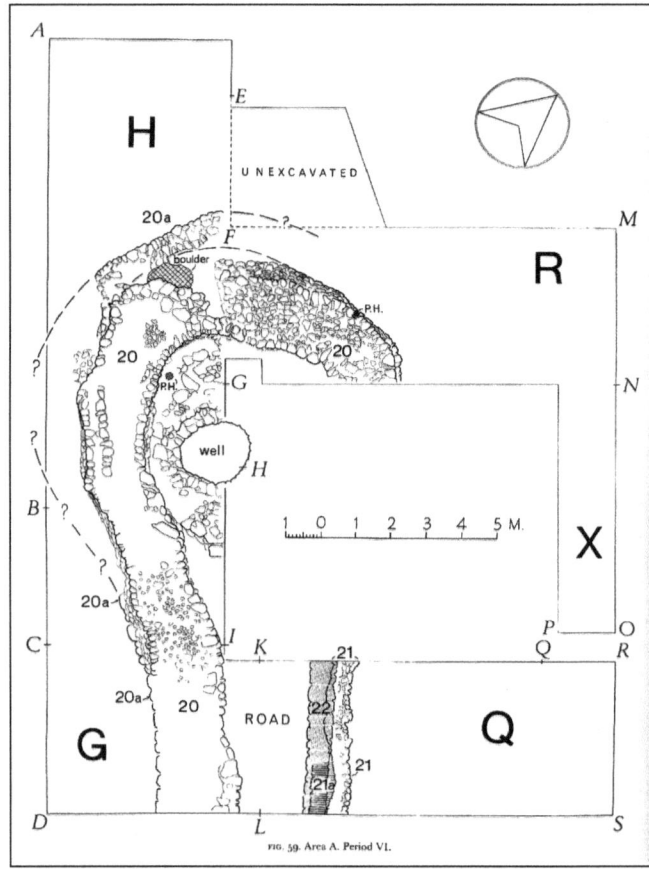

Fig. 2

balanced pole used like a crane to draw vessels of water from the well (*shaduf*) (a bucket/pot is used on one extremity of the pole, a counterbalancing weight (stone) on the other), if the post-hole, at one metre from the edge of the well, was not very close for such an arrangement (Hood 1981: 110). This simple water-lifting device cannot be used in very deep wells; attested in Classical Greece, it is still used in Greece and Asia (Hellmann 1992: 183). It was represented on Lagash seals (middle of the 3rd mill.BC) (Bethemont 1982: 10), and in 3rd millennium BC Egypt and it is mentioned in the Hammourabi code (first half of 2nd mill. BC) (Bonnin 1984: 254-256, fig. 13-3). Post-holes suggesting the use of such a device were found by a stone-lined well in Hacilar II (Aurenche 1982: 33).

V and IV may have lasted a long time and occupation apparently extended to other areas (Hood 1981: 89, 111). A path now led up to the platform round the well from the area below it to the west through a gap in the ruined wall (Hood 1981: 112, fig. 60). The spaces E and W of the well were occupied by houses in V (Hood 1981: 94); in IV they have encroached upon the area round the well (Hood 1981: 94), the doorway of House IV having direct access to it (Hood 1981: 118, 120). A narrow path between houses mounted to the platform (Hood, 1981, 124). Access to the well was now possible from the W as well as the E (Hood, 1981, 94). As the IV settlement (Thermi I-III, Poliochni Blue adv., Troy Id-IIf, Myrtos I-II: Parzinger 1993: 269, 270) was destroyed by fire (C14 2580 BC: Hood 1982: 725; 2621-2285: Manning 1995: 171), lots of vases were recovered from above the floors of the houses (Hood 1981: 94, 111): from House IV, 62 vases (apart from pithoi), among which 26 bowls and 13 jugs; from the excavated parts of Houses VII and VIII, respectively, 58 mostly fine ware vases including 45 bowls, 3 askoi and 7 jugs; and 35 complete vases, including 22 bowls and 3 jugs (Hood 1981: 354-356). Emporio V-IV jugs height varies (<20 - >30 cm, average 20 cm; Hood 1981: 386). An important number of jugs come in particular from House IV, which had direct access to the well platform.

In III (III-II/I: Poliochni Red, Troy IIg-III, Myrtos II; Parzinger 1993: 271; Manning 1995: 78) the ruins were filled with stones to make a platform in almost all the excavated area, the well being left in one corner of it (Hood 1981: 94, fig. 65). A narrow passage permitted access to the platform from the north, barred by a gate (there is a slot for a wooden beam in the wall) (Hood 1981: 94, 134). The platform was extended (II) and partly occupied by houses (Hood 1981: 94). Jugs fragments are abundant as before (Hood 1982: 447). The well was filled and closed during (I) and may have been replaced by a new well elsewhere (Hood 1981: 94, 134).

ATHENS AGORA (FN, ATTICA, CENTRAL GREECE)

Not surprisingly, considering the continuous occupation of the area, no actual prehistoric settlement was uncovered in the Agora of Athens. Evidence about the Neolithic and Early and Middle Bronze Ages comes from wells, pits and bothroi (Immerwahr 1971: vii). Neolithic traces are found essentially on the slopes of the Acropolis, particularly the south, north and northwest (Immerwahr 1971: 4). On the northwest slopes, in an area below and to the east and west of the classical Klepsydra fountain, not far from the caves of the north slope, numerous shallow wells were designed to collect water from the water table which fed the Klepsydra (Immerwahr 1971: 1, pl. 91; Camp 1977: 33). Not only the defensive capabilities of the rocky outcropping of the Acropolis but specifically the number and diversity of is water sources, and thus secure water supply, attracted settlers (Crouch 1993: 255). Pottery from twenty wells (twenty-one: Camp 2002: 8; cf. Immerwahr 1982: 60).) dates them in the latest phases of the Neolithic period (FN), ca 3200-3000 BC (Immerwahr 1971: 21; Camp 1977: 33; 3000-2800 BC: Camp 2002: 8). From the numerous attempts to insure water supply one must presume some near-by settlement, either in and around the caves just to the east (Camp 1977: 33-34) or farther down the slope, the caves possibly having been used as rock shelters, for burial or for worship (Immerwahr 1971: 1). On the hill slope below the Odeion of Herodes Atticus and near the Asklepieion several Neolithic pits gave close parallels for the pottery of the wells (Immerwahr 1971: 3).

The wells, roughly circular in plan, often tapering toward the bottom (diam.: 0,85-1,0 m., depth: 3,30-7,70 m.), were crudely cut and unlined. When a large or hard boulder was encountered, digging was abandoned or the shaft diverted (Immerwahr 1971: 1; Camp 1977: 34). The contents of the wells could not be clearly divided into use and dump fill (Immerwahr 1982: 61), both FN; the interval between them may not be long (Immerwahr 1971: 2, 9). The scrappier material may be considered dump fill, after the wells ran dry, and with this might be associated some skeletal material, at least in five wells, including three skulls from one well, one each from two others (Immerwahr 1982: 61) and possibly figurines from near-by graves, as well as animal bones and other household refuse (Immerwahr 1971: 17) from settlements. Burials must have taken place in the area, but probably not in these shafts, which did not contain complete skeletons and seem to have been cut as wells, but perhaps in the neighbouring caves (Immerwahr 1982: 62). Association of burials and domestic remains in or in the vicinity of caves is characteristic of FN deposits in caves (e.g. Kitsos, Franchthi, Alepotrypa). However, a FN grave was also found in the Agora, in a small side chamber at the bottom of a three-meter deep shaft, dug in the same way as the wells, and filled up with water. Immerwahr (1982: 54, 56, n. 12, 59) thinks that it was probably dug for the burial and not initially as a well; the water table may have changed.

Complete vases were found with human bones in several wells, but, as this is not consistent, Immerwahr (1971: 2 and n. 5) rejects the idea that the whole pots, mostly Red Burnished biconical jars, came originally from graves and suggests that they should be connected with the use of the wells, having served as containers to draw water, although their size (height ca 0,20 m) and capacity are small and the surface finer than would be expected for such use and although they were also found in non completed wells. Red Burnished local pottery, mainly biconical or ovoid jars and hemispherical or shallow bowls, occurs in all wells. Biconical jars (in seven wells) have elaborate lugs, vertically pierced, adapted for inserting strings or thongs to let down the pot. Intact vases would be left in the wells if the cord was cut when they were at the bottom or under a boulder (Immerwahr 1971: 2, 4, 5, 8). Two local coarse ware bowls may also come from use fill (Immerwahr 1971: 13 and pl. 12, 171-172).

Kastelli Phournis (FN, Eastern Crete)

Near the well (diam. 2-2,5 m., excav. depth 6 m.) there was initially a spring; the area is rich in underground water. Jars (height 17-22 cm., a few up to 28 cm., one smaller), especially high-necked jars, with vertical, horizontally perforated lugs, were the commonest shape of the homogeneous, mostly burnished, pottery from the well; 15 were intact or fully restored. There were also six jugs, two amphorae, a mug, a pyxis and a bowl. Plant cords were recorded at the time of the excavation, passing through lugs of vases (Manteli 1992).

THERMI (EBA, ISLAND OF LESBOS, NORTH-EAST AEGEAN)

Thermi is situated near the eastern coast of Lesbos, on a low mound between two streams, about half a km south-east of the hot springs which gave the district its name (Lamb 1936: 2; Kontis 1978: 12, 16). The occupied by five successive towns area, partly eroded by the sea, would have attained initially ca 1,60 hectares (Lamb 1936: 7). The region (plain and surrounding hills) is one of the most fertile of Lesbos; besides, the town population would have had maritime interests. Its location, near the shortest passage between the coast of Lesbos and the opposite Asia Minor coast, both with sandy beaches for boats, offering refuge for all weathers, had significant advantages (Kontis 1978: 202, 203). Streets identified in various periods would once have led to the sea or the harbour, such as two wide streets and an alley branching off the main street (it joins the two gateways) of Town V, or a Town II street, that running to the cliff edge, from where remains of a Greek or Roman harbour could be seen, and the prehistoric harbour should not have been far (Lamb 1936: 21, 48).

The area was occupied before the earliest excavated houses were built: a crucible found above a stream bed and below the lowest floor in area E (Lamb 1936: 157, pl. XXIV, no. 30.43) attests metallurgical activities on the spot. The first houses (C14 2923-2695 BC: Manning 1995: 28) were built close to virgin soil on the banks of the streams (Lamb 1936: 7). A channel or stream bed (areas E and N) had been partly filled before the houses were constructed, after people had inhabited the site for some time (Lamb 1936: 11). It may have been used for some time for refuse (Lamb 1936: 17). It is not clear whether several miniature vases, mostly bowls and jugs, deposited in this stream bed (Lamb 1936: 14, 17), as well as a few others, found in an open area (K) outside the town, where another stream bed was conspicuous in the landscape and also used for refuse (Lamb 1936: 13), were part of rubbish, or if they are traces of some other open air activity by the stream (Marangou 1992: 76, 238; cf. 1991; 1994). In fact, during Town II, not far from the entrance to the town between bastions, mud produced by inundations on either bank of the K stream (still open and used as a dump), was covered from time to time with pebbles in order to dry and harden the surface. Towards the end of Town II, the stream seems to have had a fence on its town-side bank. A row of stones was found there, probably trace of a hedge of wood or brushwood. One of the stones could have been a door socket, marking the position of a small gate, or have been re-used. Remains of a round platform and of parallel platform supports were found behind this fence (Lamb 1936: 20, fig. 2). During Town III, near the bed stream there was a platform and at the edge, a row of stones, the latter covered later by a floor. The pebbles of this floor reappear beyond the stream, and are embedded in the interstices of the platform stones. Below this floor the earth gets black on both sides of the stream, suggesting that mud had collected all round (the channel had got filled up?). In two places the stream bed may have been dug out after inundation with a view to drainage (Lamb 1936: 37, figs. 2, 10). Such arrangements might facilitate some activities by the stream (washing, drawing water?), or crossing (pebbles, platforms), or obstruct animals from approaching the town, or confine them in a delimited space (fence).

Three wells belong to Town I, all near the important house A. One of them, filled with black earth, sherds and stones, preceded the architectural remains of I; the second (aquifer at 1,19 m.) belonged to an early phase and contained black earth, sherds and sheep and goat bones. House A probably had an anteroom; a little doorway led from the latter to area ¢, containing the third well (aquifer at 0,80 m.); this was filled with pottery, including a few complete vases, two bowls and a jug (Lamb 1936: 15, 104). In II, a door between one of the two rooms of A and area ¢ implies again a fourth wall for the room (Lamb 1936: 22), but also, easier communication with the area of the well in ¢; the latter could be a closed space (this is not clear in the publication).

In Town IVB, from an important street in K one enters room K 9 over a wide door in its long wall, which is exceptional, apparently making access to a large well in the room easier. The well, closed during Town V, contained pottery, and in its lower part (3,60–3,25 m.) organic matter and ash (Lamb 1936: 11, 37). The second well of IV (probably also used in III: Lamb 1936, 11) is again situated in a building (Z 1), separated from the narrow street Z§ by two little rooms. Although one can enter one of these from the street, this does not facilitate communication between K and the eastern part of the town, even if people were able to pass through both rooms and each other's houses. This well contained pottery, ash, and bones of goats and pigs, probably thrown when the well was being filled up (Lamb 1936: 11 and n. 1, 41 and n. 1).

In the absence of wells (Town V), rain (average 696 mm (1945-1949): Kontis 1978: 21) water could have been collected in unroofed spaces, almost absent in V, or on flat roofs(?). In the latter case, this may have been done collectively, as roofs, and therefore construction of groups of houses and roof conservation were common (Kontis 1978:

203). Pithoi, used for storing foodstuffs, might also have contained water (Lamb 1936: 92). Among the numerous (in all three Thermi pottery classes) jugs (Lamb 1936: figs 26, 28, 29), forms 1-3 often have, at the upper part of the handle, two or three holes (Lamb 1936: 76; cf. Emporio VII - VI: Hood 1981: 341), possibly in order to insert cords; jugs forms 8-9 (class A) are almost always made in coarse clay (Lamb 1936, 78). Their use in connection with water procurement is possible.

The climate of Thermi resembles that of "windy Troy"; spindle whorls in some hearths may show that women spun by the fire: hearths are numerous and varied, many rooms being equipped with 3 or 4 of them (Lamb 1936: 55; cf. Kontis 1978: 19-20). There is plenty of evidence about humidity or presence of (undesired) water: reeds (Lamb 1936: 95), tortoises and frogs or toads (Lamb 1936: 95, 216); efforts to manage overflowing streams or covering and filling of stream beds (I); sprinkling layers of pebbles on streets, open spaces (IVA, IVB, V), or muddy banks of stream-beds (II, III); laying stones at intervals throughout the course of streets or paving them, at least partly, with cobbles and stones (V); and calcareous deposits from water seeping near house walls (IV; cf. Emporio IV: Hood 1981: 129, 130) and in some wells (Lamb 1936: 7, 31, 32, 36, 48). The sudden adoption (III-IV) and subsequent abandonment of the *bothroi* could be explained by their use for draining water from waterlogged house foundations during rainy seasons (Hutchinson in Lamb 1936: 63; Kontis 1978: 204).

POLIOCHNI (FN-EBA, ISLAND OF LEMNOS, NORTH-EAST AEGEAN)

Two streams are situated to the north and the south of Poliochni; the more important is at 160 m to the south. The aquifer is at 3-4 m. under the soil of the plain, and this facility, as well as the protected bay, must have influenced the choice of the site for settlement (Bernabo-Brea 1964: 22). A cylindrical well of Poliochni Blue (C14 2876-2584 BC: Manning 1995: 28) initial and middle phases (diam.: 1,90 m.) was excavated through strata of the Black period till 7,70 m. (aquifer at ca 8,20 m.). The chronologically homogeneous fill included several bowls, jugs and some fragments of large jars (Bernabo-Brea 1964: 51-53, 62-67, figs. 25-29).

In Poliochni Yellow (Troy IV, Emporio I: Parzinger 1993: 272), a well (fill lost) was initially situated in the NW angle of square 103 (Bernabo-Brea 1976: figs. 16, 21-24, 150). Later buildings covered parts of the surrounding pavement, and the well was in the centre of a small, polygonal space. A round coping, delimited by a small wall (ext. diameter: 5,50 m.) is covered by large stone plaques, rendering the mouth of the well smaller and pentagonal. The round shaft (diam.:1,63 m.) is lined with parallelepiped stones. A drainage channel, initially covered with plaques ends in street 102 (Bernabo-Brea 1976: 28-30). In the area around the well, a stone plaque was found, with a spiral of incised small cavities(?), "probably a primitive game-table" (*tavola da gioco*) (lost; Bernabo-Brea 1976: 57, 314). A similar plaque with cup-marks forming an ellipse on its upper face was found among the stones of a partly paved Red period corridor (or narrow dead end?) communicating with a large yard (Bernabo-Brea 1964: 319, 321, fig. 176). Another triangular plaque, with two intersecting circles of cup-marks, found between the stones of Red period street 121, near street 118, was also interpreted as a game-table or children game on the street pavement (Bernabo-Brea 1964: 369, fig. 210; 1976: 314, fig. 176).

The second Yellow period large well (attained depth: 8,50 m.) with rectangular shaft is located in the SW angle of square 106. Four large quadrangular stones delimit an almost square opening of the well mouth. They are surrounded by large stones on three sides. On the E and N a short *stradino* among the stones permits to accede to the level of the mouth. Transformations of the streets ending into the square have limited the area around the well. Some buildings looking towards the square have special characters, and could be thought of as affected to public, civil or religious uses (Bernabo-Brea 1976: 39-42).

DISCUSSION

The data examined above show continuity between the FN and the EBA, but also a number of transformations in the practices related to water.

Evidence about water procurement from surface water, such as streams, or related management, is scarce, and it comes from EBA (Thermi). There is no certain evidence for systematic collection of rainwater, but this would have been feasible, e.g. in vessels in open yards (Schofield 1995: 249; 1998: 118). Evidence about FN wells is rare, but may sometimes be assumed: by the isthmus at Kephala (Keos), a modern well provided water for grazing animals till recently. Similar wells on beaches are common on Keos and their water is drinkable. Since no other perennial water supply has been found at or near the FN site (unless this is now underwater), it is probable that the inhabitants used similar wells at least when there was no rain (Coleman 1977: 2). FN wells arrive up to a depth of 7,70 m. (Agora), EBA ones, at 8m. (Vasiliki, Crete: Zois 1976: 53), 8,50m. (Poliochni), 9,60m. and even 17, 35 m. (Corinth: Weinberg 1948; Waage 1949). Their diameter varies from 0,85/1m. (Agora) to 2,50 m. (Kastelli) in the FN, between 0,75-1m. (Crete: Zois 1976: 53-55) or 1,10/1,20m. (Corinth, Crete) and 1,90m. (Poliochni) or 2,30m. (Emporio) in the EBA. A smaller mouth insures cool water, is more easily protected against contaminants and accidents involving animals, children, or the infirm (Smithson 1982: 147). Wells are often used as rubbish pits (including from burials) after abandonment or drying up, in both periods.

Hand- or foot-holes, vertical rows of shallow cuttings on opposite sides of the shaft, exist since the aceramic in Cyprus (Peltenburg 2001). They are attested in EBA wells in Corinth (Weinberg 1948; Waage 1949) and Vasiliki (Zois 1976: 53-55) and become common since the Geometric period. They were designed to aid descent and ascent in the well, presumably both during construction as well as for subsequent maintenance and cleaning (Camp 1977: 176). The mouth of the well might have some sort of definition (Poliochni), and the surrounding the well area is taken care of (Emporio FN-EBA, Poliochni). Although not preserved, (wooden?) covers over the well mouth would be needed, in order to prevent dirt, stray objects, animals, and people from falling in (Camp 1977: 179-180). Roads/paths are constructed, including on steep slopes, in order to facilitate access to water sources (Emporio Neol.-EBA). At Ayia Irini on Keos, the only known source of fresh water on the peninsula is located in the western sector of the settlement. In all phases when the spring was active, since it started to be used in EBA II, when bedrock was cut out to create a water basin, there is evidence of careful planning of this sector in order to provide access (Schofield 1995: 250; 1998: 119). A great cobbled way was constructed, leading from the terrace of the houses down the slope of the hill, towards the spring. Such attention paid to providing access to a public water supply suggests sophisticated communal planning not only in the EBA (Schofield 1998: 119-121), but already in the FN (Emporio).

As in later periods, water was drawn from the well by means of a jar (or wooden bucket; cf. Smithson 1982: 147) tied to the end of a rope (Kastelli FN). Most often the water would be pulled up by hand, but at Emporio (EBA) a *shaduf* may have been used. The vast majority of vases were clay jars, many of which were dropped or broke and fell into the well (Camp 1977: 181, 278, note 18). This also happened with FN jars and some bowls, strikingly often intact (Agora, Kastelli) as well as a few EBA bowls (Thermi), jars and jugs (Weinberg 1948). In this respect it is notable that vast numbers of jug fragments (and not complete vases) came from the well area (not from the well itself) at Emporio (EBA, VII-VI and later), in particular after the main period of use of the jars, that is, the Chalcolithic (period VIII). Both situations might also be intentional. A height of 25-30 cm frequently occurring in our material is convenient for later buckets, while 40 cm high vases are more suited to transport (Smithson 1982: 147). Traditional water vessels of particular shapes with specific names according to specialised uses and local dialects are common in Greece (Yannopoulou *et al.* 1999: 189-191, 193).

Besides household needs, if ponds or streams are absent, herds must be brought to the village's wells, but there is no evidence about (wooden?) troughs from which cattle could drink (Toulmin 1992: 145, 147, 280). Furthermore, it would be difficult to imagine animals drinking in closed spaces (Thermi), and obstruction of access (gates, walls; Emporio) may aim to prevent them from approaching. However, it is possible that animals carried water jars. Public wells are placed so as to be accessible to a great number of people (in squares: Poliochni; on a terrace: Emporio). Some wells may be associated with particular buildings, the latter possibly having direct access to the well area (Poliochni, Emporio IV, Thermi); a semi-public use is conceivable. A gate may bar access to the well area (Emporio IV, III) or the well may be inside a building (Thermi IVB, possibly I/II); access to water is then under control. In Mali villages, the chieftaincy controls digging of wells by village households. In these cases, wells are dug, maintained, and owned by the community as a whole, used for domestic-water supplies (Toulmin 1992: 34-35). In addition, before 1960, private wells belonged to the village chief, the only one who had the right to dig wells within the village territory (Toulmin 1992: 142). In historical periods, wells are found inside workshops (Camp 1977: 181).

Providing domestic water on a daily basis is likely to have been a female responsibility, a private matter for individual households, kept within the family. As designing and constructing urban drainage systems is a masculine and communal concern, this may well explain why, though drainage plays a large part in Bronze Age Minoan and Cycladic town planning, associated with the paving of streets, little attention was paid to water supply: public wells are rarely found (Schofield 1995: 249; 1998: 118-119). In ancient Greek society, service activities using water, such as carrying drinking water, cooking, washing and washing up, were done by women and girls (although male citizens were involved with water use and management), possibly also by boys, as in Greek countryside today (Crouch 1993: 311, fig. 16.20). It may be interesting to note that miniature jars or pyxides are found in women's burials, miniature jugs both in children's and adults burials in the EBA (Marangou 1992: 242, 245-248).

Topography and distance to water sources can affect the demand for water carrying vessels (Arnold 1985: 145). When carrying over short distances, any loss of water is inconsequential because the water is close (Arnold 1985: 147). Motor habit patterns are sex-linked, possibly due to differences in role behavior (men may never carry pots) and sexual differences (hip width): women carry jars on the hip more easily than men. One arm clasps the long neck of the vessel, a flat base is easily steadied on the hip, the height of the vessel should fit comfortably between the hip and the bent arm (Arnold 1985: 147). In the "shrine" of Myrtos (period I), a hollow, painted female figurine clasps with its left arm a miniature jug. The right arm comes across the body and held the jug by the handle (Warren 1972: 86-87, 209-210, fig. 91-2, pls. 28B, 69-70) (Fig. 4). The figure was interpreted as a goddess, presumably protecting water supply, of crucial importance in the life of the settlement, since there were no wells on the hill and all water had to be carried up steep paths (Warren 1972: 86-87, 265). A woman may carry one vessel on her hip and place another on her head using the handle to steady it (Arnold 1985: 148). Two opposing vertical handles are used either for lifting a jar to the top of the head where it may rest on a coil of cloth during transport, or in order to secure the vessel with a rope for carrying it on the back using a tump-line over great distances (Fig. 3.) The long neck increases the volume of the vessel (fewer trips to water sources are needed), and prevents spills over difficult terrain; carrying on the head probably would result in more breakage (Arnold 1985: 148). Tracing motor habit patterns required for using water carrying jars could reveal the extent of populations in space or time and population growth or migration could be inferred (Arnold 1985: 233), e.g. exogamy, but there are not enough elements for the moment in our material.

Fig. 3

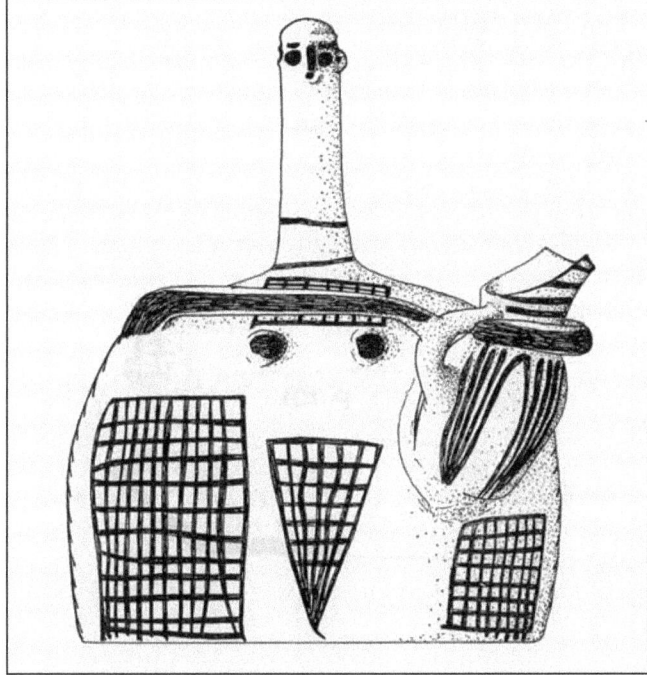

Fig. 4

opportunities for social relations and gatherings. Perhaps it is not surprising that game-tables were found in such spaces (Poliochni). A presence of children, for working (carrying water home) (Marangou 1991) or playing may be suggested by the occurrence of children's open miniature vases (bowls) in streets and squares, as well as in their tombs (Marangou 1992: 237-239).

Fig. 5

It is not surprising that many tales and customs reflect the task and itinerary of carrying domestic water, such as those mentioning "mute water"(?cf Aikatairinidis 1999), water one has to bring home without pronouncing a word on the way. In Lesbos, a girl of 12-14 years had to carry a jar full of water from the far away village fountain, without stopping nor putting it down, in order to prove that she was ready for marriage (Gratsia *et al*. 1999: 68). We are of course unable, if not to identify such symbolic and ideological matters, indeed to interpret with certainty ritual and ideological practice based solely on mute traces of archaeological material.

It is not unusual for settlements to be some distance away from their domestic water supply. Villages in the Mani (southern Peloponnese) are each at 10-15 minutes walking distance from their supplies, i.e. ca half a km (Warren 1972: 264, 282 and n. 2). Women might spend several hours each day drawing and carrying water for household requirements. At Bronze Age Gournia, where no wells are reported, at least 14 000 litres daily for a population of perhaps 700 would have been needed, and carrying it up steep, narrow, cobbled streets would have been a difficult and time-consuming task, even if the source was nearby (Schofield 1995: 249; 1998: 118). Having good water supply has several advantages, as women will not spend long hours waiting for the well to refill and consequently can spend more time on other activities (Toulmin 1992: 148). As wells are often in public places, crossroads, squares, terraces, and as probably one would not go drawing water by oneself, but accompanied by other women (Fig. 5) and/or children, there would be

Acknowledgements

I wish to thank warmly Dr. Dragos Gheorghiu for his kind invitation to participate in the UISPP Congress in Liège, as well as for his patience.

Bibliography

AIKATERINIDIS, G.N., 1999, Water in cult, magic and prediction customs. In *Water, source of life, movement, purification*. Athens: Ministry of Culture, Museum of Greek Popular Art, p. 42-46.

ALRAM-STERN, E., 1996, *Die Ägäische Frühzeit*. Wien: Österreichische Akademie der Wissenschaften.

ARNOLD, D.E., 1985, *Ceramic Theory and Cultural Process*. Cambridge: University Press.

ASLANIS, I., 1998, The first appearance of fortifications in prehistoric settlements of the Aegean area (in Greek). In Mendoni et al.. (eds.) 1998, p. 109-115.

AURENCHE, O., 1982, Préhistoire des sociétés hydrauliques du Proche Orient Ancien. In Métral (dir.) 1982, p. 31-44.

BERNABO-BREA, L., 1964 and 1976, *Poliochni. Città preistorica nell'isola di Lemnos*, volumes I-II. Roma: "L'Erma" di Bretschneider.

BETHEMONT, J., 1982, *Sur les origines de l'agriculture hydraulique*. In Métral (dir.) 1982, p. 7-30.

BONNIN, J., 1984, *L'eau dans l'antiquité. L'hydraulique avant notre ère*. Paris: Eyrolles.

CAMP, J. McKESSON, 1977, *The water supply of Ancient Athens*. Dissertation, Princeton University. Michigan: Ann Arbor.

CAMP, J., 2002, Wells and cisterns (in Greek). *Kathimerini* Special Issue Seven days "Water Supply of Athens", 24th March 2002, p. 8-9.

COLEMAN, J., 1977, *Keos*, volume I. *Kephala. A Late Neolithic Settlement and Cemetery*. Princeton: American School of Classical Studies.

CROUCH, D.P., 1993, *Water management in Ancient Greek Cities*. New York and Oxford: Oxford University Press.

GRATSIA, I. and PAPATHOMA, E., 1999, Water vases and performance of customs in Modern Greek society (in Greek). In *Water, source of life, movement, purification*. Athens: Ministry of Culture, Museum of Greek Popular Art, p. 64-72.

GUILAINE, J., 2001, Parekklisha-Shillourokambos: périodisation et aménagements domestiques. Paper presented at the Conference *Le Néolithique de Chypre*, May 2001, Nicosia.

HELLMANN, M.-C., 1992, Le vocabulaire de l'eau dans les inscriptions de Délos. In *L'eau et les hommes en Méditerranée et en Mer Noire dans l'Antiquité de l'époque Mycénienne au règne de Justinien*, edited by G. Argoud, L. Marangou, V. Panayotopoulos, C. Viallin-Gandossi, p. 181-196.

HOOD, S., 1981, 1982, *Prehistoric Emporio and Ayio Gala*, volumes I-II. Oxford: The British School of Archaeology at Athens supplementary volumes no. 15-16, Thames and Hudson.

IMMERWAHR, S. A., 1971, *The Athenian Agora, volume XIII. The Neolithic and Bronze Ages*. Princeton, New Jersey: The American School of Classical Studies at Athens.

IMMERWAHR, S. A., 1982, The Earliest Athenian Grave. In *Studies in Athenian Architecture Sculpture and Topography* presented to Homer A. Thompson, Hesperia Supplement XX. Princeton, New Jersey: American School of Classical Studies at Athens, p. 55-62, pl. 9.

KONTIS, I., 1978, *Lesbos and its Asia Minor region* (in Greek). Athens: Athens Technological Organization, Athens Centre of Ekistics.

LAMB, W., 1936, *Excavations at Thermi in Lesbos*. Cambridge: University Press.

MANNING, S.W., 1995, *The absolute Chronology of the Aegean Early Bronze Age*. Sheffield: Academic Press.

MANTELI, K., 1992, The Neolithic well at Kastelli Phournis in Eastern Crete. In *Annual of the British School at Athens* 87, p. 103-120, pls. 1-2.

MARANGOU, C., 1991, Social Differentiation in the Early Bronze Age: Miniature Metal Tools and Child Burials. In *Journal of Mediterranean Studies* 1, (2), p. 211-225.

MARANGOU, C., 1992, *Eidolia. Figurines et miniatures du Néolithique Récent et du Bronze Ancien en Grèce*. BAR International Series 576, Oxford.

MENDONI, L.G. and MAZARAKIS AINIAN, A.I., 1998, *Kea-Kythnos: History and Archaeology*. Athens: Research Centre for Greek and Roman Antiquity, National Hellenic Research Foundation.

PANTELIDOU GOFA, M., 1991, *Neolithic Nea Makri. The architectural remains* (in Greek). Athens: The Athens Archaeological Society no. 119.

PAPADOPOULOS,, S. and MALAMIDOU, D., 2002, The early habitation phases of the Neolithic settlement at Limenaria (in Greek). In *Archaeological Work in Macedonia and Thrace* 14, 2000. Thessaloniki: Ministry of Culture – TAP and Aristotle University of Thessaloniki, p. 25-32.

PARZINGER, H., 1993, *Studien zur Chronologie und Kulturgesciechte der Jungstein-, Kupfer- und Frühbronzezeit zwischen Karpaten und Mittleren Taurus*. Mainz am Rhein: Philip von Zabern.

PELTENBURG, E., 2001, The 10th-9th millennium BP wells of Kissonerga-Mylouthkia. Paper presented at the Conference *Le Néolithique de Chypre*, May 2001, Nicosia.

SCHOFIELD, E., 1995, Water supplies and water planning: a view from the Cyclades. *Bulletin of the Institute of Classical Studies* 40, p. 249-250.

SCHOFIELD, E., 1998, Town planning at Ayia Irini, Kea. In Mendoni et al. (eds.) 1998, p. 117-122.

SMITHSON, E. Lord, 1982, The Prehistoric Klepsydra: some notes. In *Studies in Athenian Architecture Sculpture and Topography* presented to Homer A. Thompson, Hesperia Supplement XX. Princeton, New Jersey: American School of Classical Studies at Athens, p. 141-154, pls. 21-22.

TOULMIN, C., 1992, *Cattle, Women, and Wells. Managing Household Survival in the Sahel*. Oxford: Clarendon Press.

YANNOPOULOU, M. and PETRAKA, E., 1999, Water vases and their use during the last two centuries (in Greek). In *Water, source of life, movement, purification*. Athens: Ministry of Culture, Museum of Greek Popular Art, p.189-200.

WAAGE, F.O., 1949, An Early Helladic well near Old Corinth. *Hesperia* VIII, p. 415-422, pls. 61-63.

WARREN, P., 1972, *Myrtos. An Early Bronze Age Settlement in Crete*. The British School of Archaeology at Athens Supplementary Volume no. 7. Oxford: Thames and Hudson.

WEINBERG, S.S., 1948, A cross-section of Corinthian Antiquities (excavations of 1940). *Hesperia* 17, p. 197-241, pls. 70-88.

ZOIS, A., 1976, *Vassiliki I* (in Greek). Athens: Archaeological Society.

WATER, TELLS AND TEXTURES: A MULTI-SCALAR APPROACH TO GUMELNITA HYDROSTRATEGIES

Dragos GHEORGHIU

Abstract: The reading of hydrostrategies should use a holistic approach, since the subject of the study is a multi-scalar natural phenomenon. Consequently, the study of hydrostrategies should cover the relationships between the social and human bodies and water from macro to micro-scale, this multi-scalar descendant reading being similar to the reading of a fractal structure. The paper discusses the hydrostrategies of Gumelnita culture, both as relationships of incorporation of water and as methods of protection against it, from macro to micro scale.

Resumé: L'étude des hydrostratégies doit utiliser une méthode holistique par ce que le sujet d'étude est un phénomène naturel a plusieurs niveaux. En conséquence, l'étude des hydrostratégies doit couvrir toutes les relations entre le corps social et le corps humain et l'eau, à partir d'une échelle macro vers une échelle micro, comme dans l'étude d'une structure fractale. L'article présent analyse les macro et micro hydrostratégies de la culture de Goumelnitza, en même temps comme relations d'incorporation et d'exclusion de l'eau.

METHOD

The geographical position of a settlement in relationship to water and landscape and the design of objects, have in common the fact that they represent "compositions", i.e. totalities involving rules of association, interdependence and transformation with spatial and temporal dimensions (Gheorghiu 2001:1). I am using this word as, in my opinion, it could suggest a structured assemblage, as well as immaterial or temporal assemblages (which involve mixtures of old and new materials and objects), and which could visualize the complexity of the archaeological record of prehistoric societies.

There are compositions that include water at a macro-level as well as at a micro-level, for example the *tell* and its ditches positioned in relation to the relief and water, or the decoration of the human body.

To understand the complexity of the relationship of a past human community with water, one should scour several overlapping levels of readings, from the far-off readings of the spatial relationships at a geographical scale to the close-up readings at the level of object design and texture of materials.

In the case of hydrostrategies, beside the classical use of macro-spatial analysis (see Clarke 1977; Clarke 1972; see also Gamble 2001:141), an analysis at a micro-scale is functional; in order to examine the *chaines-opératoires* of objects and the nature of materials that impose the shape and utility of objects.

Through experimental archaeology, a synthesis including ethnography, object replication and 3D simulation, archaeologists can obtain analogous models, at different levels, that also help to understand the hydrostrategies of prehistoric cultures.

In order to explain the hydrological contexts where the culture studied developed its hydrostrategies, the approach should begin from the macro- to the micro- level, i.e. from geography to texture.

I have chosen the Gumelnita Chalcolithic culture because, starting with the 5th millennium B.C., new hydrostrategies emerged in the Danube area and the Balkans, visualized as macro-compositions between settlement and the environment known as *tells*. In the Danube plain the passage from the Boian culture 'open-flat' settlements (Andreescu and Bailey 1999: 11ff), characterized by wide spaces left between buildings, to the Gumelnita culture agglomerated *tell* settlements, partly surrounded by rivers and partly surrounded by ditches filled with water several months of the year, is an index of a significant cultural change that is very important for the understanding of hydrophilic Chalcolithic "clay-cultures", totally dependent on water.

MACRO-LEVEL READING HYDRO-CONTEXT

A first level of interpreting Gumelnita hydrostrategies would be the following: Gumelnita culture (Dumitrescu 1924; 1925; Stefan 1925; Nestor 1933) (named Karanovo VI - Kodjadermen in Bulgaria), developed during the Atlantic climatic optimum in central, eastern and south eastern Bulgaria, up to the northern shore of the Aegean Sea, the Lower Danube basin (between the Olt and the Danube branches), and Dobroudja in south-eastern Romania, and south-east Moldavia (here mixed with Precucuteni III), up to the Dniester river (Ursulescu 1998: 124).

The present text will discuss only a part of the northern area of this culture, including the Danubian plain and Dobroudja, whose hydrological structure is characterized by a main collector channel (the Danube) (Fig. 1) that unites a series of

Fig. 1 The Danube flood-basin near Corabia. (Photo. Dr. Alex Gibson)

tributaries springing from the Carpathian mountains and the sub-Carpathians, and flowing to the Black Sea, which coastline also unites a series of small rivers and estuaries.

Due to the heavy rains and the melting of the snow from the Carpathians mountains, the Danube and its tributaries produced major floods every year (in early spring and autumn): sometimes disastrous ones. This phenomenon was also repeated in mid-summer, but over a very short period of time. (Zavoianu 1999: 179, 190-191). The annual floods of the Danube were collected by the large lakes bordering the river's left bank (today all drained), which used to have the effect of buffers. One of the major results of the floods was the layer of fertile mud left in the inundated valleys, for example that of the Calmatui river. (See Pandrea et al 1997:204.)

In this hydrological context, the Gumelnita settlements occupied locations with high ground water (see Sherratt 1980: 314), on marshes, lakes (on 'turtlebacks', Fig. 2), estuaries (see Lazarov 1993; Ivanov 1993), high terraces (see Hasotti 1997), or near the seashore, being always in a direct proximity to water[1].

Fig. 2 The site of Gumelnita positioned on a 'turtleback', surrounded by marshes. View from the north.

Sometimes the settlements positioned in the flood area, such as the Cascioarele *tell* (see Dumitrescu 1986: 76 ff), endured repeated inundations, being settled on again each time.

Such proximity to flood water (a risk factor to Western thinking) can be explained only if the communities used water as a symbolic, trade, and protective medium. For prehistoric populations the risk factor from close proximity to water could be perceived in a completely different way, possibly even as "a celebration (...) [or] as the will of (...) Gods" (Brown 1997:293).

---

[1] A special case in Dobroudja are the settled caves "Gura Dobrogei" and "La Izvor" ("At the Spring")–Cheia (see Hasotti 1997: 83), both situated in the proximity of rivers.

ECOSYSTEM

River valleys, lake and estuary shores, were covered by dense vegetation, mostly of willow, bulrush and reeds. Ethnographic examples show that all three plants were primarily used for wickerwork and plaited baskets and mats.

Vitis silvestris was common in the forests along the Danube, and was collected by Gumelnita communities (Monah 1998-2000: 73).

The river valleys and forests bordering the lakes (Fig. 3) were populated with abundant fauna of mammals (Balasescu 1977: 52-53; Moise 2000 – 2001: 1957) and fowl; many species of fish and mollusc inhabited the waters.

Fig. 3 Oak forest and reeds on the shores of lake Cernica, near Bucharest.

THE GEOGRAPHICAL-SPATIAL ORGANIZATION

The spatial organization of the settlements in the Danube plain and Dobroudja was imposed by the orientation of the hydrographic network of the Danube's tributaries and branches, as well as by the estuarine structure of the Black Sea coast (see Lazurca 1995: 21). In the Danube plain the river and its tributaries formed one articulate system of communication. In this spatial organization the Danube acted as a main artery, connecting the clusters of settlements of each tributary. One may infer that settlements acted as a spatial composition, being in a permanent relationship of contact.

A second similar system was formed by the Black Sea coastline, and connected the clusters of settlements positioned along the shores of the lakes, estuaries and rivers. The two systems mentioned were in close contact, connected as they were by two branches of the Danube and the Carasu valley.

Some of the Gumelnita settlements were positioned in special locations on river mouths in relationship to the Danube, for example the eponymous Gumelnita settlement (Dumitrescu 1925) near the Arges river mouth, the Sultana settlement near the Mosistea river mouth (Andriesescu 1929), and the two settlements at Harsova (town and Dealul Lacului; see Hasotti 1997: 85) at the junction of the two branches of the Danube in front of the Ialomita river mouth, and near the Carasu valley that crosses Dobroudja. The last location could have functioned as a link between the sub-Carpathians and the Black Sea coast. Such a strategic positioning, at the crossroads of many water routes, could explain the large amount of exotic items, such as *Spondylus gaederopus* shells, discovered at Harsova (town). (Fig. 4)

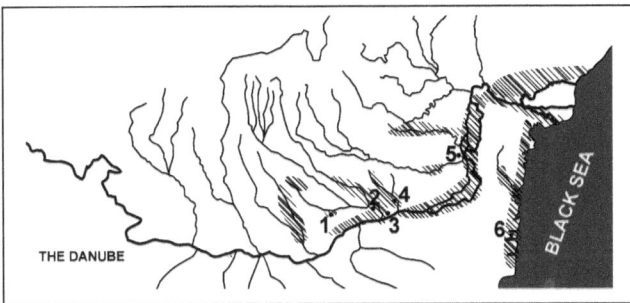

Fig. 4 Clusters of Gumelnita settlements on the Danube tributaries and the Black Sea paleo- coast. The main settlements discussed in the text are:
1.Uzunu, 2.Radovanu, 3.Gumelnita,
4.Sultana, 5.Harsova, 6.Limanu.

In the Danube plain a change in dynamic relationships with the environment could be detected between Early Chalcolithic (Boian culture) and Middle Chalcolithic (Gumelnita culture), as Gumelnita settlements became more lasting, developing a long-term connection with water on definite places.

At present in Romania, the data is still insufficient to establish rules governing the distances between settlements because of the absence of satellite images, the scarcity of aerial photographs, and the deficiency of systematic field research (for the list of the known Gumelnita settlements see Comsa 1991: 173; Hasotti 1997: 85), and because some of the sites identified in the middle of the last century had already been destroyed by urbanization and industrialization (to cite only Mangalia, Costinesti, Medgidia and Limanu) before any systematic archaeological survey had been undertaken to identify the type of settlement and its dimensions.

It is hoped that satellite investigations will add a large number of new *tells* to the map, and in particular concentrations of occupational debris from flat settlements (see Philip et al. 2002), especially on the submerged north coastline of the Black Sea, in the area between the two branches of the Danube, along the southern coastline of the Delta, and on the northern area of the Danube Delta. These regions, not yet fully investigated, represent the link between the two systems mentioned.

LANDSCAPE AND *TELLS* VISIBILITY AND POSITIONING IN RELATIONSHIP WITH WATER

Recent studies on prehistoric landscape insisted on the concept of visible dominant locales, such as mountains or hills. In the case of the Danube's landscape, or its main tributaries, the dominant locale (i.e. the river) has developed over a flat, horizontal surface, and cannot be seen from any distance. As a result, the Danubian landscape is characterized by a total absence of vertical dominants. The anthropogenic intrusion of *tells* did not change these flat landscape settlements, although the general perception is that *tells* represented a type of dominant locale.

In the Gumelnita culture, the siting on a special place near the water (see Hasotti 1997: 77; Bailey 2000:157) (for symbolic, economic or defensive reasons), and the observance of the palisade and ditch perimeters (Morintz 1962) surrounding some settlements, in time led to vertical growth, producing *tells* (Chapman 1989, 1990, 1991, 1994, Gheorghiu 2001a). The presence of *tells* indicates a long-term relationship with the ecosystem as well as with other settlements in a network. To the south of the Danube, *tells* of up to 15,000 square meters (Todorova 1978: 55), built according to a set plan (Todorova 1978: 48), were sometimes surrounded by earth walls and ditches and palisades (simple or double) (Perniceva 1978: 164-165). (Fig. 5) To the south of the Danube a visible difference in dimensions, and probably in functions (Lichardus 1988: 91), between settlements suggests an inter-settlement hierarchy. An example would be the agglomeration of settlements and necropoleis on the shores of lake Varna (for a possible relationship between the immersed settlements and the excavated Varna necropolis, see Ivanov 1993: 24), compared to the settlements on lake Limanu.

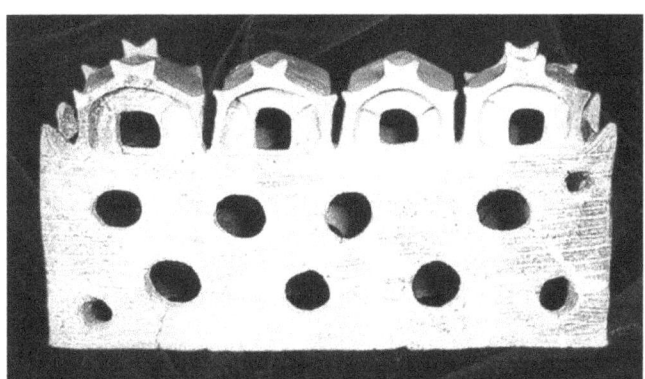

Fig. 5 Brazier in the form of a tell with palisade.

Studies of the Gumelnita settlements (Morint 1962) identified three types of positioning of *tells* in relation to water (i.e. three kinds of compositions): on terraces, islands, and flat surfaces.

Island of Ostrovel, Lake Cascioarele. (National Museum of Archaeology, Bucharest.)

LEVEL II
SETTLEMENT SPATIAL ORGANIZATION: *TELLS* AND OPEN SETTLEMENTS

The above-mentioned constraints on the growth of settlements produced, over time, demographic fissions that led in places to the emergence of flat settlements in the proximity of some *tells* (as at Radovanu [Comsa 1990], Uzunu [unpublished, discovered by the author in 2000], Burdusani-Popina, Valea-Argovei-Vladiceasca [Marinescu-Bilcu 1997: 36-37]; Teiu [Nania 1967; Comsa 1997:150]), probably subordinate to the *tell*, and probably seasonal due to cyclical flooding. This pattern becomes visible for the first time at Radovanu (Fig. 6), a site belonging to the late phase of Boian ("the transitional phase to Gumelnita"[2], Comsa 1990; 1997; for off-*tell* structures see also Bailey *et al.* 1998).

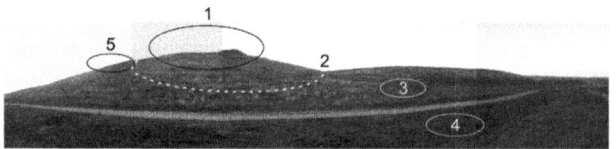

Fig. 6 The Radovanu tell positioned on a terrace (1), surrounded by a ditch (2) with one open settlement at its base (3,4) and a workshop (5). View from the East.

Not every settlement positioned in an advantageous position near water would transform into a *tell*, *e.g.* the sites at Costinesti (Hasotti 1988-1989), Largu, Liscoteanca-Santoieni, Scarlatesti-Popina (Pandrea *et al.* 1997), Brailita (Hartuche and Dragomir 1957) or at Panduru (V. Lungu *pers. comm.*). The settlement at Panduru, positioned at the intersection of two rivers and near the Altan-Tepe copper source (see Radulescu and Dimitrescu 1966:119), has only one layer of occupation, despite its extremely favourable position. Until today, only five *tells* have been recorded in Dobroudja.

A variant to the double-settlement pattern is that with one site positioned inland while the other is out in the middle of still water; this is the case at Limanu (with a settlement situated near a spring, on a high terrace dominating the lake, and a second one positioned on an island at 500 m distance, in the middle of the lake) (Fig. 7), or at Sultana.

Fig. 7 Two settlements at Limanu: on a terrace (right) and on an island (centre, background). At the base of the terrace there is a spring. View from the North.

---
[2] Periodisation criticized by Morintz and Preda (1959: 165-7) and Dumitrescu (1963: 61-2). Pandrea (2000: 42) believes that Radovanu belongs to Gumelnita A1 phase.

LEVEL III
DITCHES

A large quantity of water, required for building and repairing houses, could be obtained from the nearby river or lake. An effortless source of water for construction and maintenance would be the ditches that surrounded some of the inland settlements (Fig. 8). For archaeologists their role is still ambiguous (Comsa 1963; Florescu and Florescu 1983; Dragomir 1996; Comsa 1997; Hasotti 1997; Pandrea et al 1999; Bailey 2000); their dimensions seem not to have been very efficient for defensive purposes (see Marinescu-Bilcu 1974: 20; Hasotti 1997: 77) (Fig. 9). What may certainly be inferred from their dimensions is that ditches were the result of controlled labour. (Some ditches discovered in Cucuteni, a neighbouring culture, had a volume of 1500 cubic metres over a length of 300 metres (Marinescu-Bilcu 1974: 20.)

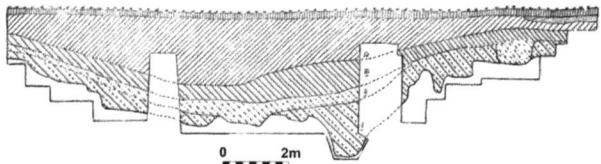

Fig. 8 Section through the ditch at Radovanu. (After Comsa 1990: 79, fig.41.)

Fig. 9 A drain separating Sultana tell (left) from the terrace. It collected water from the ditch (3m deep x 2m wide) dug in front of the settlement, and from the slopes of the tell. View from the North.

A possible additional role for these ditches, as well as for the palisade, could have been to prevent the phenomenon of soil erosion, frequently occurring on the slopes of *tells*, by interrupting the tensions in the soil layer. (Fig. 10)

A symbolic role for these ditches could have been the defining of the boundaries of a social group; the ditch could have had the function of fixing the sacral limits of the settlement (acting as a sort of *temenos*), the soil resulting from the digging being used to build the first houses. (I am using here as an inspirational model the foundation of Rome; see de Coulanges 1908.) After the rainy season, in early spring and autumn, as well as sporadically in mid-summer when the absence of water in the Danube plain is acute, these ditches were filled

Fig. 10 Natural ditch at Sultana, produced by the sliding of the soil layer.

Fig. 12 The Uzunu tell, positioned to the south of a small tributary of the Danube. A flat settlement is 30 m to the left. View from the North.

with water and could become enormous reservoirs for the use of the *tell* community. The positioning of numerous *tells* on slightly convex surfaces (see Todorova 1982: 184 ff) allowed better drainage of water towards the ditch. By controlling the drainage, small-scale irrigation would have been possible at the base of the *tell* for a limited number of days. At the same time, a ditch could have acted as a strategic water reservoir for the *tell* community, the water collected being used for animals (especially in winter) and for *tell* formation, a process where the relationship between clay and water is essential, or for the extinction of fires. The fired habitation layers, considered by some archaeologists as intentional (Tringham 1992), could be an additional reason for the existence of water reservoirs that could control the spreading of a deliberate fire.

ORIENTATION TOWARDS SUN AND WATER

The same level of interpretation, allows for the study of *tell* positioning in relation to sun and water, that seems to have observed in many cases the same rule of orientation, the river being in most cases to the north of the tell, or flat settlement. (Examples from the Danube Plain are at Sultana, Uzunu, Limanu, Panduru, Scarlatesti-Popina, Tangaru and Radovanu (Figs. 11-12), and from the south of the Danube at Kalajazidere, Ovcarovo, Teketo, Bajacevo, Targoviste, Dalgac, Goljamo-Delcevo); this composition being probably determined by the dominant winds, by efficient solar exposure in winter, and also, probably, by symbolism. In some settlements from the southern zone of the Danube, an East-West oriented narrow corridor, probably with solar symbolism, separated the group of houses.

Fig. 11 The Sultana tell, on the Mosistea river terrace near the Danube.

DWELLINGS

As remains of foundations and walls show, Gumelnita houses were built of wattle-and-daub, using a structure of wooden posts. Surface dwellings become common at the end of Boian culture, when they replaced semi-subterranean houses. An explanation for this could be the increase of the degree of sedentariness of Gumelnita communities near water, on wet soil, the difficulties of overlapping semi-subterranean houses during the growth of the *tell*, and the large quantity of water accumulating from the roofs of the neighbouring houses, in a very compact group of dwellings, that soaked into the ground whenever it rained heavily.

The orientation of most of the *megaron* houses (Berciu 1937:5, fig.3/2), with entrances to the south, was to allow winter sunlight to reach the interior and therefore combat cold and humidity, as well as the dominant northern winds.

FOUNDATION TRENCHES

The archaeological record reveals that one of the first operations in building surface dwellings would have been the digging of "foundation trenches" (see Marinescu-Bilcu 1997: 68; Randoin *et al.* 1998-2000: 231, Plate V), of variable width and depth, and whose functionality I have tried to define by means of experiments. The basic wooden structure of the house consisted of posts of different sizes thrust into the base of the trenches (see Todorova 1982: figs.89; 92), followed by the construction of wattle-and-daub walls. The digging of a foundation trench is not justified structurally as posts could be thrust directly into the ground, or in separate foundations dug for each of them, consequently trench-digging could have had a diverse role, at the same time functional and symbolic.

For the experiments to identify the function of the trenches, I was inspired by the traditional method of construction from Dobroudja that used water for the driving and fixing of the posts into the soil. The experiment consisted of repeated watering of the base of a ditch whose dimensions were scaled with those of the Gumelnita houses, and of rotating a sharpened post until it penetrated deep into the ground. A second experiment took place after rain had filled the trenches and when the posts could be fixed with less effort than in the previous experiment. (A similar method could have been used for any wooden structure built on a wet surface, using posts.) The space left in the trench after fixing the posts allowed for the insertion of rods and the plaiting of twigs or reeds to hold the clay. To then 'cement' the wooden structure and fill the empty spaces, mud could be taken from the trenches and used as a primary material. (Figs. 13-16)

Fig. 13 Watering the base of the post.

Fig. 14 Rotating the post.

Fig. 15 Post and rods fixed in the soil by using the watering method.

Fig. 16 The foundation trenches with excavated soil.

It is likely that the symbolic role of the Gumelnita foundation trenches could be analogous to that of the foundation trenches mentioned by ancient authors (see de Coulanges 1905), having the function of symbolic separation of the interior space of the house. Analogies, both functional and symbolic, could be made between the trenches and the ditches that surround the settlements.

WOODEN FLOORS

Common houses had the floor made of a layer of insulation from diverse recycled materials and small stones, covered by a secondary layer of compacted soil (Popovici *et al.* 1998-2000: 14).

A number of surface buildings used to have a wooden floor made of split trunks (see Popovici and Railland 1996; Randoin *et al.* 1998-2000: 226, plate I; Todorova 1982), whose surface was covered with a layer of clay to protect the interior of the house from humidity coming from the soil or walls.

Another insulating function of the floor was to collect the water used in the household in the empty spaces left under the planks (see Popovici and Railland 1996).

ROOFS

Clay models represent Gumelnita houses as having the inclination of the roof at *c.*45 degrees, an angle that allowed a good run-off of water or snow. These roofs we imagine as having been covered with reeds (Pandrea *et al.* 1997: 206; Popovici *et al.* 1998-2000: 17), an abundant material in the ecosystems of a culture that developed in close relationship with water. The layers of reed, plain or coated with clay, produced a good insulating material due to the air in the stems and to the property the stems had of letting water run away. (Figs. 17-18).

Fig. 17 A contemporary wattle-and-daub stable in the village of Vadastra, near the Danube, using bent reeds for the roof. The attic is used to store fodder.

Fig. 18 Side view of the house in Fig. 17.

Probably the most important functions of roofs in any *tell* (a settlement with a high degree of agglomeration of houses; Chapman 1989) was to collect water for household needs and to direct rainfall in the direction of the perimeter ditch, or away from the settlement. The relationship between built and unbuilt space (Chapman 1990), occasionally allowed for a drain to collect rainwater (see Todorova 1982: 155; Comsa 1990: 73).

There seems to have existed a design relationship between the systems of collecting rain and snow water and the openings to the perimeter palisade, as one may see from virtual reconstructions of house roofs from the settlements excavated in Bulgaria. (Fig. 19) In spite of the changes in the orientation of the houses during the *tell* growth (Gheorghiu 2001 a: 99, fig. 6/10), the streets that collected atmospheric water lead always to the entrances of the palisade or walls, fact that made the draining of water easier.

Seen from this perspective, the roofs, streets, entrances, the slight convex or inclined surfaces of the settlements, and the ditches, all seem to have formed a coherent network for the control and exclusion of atmospheric water; the entire *tell* acting as a system for water collecting and dispersal away the settlement, towards the perimeter ditches.

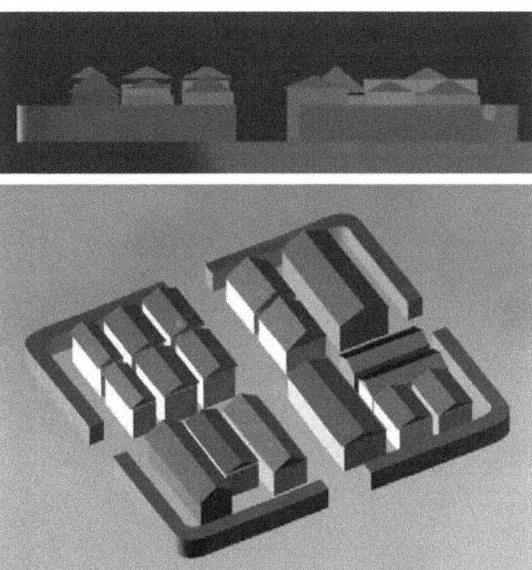

Fig. 19 3D reconstruction of the volumes of *tell* Poljanica, level I. (Plan after Todorova 1982: 207; drawing by Corina Sarbu.)

TELLS: A COMPOSITION BETWEEN CULTURE AND NATURE

The positioning of *tells* on terraces and islands (i.e. on the bank or in the middle of the water), the orientation towards water, as well as the positioning of ditches and the orientation of houses and entrances to the palisades of many of the Gumelnita *tells* could demonstrate the existence of a standardized composition between culture and Nature, in other words of a design with the sun, valleys and water. At the same time, the composition is temporal (see Gheorghiu 2001: 1) as it implies a relationship with the past (see Chapman 1989, 1990, 1994) that I have labeled a "composition with the living, the dead, and Nature".

Tells are generally visible from the waterside (as Radovanu, Sultana, Harsova), because, seen from the land, they were camouflaged by vegetation. Even *tells* positioned on islands (as Limanu) were only visible from a short distance, being hidden by the surrounding terraces.

In the present text I have tried to evoke the composition of the Radovanu *tell* with the valley and the river through the visualization of a journey from the north, along the river. (Fig. 20) Positioned as a central point of the perspective, the *tell* dominates visually the river valley, being visible from one mile away, inferring the existence of visual control over the wetland area.

MICRO-LEVEL INTERPRETATION
LEVEL I
CHALCOLITHIC ECONOMY

The economy of the Gumelnita culture may be divided into three major sectors: 1) dry harvest, represented by agriculture, gathering and hunting in the river valleys and marshes, 2)

Fig. 20 The Radovnu tell, seen from the river valley.

wet harvest, represented by fishing and riverine, lacustrine and marine gathering, and 3) animal breeding, in the river valleys and marshes.

A decisive influence on economy was the climate, with its two distinct seasons, which led to a seasonal economy and the development of a storage strategy for the wet period.

Agriculture (whose storage strategy [Nania 1967: 19; Galbenu 1962: 303] materialized as barns and ceramic large amphorae up to 200 litres (Bailey 1991)) was practiced with the help of the plough (Hartuche 1987: 20, fig.59; Dumitrescu and Banateanu 1965: 61), and wheat, barley, oat, and rye (Comsa 1996: 25-26; Hartuche 1987: 41; Carciumaru 1996: 90) were cultivated. The maritime communities could have used *Elymus Sabulosus* as a substitute for cereals, growing in abundance on the sandy dunes of the Black Sea.

Because, so far, there is no archaeological evidence for irrigation channels, one may infer that the Gumelnita culture is to be characterized by a dry-farm economy, dependent on soil moisture and rainfall, analogous to those existing at the same time in the Middle East. A second argument for the absence of irrigation channels could be the fact that periodic floods of the Danube and its tributaries could generate "flood-water farming" (see Sherratt 1980: 322) on the alluvium. It seems likely, at least for the system of communities in the proximity of the Danube, that there existed just such a flood economy, dependent on the cyclic inundation of the river.

This is evidence for the cultivation of *Vicia ervilia* and *Lens culinaris* (Renfrew 1973: 113, 116; Janusevic 1983: 112; Monah 1998-2000: 72) in the Danubian area and in the Balkans.

Fishing was performed in lakes, rivers (for Burdusani tell see Radu 1997: 98-101, for the Harsova *tell* see Hasotti 1997: 106), the sea (Radu 2000-2001: 166), as well as the collecting of shells (Hasotti 1997:107; Popovici *et al.* 1998-2000: 24). According to the data from the Harsova *tell*, the capture of *Cyprinus carpio* and *Stizostedion lucioperca* was practicised in summer and autumn (Radu 1998-2000: 75 ff), the fish being smoked and salted for winter food. *Unio* shells were amassed in large quantities between May and June (Popovici *et al* 1998-2000: 24).

The Gumelnita economy was context oriented, the wet harvest being more important for the communities along the Danube (for Harsova, see Hasotti 1997: 106), and the dry harvest for the inland ones. For both type of communities animal breeding and hunting were complementary sources of food. Sheep, goats, pigs and cattle breeding varied from settlement to settlement, depending on local factors (Balasescu 1996-98: 102).

The spatial distribution of settlements along the rivers, beside the wet-harvest efficiency could have also a secondary economic reason. It is significant to note that this positioning of the settlements on the Danube tributaries coincides with the later "salt roads" that started off from the forested sub-Carpathians mountains rich in salt deposits, and come down to the Danube.

PREPARATION OF MATERIALS OR AMORPHOUS COMPOSITIONS

Water was essential in the construction of every ceramic object, as well as playing a basic role as a bond for architectural materials in the cyclical ritual process of construction – reparation – deconstruction – reconstruction of wattle-and-daub houses (Gheorghiu 2001: 21), by fixing the clay mixed with recycled fragments of pots, walls, ovens, ashes and refuse (see Haita 1997: 88).

The large volume of wattle-and-daub constructions and repair/maintenance procedures from successive plastering of houses in the *tell*, were water-consuming processes, as scientific research (see Haita 1997: 90), ethnological examples and experiments prove. During the summers of 2001 and 2002, I took part in the construction of several large architectural clay objects (up-draught kilns, house walls) in the village of Vadastra, near the Danube, and I witnessed the use of a large quantity of water to prepare the material (Fig. 21) to fix it, and to finish the exterior and interior surfaces. For a wattle-and-daub building of 2.5 x 2.5 x 1.90m, 250 litres of water were necessary for the entire process, from the beginning to the finishing of the wall surfaces. (Fig. 22)

Fig. 21 Mixing clay and straw with water.

Fig. 22 Plastering the walls of a kiln. Note the quantity of water needed for half of the task.

At a different level, the construction of *tells*, using alluvial clay, organic substances, and recycled materials (see Haita 1997: 89) deposited in layers, could not be achieved without using a large quantity of water used with the bonding.

Clay mixed with straw was one of the first composite materials, and its property of 'cementing' different substances into a stable shape puts it into the category of amorphous "compositions".

FISHING MATERIALS

A close reading of the Gumelnita economy reveals a diversity of fishing instruments whose materials were preserved in the archaeological record, for example clay net-weights (Berciu 1956: 523; Berciu 1935: 31), stone net-weights (Marinescu Bilcu *et al.* 2000-2001: 126), bone harpoons (Hasotti 1997: 106; Comsa 1986: 43 ff; Dragomir 1983: 142; Dumitrescu 1965: 227; Galbenu 1962: 301; Popescu 1938: 117; Nestor 1937: 13; Berciu 1935: 33; Dumitrescu 1933: 152; Christescu 1925: 284; Dumitrescu 1925: 94; Stefan 1925: 191) for capturing large fish (*Cyprinus carpia, Silurus glanis* and *A. ruthenus*), and cooper hooks (Dumitrescu 1925: 103; Berciu 1956: 523).

The use of harpoons for capturing large fish could also be an indicator of fishing from the ice during the cold season.

One could infer by analysing the construction techniques of palisades and walls, and by making use of ethnological examples from the Danube area, that the Gumelnita communities could have used a system of fishing weirs to catch fish after periodic floods. Moreover one could infer that all the communities living on islands, or along the Danube, made use of boats, although these have not yet been discovered by archaeologists. Anchors made of perforated stone boulders (Popovici and Railand 1996: 42) are the only evidence for the presence of boats.

Ethnological examples involving such social activity as collective fishing with pound nets could suggest a possible model towards understanding the methods of fishing in the Gumelnita communities. (Fig. 23)

Fig. 23 Collective fishing with pound nets on a tributary of the Olt river, summer 2001.

CERAMIC OBJECTS FUNCTIONAL SHAPES AND TRANSPORTABILITY

The shape of a ceramic vase designed to carry water reveals specific details due to the factor of transportability: the relationship between the dimension of the mouth and the central diameter, the position of the centre of gravity near the base, increased ergonomics, the presence of perforations to introduce cords or ropes, the representations of rope fastenings for transporting (Fig. 24a). When the distance between the source of water and settlement was far, the vase would have an ergonomic shape so that it could be carried on the hip (see Arnold 1993: 124, fig.6.2), or on the back by using ropes (see Arnold 1993: 125, fig.6.3), on the shoulder or head.

Fig. 24a A Gumelnita vase for carrying water, with skeuomorphs of cords (National Museum of Archaeology, Bucharest). The perforations on the neck of the vase were to fix the cords.

Fig. 25 Experimenting with the ergonomics of the arched base. Replica made by Florentina Mititelu.

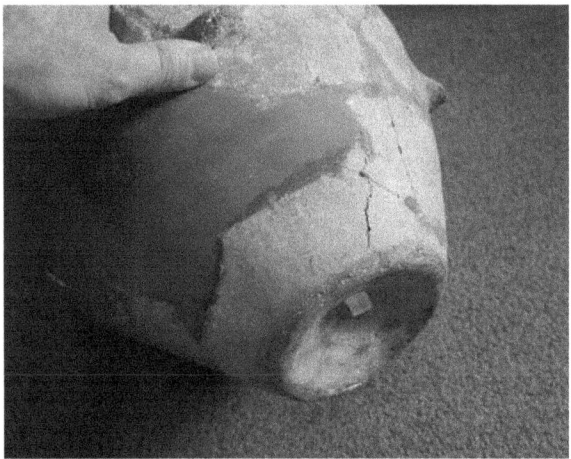

Fig. 24b The base of the vase in Fig. 24a.

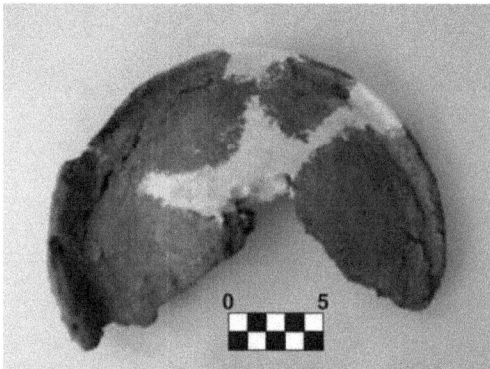
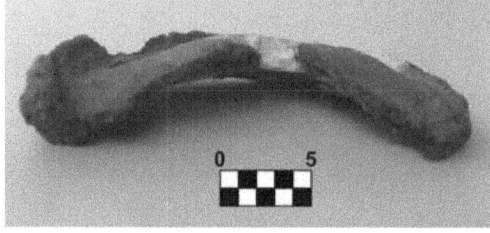

Fig. 26 The arched base of a water jar from Panduru (Archaeological Museum, Tulcea).

Gumelnita vases that I presume to have been designed to extract and carry water, were fixed and carried by means of cords and ropes, as the perforated protuberances and hook-like protuberances infer. The special shape of the base, very arched, (Figs. 24-26) demonstrate a good multifunctional design, because the object could be very well fixed on the shoulder (Fig. 27), on the head (Fig. 28) and very well handled when used, as experiments and ethnologic examples showed (see Arnold 1997: 148). Additionally, the angle resulting from the connection of the large median diameter with the base and mouth allows for a good positioning of the hands on the vase surface when carried on head (Figs. 28-29), as ceramic figurines illustrate (Rosetti 1938: fig.25; Miclea and Florescu 1980: fig.227), and also on the back, when carried with the help of ropes. Small handles, with the dual role of portability, for hands and ropes also indicate the function of the vases.

Since analysis of the profiles of the vases from a settlement reveals a small number of arched bases, one may infer that the transporting of daily water from source to settlement was carried out using leather bags, this hypothesis being supported by several ceramic skeuomorphs.

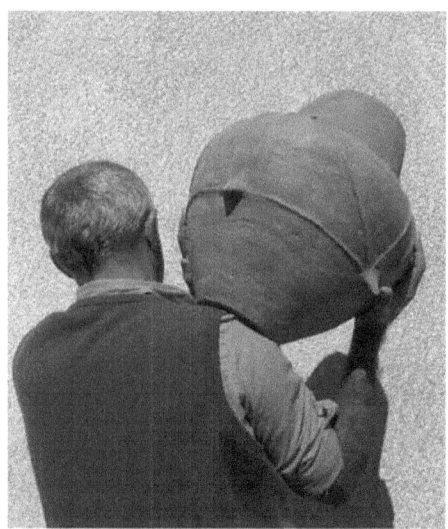

Fig. 27 Experimenting with the ergonomics of the arched base.

Fig. 28 The positioning of hands on the vase surface.

WELLS

The use of cords and ropes, as skeuomorphs indicate, could also suggest the existence of wells, dug near the shore (as contemporary examples from traditional society show (Fig. 31), from which water was extracted by immersing the vase. Although not yet proved by the archaeological record, wetland wells could have acted as filters for the standing water of lakes and marshes.

Fig. 31 A well near the shore of the lake Mosistea, near the Sultana *tell*.

RITUAL AND TRANSPORTABILITY

One may suppose that the daily transportation of water to the settlement, or its transportation in various rituals, created motor-habit patterns with a strong ceremonial and symbolic significance.

Figurines carrying a vase on the head were found in several Gumelnita settlements (see Miclea and Florescu 1980: fig. 227; Rosetti 1938: fig. 25/1; Marinescu-Bilcu and Ionescu 1967: 21,22; Micu and Micu 1995-1996), some of them re-utilized after breakage as stands. In Mangalia (south of Dobroudja, on the seashore near Limanu), I discovered a fragment of the above type of figurine (with the edges rounded), showing a hand holding a vase. The hand was adorned with two bracelets, which we may imagine as being made of *Spondylus gaederopus* shell, gold, or copper, indicating a special status. (Fig. 32)

Fig. 29 Human figurine carrying a vase, from the Gumelnita site (National Museum of Archaeology, Bucharest).

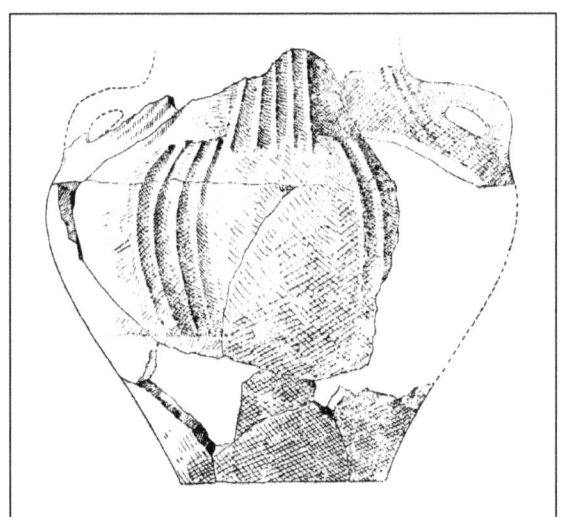

Fig. 30 Vase with small handles, from Sultana (Andriesescu 1929: 76, fig.10).

Fig. 32 Fragment from an anthropomorphic figurine carrying a vase, from Mangalia.

Mention may also be made here of the miniature vases that copy the shape and decoration of a special category of vases (as those with shell-decoration), and are less at risk when transported, as well as the *askos* (specific to the Gumelnita culture, Ursulescu 1998:125), that replicate skin containers and their cord handles.

VASES DECORATED WITH SHELL

Beside the ropes on vases, a possible symbolic relationship between ceramic containers and water could be discerned in the treatment of the surface of vases made with the help of shells (Figs. 33-35) (and see also Andriesescu 1929: 81, plate.XXV; 83, plate XXVIII; 84, fig.XXIX). The incised decoration suggesting waves on water surface (an interpretation inspired by the meaning of analogous patterns in traditional culture), or the texture of some exotic shells (this interpretation being suggested by pre-Columbian vases copying *Spondylus* shells), was composed in parallel rows with an alternating pattern position.

Fig. 35 Fragment of vase decorated with shell, from Sultana.

Fig. 33 Student Oana Veiner experimenting with incised shell decoration.

Fig. 36 Vase from Sultana Museum of Archaeology, Giurgiu).

Fig. 34 Fragment of vase decorated with shell, from Sultana.

Fig. 37 Fragment of a miniature vase, copying a vase decorated with shell, from Sultana.

This pattern is also found on miniature vases (Fig.36). When reduced, the incised decoration resembles very much the textured surfaces of exotic shells, ornamented with spikes and covered with organic concretions. (Fig. 37)

EXOTIC SHELLS

A workshop for processing *Spondylus gaederopus* shell was discovered at Harsova (town) (Galbenu 1963), on a *tell* positioned near the Danube (Fig. 38)

Fig. 38 Part of the Harsova (town) tell seen from the Danube. One of the largest Chalcolithic tells from Europe (200 m in diameter and 11 m height). The stratigraphy of the base (in the area of flooding) demonstrates a high frequency of levels of destruction as well as a small number of wattle and daub constructions, compared to the higher levels of the tell, that were above the flooding level.

For prehistoric populations the *Spondylus gaederopus* shell (Fig. 39) was an exotic and prestigious product, imported over long distances (Childe 1929).

Fig. 39 *Spondylus gaederopus* shell.

In the Danube plain, Boian populations used local as well as imported shells - *Ostrea edulis, Pectunculus, Dentalium* or *Spondylus gaederopus* - in their funerary rituals (see Cantacuzino 1968), a practice continued by Gumelnita populations that used *Spondylus gaederopus* and *Denatalium* (Ivanov 1992; Whittle 1996: 98) as a prestigious material; this tradition confirming the persistence in Gumelnita of old trade routes from the Aegean to the Danube, although they could not cover up the great demand for exoticism, a reason for the appearance of a skeuomorph, gold, that partially replaced the exotic material. (Fig. 40)

Pecten and *Cardium* shells with central perforations (*cf.* the *Cardium* shells from Thermi, with 5 to 9 mm perforations, displayed in the Museum of Archaeology, Tessaloniki), resemble perforated gold pendants specific to the Gumelnita culture, found at Sultana (Halcescu 1995: 16, figs. 1 and 2) and Varna (Ivanov 1992).

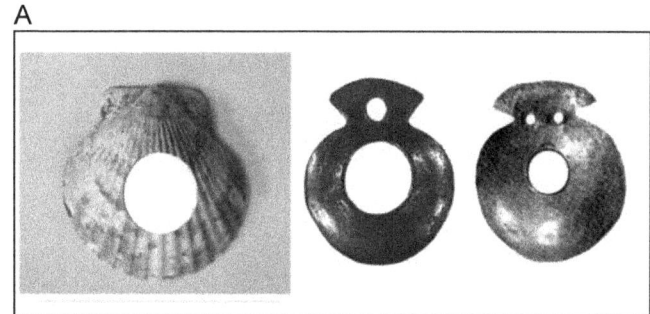

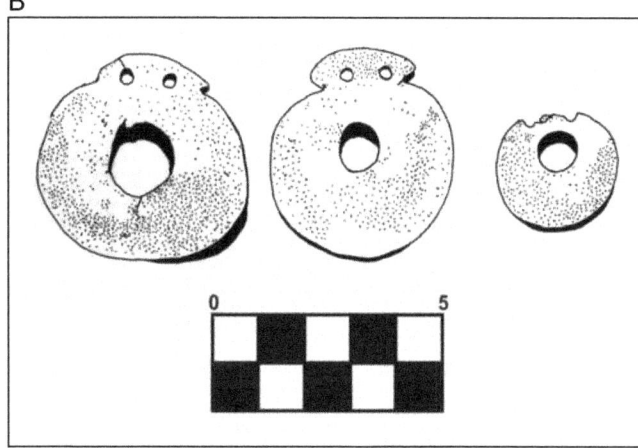

Fig. 40 A) Perforated *Pecten* shell and gold skeuomorphs (gold pieces from the Varna cemetery, Ivanov 1992, and B) from the Sultana hoard, Halcescu 1995).

SHELLS AND VASE COLOUR

Probably the most fascinating colours in relation to water are those of *Unio* shells, with a glossy dark exterior and mother-of-pearl interior. This colour composition is to be found on some prestige ceramic vases with a glossy dark surface (resulting from firings in a reduced atmosphere) painted on exteriors and interiors with graphite. It is supposed that these glossy surfaces, decorated with graphite, appeared even better in artificial light, as experiments seem to confirm, the visual effects being similar to those produced by shells or glittering water. (Fig. 41)

GOLD

Gold was in a relationship of substitution (see Renfrew 1992: 148; Whittle 1996: 119) with diverse materials, such as stone, copper, or ceramics, as may be see from the Varna cemetery.

Among the first gold objects of the Gumelnita culture (see Dumitrescu 1961; Ivanov 1988 a, 1988 b) were skeuomorphs copying *Spondylus gaederopus* and *Pecten* shells. The latter were produced in the shape of calotte pendants, sometimes perforated in the middle, with two protuberances that copied the shell's body and "ears". (Fig. 40)

I believe that twisted gold bands or *saltaleones,* such as those discovered at Sultana (Halcescu 1995: 17, fig.3), could be

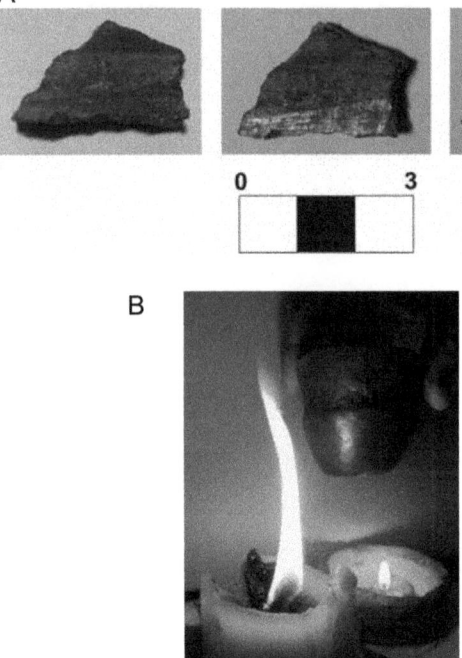

Fig. 41 Illuminating a shard painted with graphite (A) and an experiment with a Gumelnita vase replica (B).

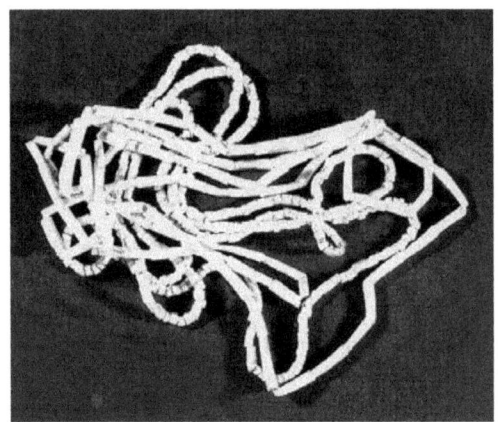

Fig. 42 Beads made of *Dentalium* shell. Varna necropolis (after Ivanov 1992).

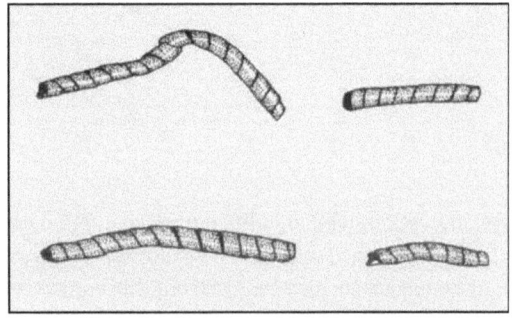

Fig. 43 *Saltaleones* from the Sultana hoard (after Halcescu 1995).

skeuomorphs of *Dentalium* shells (Fig. 42), whose cylindrical curved shapes could be easily copied by spiraling a narrow strip of metal (Fig. 43). The dimensions of *saltaleones,* as well as their slightly curved shape, correspond to those of the *Dentalium* shells found in tombs at Varna (see Ivanov 1992), and their modules to *Dentalium* cylindrical beads.

Other gold pendants in the shape of horns, I assume to represent ovine forms, and symbolize also a relationship with water. It is well known that in traditional societies, collecting alluvial gold required sheep fleeces to be secured to riverbeds (see Koleseri 1780; Roman *et al.* 1982). The presence of gold along the Danube tributaries - the Olt, Arges, and Dambovita (i.e. the area covered by the Gumelnita culture north of the Danube) has been reported since the 18th century (see Koleseri 1780), therefore part of the Chalcolithic gold used in this area could be of local origin (for a foreign origin of the Gumelnita gold see Hartmann 1978).

From this perspective, I believe the metaphor of "the Golden Fleece" may be illustrated for the first time in the Varna cemetery in the form of gold rams' horns, astragal and silhouettes, this symbol of gold being related to water.

Another link between horns and liquids is to be found in the use of rhytons, a type of vase specific to the Gumelnita culture. (Fig. 44)

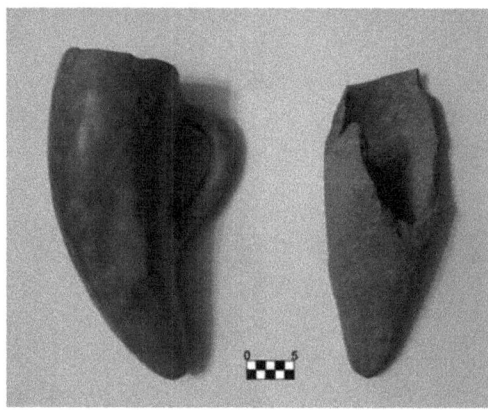

Fig. 44 Rhyton from Uzunu, right (Calugareni Museum). Replica with handle on left.

LEVEL II
COATING WITH CLAY

At a more detailed reading of micro-hydrostrategies, that of micro-morphology, one may re-encounter the phenomenon of water exclusion, on this occasion by the use of waterproof coatings.

The structure of the composite material resulting from the mix of clay, straw, and dung with water, permits a good thermal insulation and a relatively dense material, even though its waterproofing qualities are not good (Fig. 45). Such composite material can be protected from atmospheric water by coating it repeatedly with thin, but dense, layers of clay mixed with dung: an operation that again requires the use of water. This is why Gumelnita wattle-and-daub walls and floors were plastered regularly with waterproofing layers (Haita 1998-2000: 52) to prevent rainwater and humidity to penetrate inside the house. (Fig. 46)

Portable braziers, with various shapes (as the one shown in Fig. 5, representing a model of a settlement with palisade) supplemented the hearth in producing heat and fighting damp.

Fig. 45 Wall fragment from Sultana showing the straw inner structure.

Fig. 46 Coated surface of a wall fragment from Sultana. Such clay surfaces needed periodic maintenance, due to shrinkage that produced visible cracks.

COATING WITH ORGANIC SUBSTANCES

The storage of grains in large ceramic amphorae used the properties of clay fired at low temperatures in dung bonfires to be water absorbent; this protected the grains from damp. In the case of water containers such phenomenon of porosity would produce, beside the loss of a large quantity of water, a cooling of the liquid.

The phenomenon of porosity, and consequently of water loss (Fig. 47), could be neutralized by sealing the pores of the ceramic vases through a process of polishing and, probably, by greasing the vases after firing with organic substances such as fat, whey, fish, meat, residues from beehives, or by boiling any organic substances in them.

FOOD PREPARATION

Among the coarse kitchenware vases, I believe that the most eloquent example showing a direct relationship between liquid and fire in the process of food preparation is the vase with inside loops. The positioning of the inside loops allows very good control of the vase, if cords are passed through them, when suspended over fire. Therefore the vase, when filled with hot liquid, could only be manipulated with the help of cords.

A

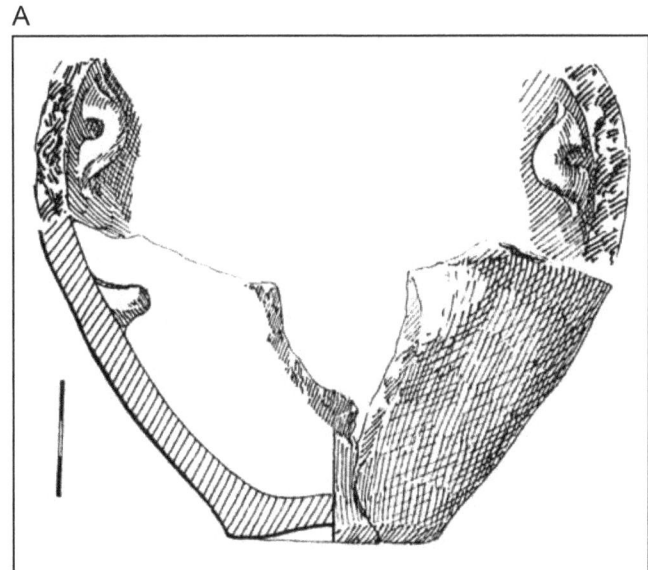

Fig 48 A) Vase with inside loops (Isacescu 1984:32, Pl.III/7) for positioning over fire and pouring hot liquid.

B

Experiment with vase in Fig. 48 A).

Fig. 47 Experimenting the porosity and water loss of a ceramic vase from Sultana.

FIRST CONCLUSION: RELATIONSHIPS BETWEEN MULTI-SCALAR LEVELS

In addition to a separate analysis of the interpretation of the several levels of compositions, all the above multi-scalar levels may be condensed into a syncretistic reading when archaeologists come to investigate religion.

RELIGION

The multiple roles of water at different levels in the life of the Gumelnita communities raise the question if this element was not the subject of a cult, resulting from the phenomenon of settling in close relationship with water. The fractality of the overlapping layers of wet clay (part anthropogenic and part natural, due to periodic floods) forming a *tell* might be perceived as a metaphor of flooding, or as an incorporation of flood (i.e. of "wild" water), whose significance was probably related to fertility. A ritual (i.e. repetitive and seasonal) action of covering the ground of the settlement, or the walls of the houses, with overlapping layers of organic and inorganic materials mixed with clay (by using water as a bond), could have had an analogous meaning to that of the overflowing, fertilizing waters of the rivers, or of the rain. In the same way, the periodic repairing of houses, or the regular demolishing and reconstruction of them (the cultural cyclic phenomenon that produces a *tell*), might be perceived as a metaphor for the fertilizing inundation, and a succession of rites of connection and separation.

The river positioned to the north of the settlement, the ditch with water positioned (sometimes) at the south, and the foundation trenches, could all be seen as belonging to a symbolic system with rites of separation and aggregation, using water as the ritual element: the *tell* separated from the rest of the world by a river and a ditch (seasonally with water) has correspondences to the first stages of house building, whose foundations separate the interior space from the exterior.

I believe the fertility cult, assigned so far to female figurines (the so called "goddesses"), could be extended to hydrostrategies, to cite only the location (and orientation) of settlements close to water, the architectural structures (i.e. the ditches and trenches) in relation to with water and the hydrophilic formative processes of tells, houses and objects (as the formation of wattle and daub and the covering with overlapping layers of slip of all architectural clay structures) that could be interpreted as ritual actions.

The Janus-like human figurine carrying a vase, the human couple positioned in the centre of a dish, the female-vases or the vases with double mouths, are additional indicators of a cult of the liquid, in relation to the human body or couple.

Ceramic containers for carrying water, pots decorated with shells, or the micro-vases, might also be perceived as belonging to the same water cult of fertility, as well as the exotic shells and gold pendants.

The marine shells from the Aegean, and their gold skeuomorphs, demonstrate a symbolic, and probably a cultic, bond to the southern waters of a faraway sea, and could be ascribed to the same cosmic symbolism related to the cardinal points that shaped the ordered *tell* settlements.

FINAL CONCLUSION: WATER THAT BINDS AND SEPARATES, OR THE COMPOSITION WITH NATURE

As an element of composition, the role of water was to act as a bond, and simultaneously as a separator, from the macro-level of geographical compositions to the micro-level of rituals, design of objects and textures.

From the multiple levels of the multi-scalar interpretation mentioned above, one may notice that water was at the same time an inter-community and intra-community social bond, a physical bond for raw and recycled materials, as well as asocial and physical separation factor.

The fertility water-cult, using equally the rites of connections and rites of separation, seems to have been the cultural link between the macro- and the micro-worlds of Gumelnita culture, relating the shape of the settlement to flooding and rains, objects to objects, objects to micro-objects as well as materials to materials.

Acknowledgements

I would like to thank very much all who helped me with the elaboration of the present text: Dr. George Trohani, Dr. Vasilica Lungu, Dr. Cristian Schuster, and M. Cristian Micu, for allowing me to photograph ceramic objects from the National Museum in Bucharest and the Archaeology Museum in Giurgiu and Tulcea; Corina Sarbu and Cornelia Catuna for editorial work and technical support. Thanks also to potter Ion Cococi, from the village of Vadastra, for the help provided in experiments.

The experiments in Vadastra were made possible thanks to a CNCSIS – World Bank Grant (No.112).

Thereconstructed Gumelnita vases were by Florentina Mititelu and Oana Veiner, and the house foundations by Corina Sarbu and Ion Cococi.

Bibliography

ANDREESCU, R. and BAILEY, D., 1999, Observatii preliminare privind locuirea neo-eneolitica pe valea Teleormanului, pp. 11-13. *The Boian civilization on Romania's territory* [cat.], Calarasi.

ANDRIESESCU, J., 1929, Sultana, *Buletinul comisiunii monumentelor istorice*, XXII, Fasc. 60, pp. 71-87.

ARNOLD, D.E., 1993, *Ecology and ceramic production in an Andean community*, Cambridge University Press, Cambridge.

ARNOLD, D.E., 1997, *Ceramic Theory and Cultural Process*, Cambridge University Press, Cambridge.

BAILEY, D.W., 1991, The social reality of figurines from the Chalcolithic of northeastern Bulgaria: the example of Ovcarovo, *unp.PhD diss.*, Cambridge University.

BAILEY, D.W., 2000, *Balkan prehistory. Exclusion, incorporation and identity*, London and New York: Routledge.

BAILEY, D, TRINGHAM, R., BASS, J., STEVANOVIC, M., HAMILTON, M, NEWMANN, H., ANGELOVA, I., and RADNUCHEVA, A., 1998, Expanding the dimensions of early agricultural tell: the Podgoritsa Archaeological Project, *Journal of Field Archaeology* 25,4, pp.375-396.

BALASESCU, A., 1996–1998, Consideratii preliminare asupra faunei eneolitice, *Buletinul Muzeului Teohari Antonescu*, Giurgiu, II-IV, 2-4, pp.99-102.

BERCIU, D., 1935, Sapaturile arheologice de la Tangaru (1934). Raport preliminar, *Buletinul Muzeului Jud. Vlasca "Teohari Antonescu"*, I.

BERCIU, D., 1937, Sapaturile de la Petru Rares (1933-1934), *Buletinul Muzeului Jud. Vlasca "Teohari Antonescu"*, II, Giurgiu.

BERCIU, D., 1956, Cercetari si descoperiri arheologice in regiunea Bucuresti, *Materiale*, II.

BROWN, A.G., 1997, Alluvial Archaeology. Floodplain Archaeology and Environmental Change, Cambridge: Cambridge University Press.

CANTACUZINO, 1968, Necropola neolitica, *Materiale de istorie si muzeografie*, Muzeul de Istorie a Municipiului Bucuresti, pp. 15-26.

CARCIUMARU, M., 1996, *Paleobotanica.Studii in preistoria si protoistoria Romaniei*, Iasi.

CHILDE, V.G., 1929, *The Danube in Prehistory*, Oxford: Oxford University Press.

CLARKE, D.L., 1977, Spatial information in archaeology, pp. 1-32. In D.L.Clarke (ed.), *Spatial Archaeology*, London: Academic Press.

CLARKE, D.L., 1972, A Provisional model of an Iron Age society and its settlement system, pp. 801-869, In D.L.Clarke (ed.), *Models in Archaeology*, London: Methuen.

CHAPMAN, J., 1989, The early Balkan village, *Varia Archaeologica Hungarica*, 2, pp.33-53.

CHAPMAN, J., 1990, Social inequality on Bulgarian tells and the Varna problem, pp. 49-92, In R.Samson (ed.), *The Social Archaeology of Houses*, Edinburgh: Edinburgh University Press.

CHAPMAN, J., 1991, The creation of social arenas in the Neolithic and Copper Age of South East Europe: The case of Varna, pp. 152-171. In Garwood, P., Jennings. P., Skeates, R., and Thoms, J. (eds.) *Sacred and profane*, Oxford Committee for Archaeology Monograph No. 32, Oxford: Oxbow.

CHAPMAN, J., 1994, The living, the dead and the ancestors: time, lifecycles and the mortuary domain in later European prehistory, pp. 40-85, In Davies, J. (ed.) *Ritual and Remembrance: Responses to Death in Human Sciences*, Sheffield: Sheffield Academic Press.

CHRISTESCU, V., 1925, Les stations prehistoriques du lac de Boian, *Dacia*, II.

COMSA, E., 1997, Tipuri de asezari din epoca neolitica din Muntenia, *Cultura si civilizatie la Dunarea de Jos*, pp.144-164.

COMSA, E., 1996, Viata oamenilor din spatiul carpato-danubiano-pontic in mileniile 7-4 I.Hr., Bucharest: Editura Pedagogica.

COMSA, E., 1991, Ensembles neolithiques pres du littoral roumain de la Mer Noire, *Thracia Pontica*, IV, pp.167-176.

COMSA, E., 1990, Complexul neolitic de la Radovanu, *Cultura si Civilizatie la Dunarea de Jos*, VII, Calarasi.

COMSA, E., 1986, Date despre harpoanele din epoca neolitica din Muntenia, *Cultura si Civilizatie la Dunarea de Jos*, II, pp.43-49.

COMSA, E., 1963, Unele probleme ale aspectului cultural Aldeni II, *Studii si Cercetari de Istorie Veche*, 14, I, pp. 10-11.

DE COULANGES, F., 1908, *La Cite antique*, Paris, Hachette.

DRAGOMIR, I.T., 1983, *Eneoliticul din sud-estul Romaniei. Aspectul cultural Stoicani-Aldeni*, Bucharest: Academiei.

DRAGOMIR, I.T., 1996, Monografia arheologica a Moldovei de sud, I, *Danubius*, 16.

DUMITRESCU, VL., 1924, Decouvertes de Goumelnita, *Dacia* I, pp.325-342.

DUMITRESCU, VL., 1925, Fouilles de Goumelnita, *Dacia*, II, pp.29-103.

DUMITRESCU, VL., 1963, Originea si evolutia culturii Cucuteni-Tripolye (I), *Studii si Cercetari de Istorie Veche*, 14.

DUMITRESCU, VL., 1965, Principalele rezultate ale primelor doua campanii de sapaturi din asezarea neolitica de la Cascioarele, *Studii si Cercetari de Istorie Veche*, 16, 2.

DUMITRESCU, VL., 1986, Stratigrafia asezarii-tell de pe ostrovelul de la Cascioarele, *Cultura si civilizatie la Dunarea de Jos*, II, pp. 73-81.

DUMITRESCU, VL and BANATEANU, T., 1965, A propos d'un soc de charrue primitive en bois de cerf, découvert dans la station Néolithique de Cascioarele, *Dacia* IX, pp 59-68.

DUMITRESCU, H., 1933, Rapport sur les sondages de Gradistea Fundeanca, *Dacia*, III-IV, 1927-1932.

DUMITRESCU, H., 1961, Connections between the Cucuteni-Tripolye cultural complex and the neighbouring Eneolithic cultures in the light of the utilization of golden pendants, *Dacia* NS, V, pp.68-93.

FLORESCU, M. and FLORESCU, A., 1983, Observatii recente cu privire la sistemul de fortificatii al statiunii de la Manastioara-Fitionesti (jud.Vrancea), *Materiale*, 15.

GALBENU, D., 1962, Asezarea neolitica de la Harsova, *Studii si Cercetari de Istorie Veche*, 13, 2.

GALBENU, D., 1963, Neoliticeskaya musterskaya dlya obrabotki ukrashenii v Hirsove, *Dacia*, NS, pp. 501-509.

GAMBLE, C., 2001, *Archaeology – The Basics*, London Routledge.

GHEORGHIU, D., 2001, On Palisades, houses, vases and miniatures: The Formative processes and methaphors of Chalcolitic tells, pp 93-117. In Gibson, A (ed.). *Behind wooden walls: Neolithic palisaded enclosures in Europe*, Oxford: BAR International Series 1013.

HAITA, C., 1998-2000, Sedimentologie, *Cercetari arheologice*, XI, pp.48-55.

HALCESCU, C., 1995, Tezaurul de la Sultana, *Cultura si civilizatie la Dunarea de Jos*, XIII-XIV, pp. 11-18.

HARTUCHE, N., 1987, Cercetarile arheologice de la Liscoteanca I, Asezarea "Movila Olarului" (1970-1976), *Istros*, pp. 36-41.

HARTUCHE, N and DRAGOMIR, I.T., 1957, Sapaturile arheologice de la Brailita, *Materiale*, III.

HARTMANN, A., 1978, Ergebnisse der spektralanalytischen Untersuchung aeneolithichen Goldfunde aus Bulgarien, *Studia Praehistorica*, 1-2, pp. 27-45.

HASOTTI, P., 1997, *Epoca neolitica in Dobrogea*, Constanta, Muzeul de Istorie Nationala si Arheologie.

ISACESCU, C., 1984, Sapaturile de salvare de la Sultana, Com. Minastirea, Jud. Calarasi, *Cercetari Arheologice*, VII, pp. 27-43.

IVANOV, I.S., 1988a, Das Graeberfeldes von Varna – Katalog, pp. 183-208. In Fol, A and Lichardus, J (eds.), *Mach, Herrschaft und Gold: Das Graeberfeld von Varna und die Anfaenge einer neuen europaeischen Zivilisation*, Sarbruechen: Modern Galerie des Saarland – Museums.

IVANOV, I.S., 1988b, Die Ausgrabungen des Graeberfeldes von Varna, pp. 49-66. In Fol, A and Lichardus, J (eds.), *Mach, Herrschaft und Gold: Das Graeberfeld von Varna und die Anfaenge einer neuen europaeischen Zivilisation*, Sarbruechen: Modern Galerie des Saarland – Museums.

IVANOV, I.S., 1992, *El nacimiento de la civilizacion europea*. Sofia: Borina.

IVANOV, I.S., 1992, La question de la localisation et des etudes des sites submerges dans le lac de Varna, *Pontica*, XXVI, pp.19-26.

JANUSEVIC, Z.V., 1983, Nakhodki kulturnykh rastenij iz pozdeneeneoliticeskikh sloev s.Ovcarovo, In Todorova, H., Vasiliev, V., Janusevic, Z., Kovacheva, M., and Valev, P., *Ovcharovo*, Sofia: Bulgarskata Akademiya na Naukite.

KOLESERI, 1780, Historico-Physico Topographica Valachiae Austriacae Svbterraneae Descriptio", In *Auraria Romano-Dacica una cum Valachiae Cis-Alutanae Subterraneae Descriptione*, Bratislava: Ed. Ioannis Seivert.

LAZAROV, M., 1993, Les sites submerges le long du Pont Ouest dans le contexte de l'histoire pontique mediteraneenne, *Pontica*, XXVI, pp. 7-18.

LAZURCA, E., 1995, Trestenic – o noua asezare neolitica pe teritoriul judetului Tulcea, *Peuce*, XI, pp.7-48.

LICHARDUS, J., 1988, Der Westpontische Raum und die Anfaenge der Kupferzeitlichen Zivilisation, pp. 79-129. In *Macht, Herrschhaft und Gold: Das europaeischen Zivilisation*, Saarbrucken.

MARINESCU-BILCU, S. and IONESCU, B., 1967, *Catalogul sculpturilor eneolitice din Muzeul Raional Oltenita*, Sibiu.

MARINESCU-BILCU, S., 1974, *Cultura Precucuteni pe teritoriul Romaniei*, Academia RSR, Bucharest.

MARINESCU-BILCU, S., VOINEA, V., DUMITRESCU, S., HAITA, C., MOISE, D., and RADU, V., 1999-2000, Asezarea eneolitica de pe insula "La Ostrov", lacul Tasaul (Navodari, Jud. Constanta), Raport preliminary – Campaniile 1999-2000, *Pontica*, XXXIII-XXXIV, pp. 123-133.

MICLEA, I. AND FLORESCU, R., 1980, *Arta neolitica in Romania*, Meridiane, Bucharest.

MICU, C. and MICU, S., 1995-1996, Despre un tip de statueta antropomorfa gumelniteana, *Pontica*, XXVIII-XXIX, pp.7-11.

MOISE, D., 2000-2001, Studiul materialului osteologic de mamifere, *Pontica*, XXXIII-XXXIV, pp.155-164.

MONAH, F., 1998-2000, Raport preliminaire sur les macrorestes vegetales du Complexe menager 521 – le tell eneolithique Harsova (Dep. de Constanta). La campagne de 1998, *Cercetari arheologice*, XI, pp. 66-74.

MORINTZ, S., 1962, Tipuri si sisteme de fortificatie si de imprejmuire in cultura Gumelnita, *Studii si Cercetari de Istorie Veche*, XIII, 2, pp.273-284.

MORINTZ, S.and PREDA, C., 1959, Sapaturile de la Spantov, *Materiale*, 5.

NANIA, I., 1967, Locuitorii gumelniteni in lumina cercetarilor de la Teiu, *Studii si articole de istorie*, IX, pp.7-23.

NESTOR, I., 1933, Stand der Vorgeschichtsforshung in Rumanien, *Ber.Roem.-Germ. Komm*, pp. 56-61.

NESTOR, I., 1936, Cercetari preistorice la Cernavoda, *Analele Dobrogei*, XVIII.

PANDREA, ST., SARBU, V. and MIREA, M., 1997, Etablissements Gumelnita dans la Valee de Calmatui, *Prehistorie du Bas Danube*, Calarasi, pp.202-218.

PANDREA, S., SARBU, V., NEAGU, M., 1999, Cercetari arheologice in asezarea gumelniteana de la Insuratei-Popina I, Jud.Braila. Campaniile 1995-1999, *Istros*, 9.

PANDREA, S., SARBU, V., NEAGU, M., 1999, Cercetari arheologice in asezarea gumelniteana de la Insuratei-Popina I, Jud.Braila. Campaniile 1995-1999, *Istros*, IX.

PANDREA, S., 2000, Cateva observatii referitoare la periodizarea culturii Boian, *Istros*, X, Braila, pp.32-70.

PERNICEVA, L., 1978, Sites et habitations du Chalcolithique en Bulgarie, *Studia Praehistorica*, 1-2, pp. 163-170.

PHILIP, G., DONOGHUE, D., BECK, A., and GALIATSATOS, N., 2001, Corona sattelite photography: archaeological application from the Middle East, *Antiquity*, 76, 291, pp. 109-118.

POPESCU, D., 1938, Les fouilles de Cunesti, *Dacia* V-VII, 1935–1936.

POPOVICI, D. and RAILLAND, Y., 1996, *Vivre au bord du Danube il y a 6000 ans*, Saint Jean de la Ruelle: Editions Caisse Nationale des monuments historiques et des sites.

POPOVICI, D. RANDOIN, B., RAILLAND, Y., VOINEA, V., VLAD, F., BEM, C., and HAITA, G., 1998-2000, Les recherches archeologiques du tell de Harsova (Dep. de Constanta). 1997 – 1998, *Cercetari arheologice*, XI, pp. 13-33.

RADU, V., 1997, Archaeozoology, Pisces, *Cercetari arheologice*, X, pp.96-105.

RADU, V., 1998-2000, Sur la duree d'utilisation d'une zone de rejet menajer appartenant a la culture Gumelnita A2 du tell Harsova. Etude archeologique preliminaire, *Cercetari arheologice*, XI, pp.75-83.

RADU, V., 2000-2001, Studiul materialului arheologic, *Pontica*, XXXIII-XXXIV, pp. 165-170.

RADULESCU, D., and DIMITRESCU, R., 1966, *Mineralogia topografica a Romaniei*, Bucharest: Editura Academei.

RANDOIN, B., POPOVICI, D., and RAILLAND, Y., 1998-2000, Metoda de sapatura si inregistrarea datelor stratigrafice intr-un sit pluristratificat: Tell-ul neo-eneolitic de la Harsova, *Cercetari arheologice*, XI, pp.199- 233.

RENFREW, J.M., 1973, *Palaeoethnobotany. The Prehistoric food plants of the Near East and Europe*, London.

ROMAN, P., SANTIMBREANU, A, and WOLLMANN, V., 1982, *Aurarii din Muntii Apuseni*, Bucharest: Sport-Turism.

ROSETTI, D., 1938, Steinkupferzeitliche Plastik aus einem Wohnhuegel bei Bukarest, *JPEK*, 12.

SHERRATT, A., 1979, Water, Soil, and Seasonality in Early Cereal Cultivation, *World Archaeology*, 11,3, pp.313-341.

STEFAN, GH., 1925, Les fouilles de Cascioarele, *Dacia* II, pp.138-197.

TODOROVA, H., 1982, *Kupferzeitliche Siedlungen in Nordostbulgarien*, Muenchen : C.H.Beck.

TODOROVA, H., 1978, *The Eneolithic in Bulgaria in the Fifth Millennium B.C.*, Oxford, BAR International.

TRINGHAM, R., 1992, Houses with faces: The Challenge of gender in Prehistoric architectural remains. pp. 93-131. In J.Gero and M.Conkey (eds.). *Engendering Archaeology. Women and Prehistory*, Oxford, Massachusetts, Blackwell.

URSULESCU, N., 1998, Inceputurile istoriei pe teritoriul *Romaniei*, Iasi: Demiurg.

WHITTLE, A., 1996, Europe in the Neolithic. The *creation of new worlds*, Cambridge, Cambridge University Press.

ZAVOIANU, I., 1999, *Hidrologie*, Bucharest: Romania de Maine.

THE CHALCOLITHIC AND EARLY BRONZE AGE HYDROSTRATEGY IN THE BLACK SEA STEPPE AREA

Yuri RASSAMAKIN

Abstract : The study of the steppe and forest-steppe populations is the study of the formation of the first forms of pastoralism. The hydrostrategies of these populations, in Eneolithic and Early Bronze Age, was, with small differences the following: exploitation of the river resources, proximity to water, the development of a specific design, ritual in relationship to water, and the use of water as a way of communication. In Early Bronze Age, due to the spreading out of wheeled vehicles this form of transport decreased in importance.

Resumé : L' étude des populations des steppes et des fôrets-steppes est en faît l'étude des premières formes de pastoralisme. Les hydrostrategies de ces populations au temps de l'Éneolithique et de l'Âge du Bronze Ancien ont été, avec des variations régionales, les suivates: éxploatation des resources des rivières, proximité de l'eau, developpement d'un design spécifique des objets quotidiens, l'éxistence d'un rituel en relation avec l'eau et l'utilisatiomn de l'eau comme support de communication. Au temps de l'Âge du Bronze Ancien, a cause du developpement des vechicule à roues cette manière de transport a décru en importance.

1. THE "HYDROSTRATEGY" CONCEPT AS AN OBJECT OF RESEARCH

Dragos Gheorghiu invited me to prepare a paper on this topic for the session "The Hydrostrategies of Chalkolithic Cultures" at the XIVth Congress of the International Union of Prehistoric and Protohistoric Sciences (Liège, Belgium, September 2-8, 2001). At first this proposal confused me because I was skeptical of its viability. But my skepticism became the reason for me to work on this project though I had little time and few archaeological facts with which to explore the idea.

First of all there was the main question of what to focus on when studying hydrostrategy of the Northern Pontic Area in Eneolithic and Early Bronze Age. Is it possible to formulate a "hydrostrategy" concept and to determine its structure?

Obviously, it is necessary to consider hydrostrategy as one of the most important directions of the general economic strategy of the steppe population. Many experts consider this general economic strategy as a development of the different forms of pastoralism. It includes, at least, two aspects:

a) – A way of life or housekeeping of the steppe population;

b) – The forms of economy, which depend on natural resources of the local ecological niches occupied by these populations (Bunyatyan 1994: 1997).

In this context, I would suggest that the "hydrostrategy" concept is multifaceted. I see four main aspects of a broad understanding of hydrostrategy, which may seem rather eclectic when presented schematically (Table 1):

1 – river systems and seacoast as a communication network;

2 – river and sea resources and resources of river valleys as an important part of the steppe population diet and maintenance of its economic needs;

3 – drinking water as the main means of life-support of a society;

4 – water - river/sea - water elements in a context of sacral, magic, ritual functions in social life.

It is possible to develop an additional scheme that shows some aspects of the general model in more detail (Table 2).

Naturally, it is possible to expand both schemes during the occurrence of new archaeological sources, results of special researches, and also on the basis of the ethnographic dates. But in any case, hydrostrategy can be determined as a system of development and use of river and sea resources, which defined the features of economic activities and way of life of the Pontic steppe societies.

1.1. GENERAL INTRODUCTION AND SOME METHODOLOGICAL PROBLEMS

In this research the question is about steppe and partial forest-steppe zones of the Northern Pontic area limited from the west by the Danube and from the east by the Don (Fig. 1). This territory represents the northern part of the so-called Circumpontic zone, which is of special interest to researchers investigating the development of metallurgy to the search of the homeland of the Indo-European people.

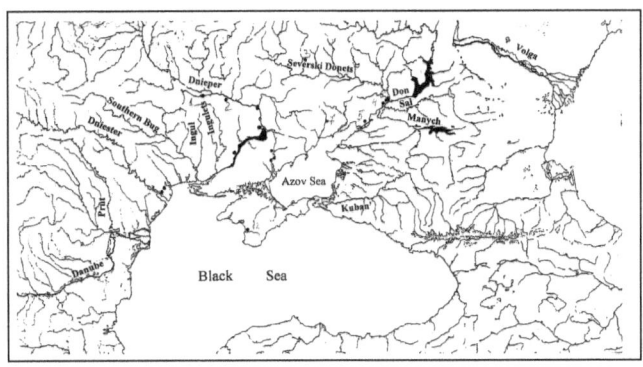

Fig. 1

Tabl. 1. Hydrostrategy of the steppe population in Eneolithic and Early Bronze Age (basic model):

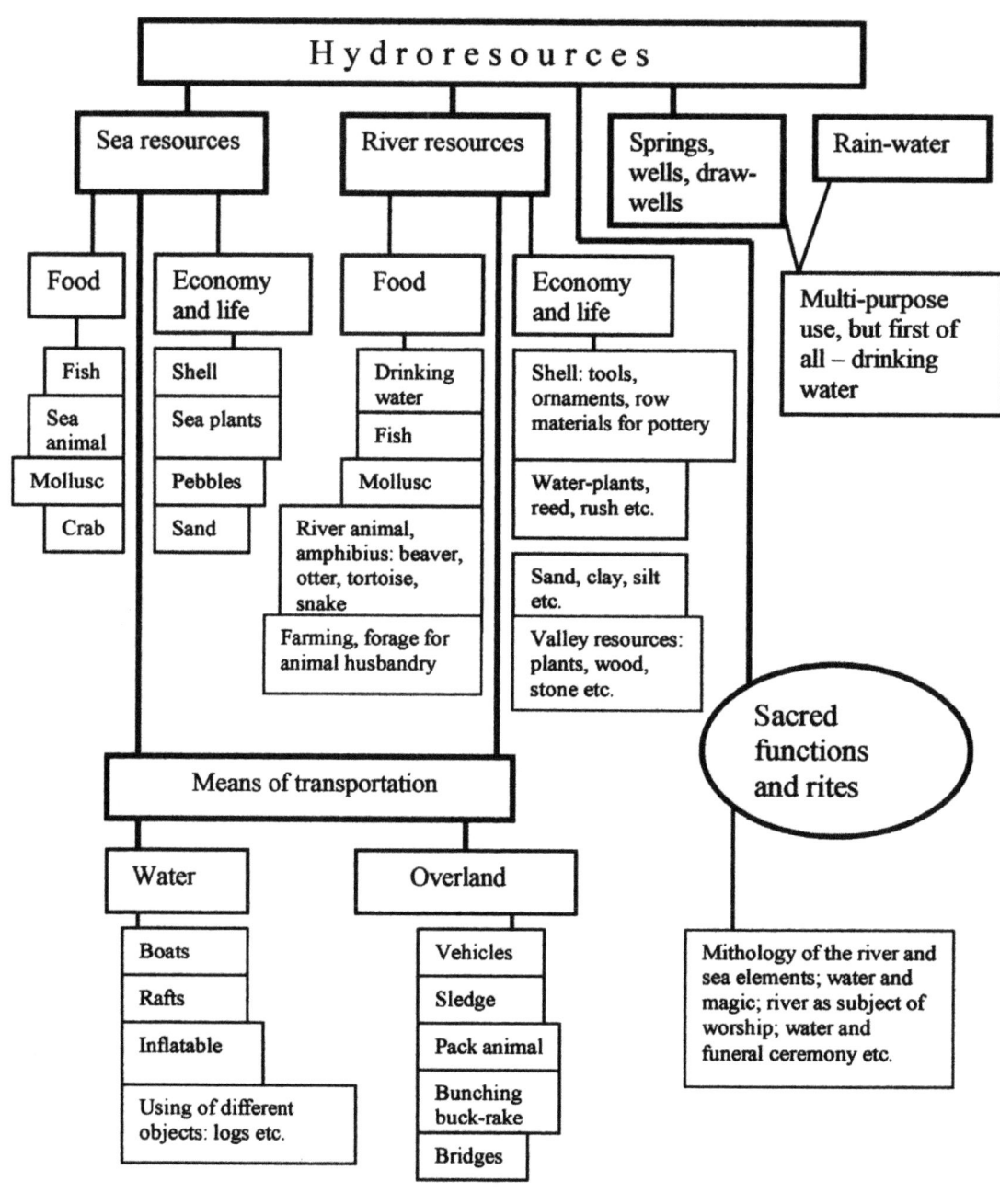

1.1.1. NEOLITHIC

The archaeological characteristics of steppe societies in Eneolithic (the first half of the 5th - the end of the 4th millennium B.C.) are very different from those of the previous Neolithic societies or local cultures of the Mariupol cultural-historical unity, among which the Dnieper-Donetsk Culture is best known (Danilenko 1969: 9-18, 30-37, 189-192; Telegin 1968: 1985)[1]. The economic strategy of these societies, undoubtedly, was connected to the rivers and river resources, the basic role of which was to allow for fishing and river gathering (Telegin 1968: 204 - 207; 1985: 171; Danilenko 1969: 36; Neprina 1988: 30-31; Mallory 1987: vii). Therefore hydrostrategy was a key part of the general fishing-hunting economic strategy both in the forest-steppe and steppe zone, though in the steppe zone the first developments of cattle breeding as a special economic form appeared at this time (Danilenko 1969: 9 - 18, 179-180; Telegin 1968: 208 - 210; 1985: 171; Zhuravlev and Kotova 1996: 11).

J. Mallory, in his introduction to Telegin and Potekhina's *Neolithic Cemeteries and Populations in the Dnieper Basin*

---

[1] The interpretation of this culture is disputed. D.Ya. Telegin considers it as one culture with its local variants (Telegin 1968; 1985). V.N. Danilenko considered the Dnieper-Donets culture as a separate forest-steppe and forest culture differed from the steppe Azov-Dnieper culture (Danilenko 1969 30-37). N.S. Kotova has a similar opinion (Kotova 1994).

Table 2. Storage of water, using of river/sea recources and their archaeological equivalents:

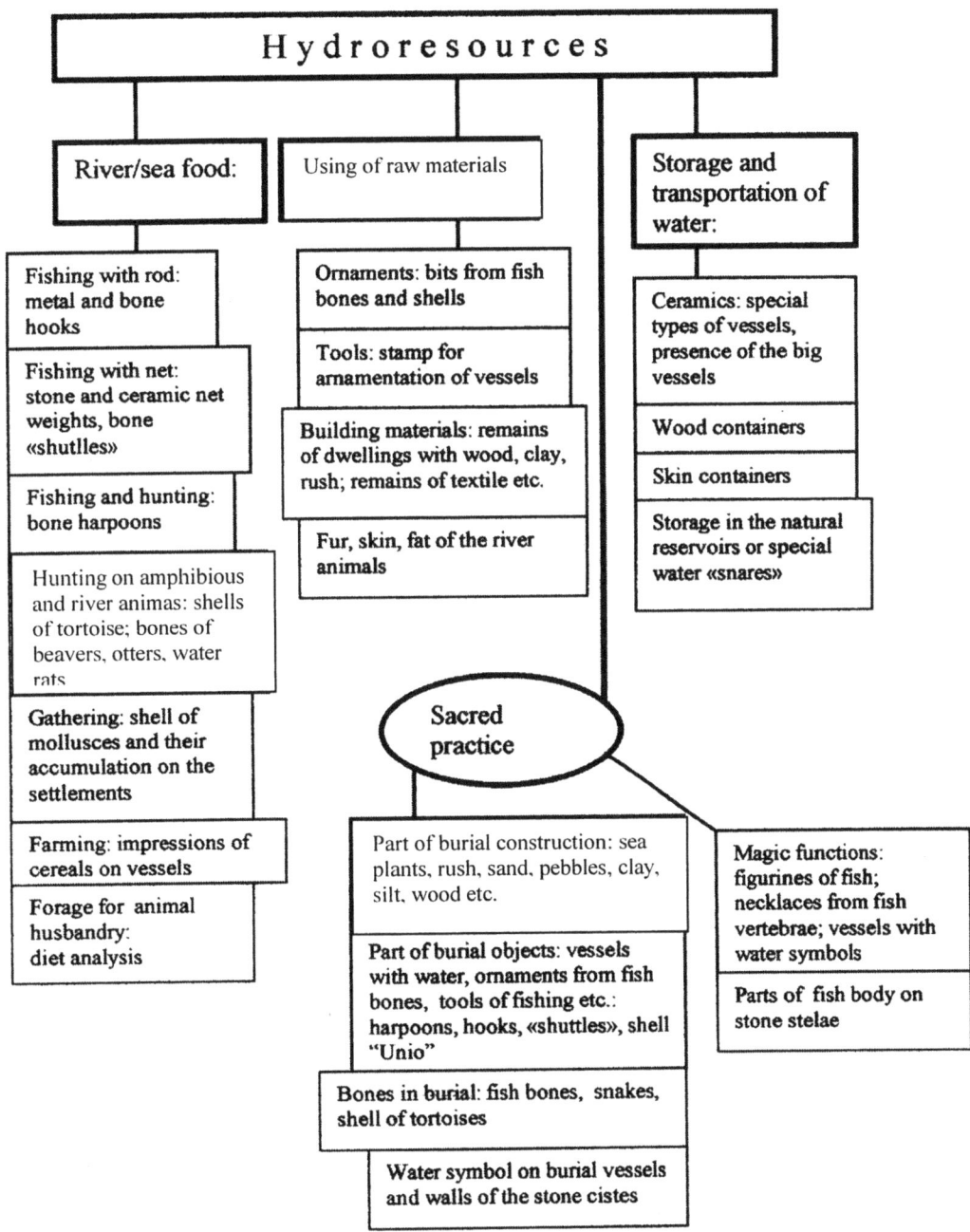

(Telegin and Potekhina 1987), directly writes that a strong dependence on fishing was basic to the economy of the population with cemeteries of the Mariupol type. Moreover, the researcher adds to this: "Ethnographical date suggests that fishing-based economies is one of the few forms of hunter-gather subsistence that may develop both substantial long term settlement and territoriality" (Mallory 1987: vii)[2].

D.Ya. Telegin writes about an emphasis on fishing in the Dnepr-Donetsk Culture. The localization of the settlements on the banks of rivers and lakes, in Telegin's opinion, also reflects the important role of fishing. D.Ya. Telegin especially marks "Nadporizhzh'a" area on the Dnieper where, in his opinion, it was possible to fish without special tools during fish spawning. In other areas diverse fishing tools were used. Telegin also assumes the use of fishing nets. The stone net weights found on the settlements confirm this opinion. In

---

[2] See other problems about it: Anthony 1994; Potekhina and Telegin 1997.

addition, bone hooks demonstrate the use of the fishing rod (Telegin 1968L 205-206).

The numerous fish bones found on the settlements provide, according to Telegin, important evidence for intensive fishing. The use of fish teeth as ornaments of clothes in the numerous burials of the Mariupol cemeteries is especially indicative of a fishing economy of the local Neolithic societies. These teeth are present in all cemeteries of the Dnieper-Donetsk culture. The fishes represented are carp and pearl roach (*Rutilus frisii*). So, for example, in the Vovnigi cemetery on the right-bank of the Dnieper (31 burials), teeth belonging to 76 carps and 16 pearl roaches, reaching up to 20 kg in weight, were found (Telegin 1968: 155, 206-207; Shpet 1956; Mallory 1987: vii). But fishing reflects only one part of the Neolithic hydrostrategy of the steppe and forest-steppe population. A similar role for fishing can be found in many cultures of different epochs (Neprina 1988).

In general, the questions about Neolithic hydrostrategy as a system in the Pontic steppe have not received special attention despite the presence of rich archaeological sources for this topic. Without specific investigation it is difficult to evaluate the Eneolithic and Early Bronze Age hydrostrategy.

1.1.2. ENEOLITHIC

The Eneolithic in the Black Sea steppe and in part of the forest-steppe can be considered as the period of formation and development of the first forms of pastoralism. This process developed within the local economic systems of settled populations. We know various cultures in the Northern Pontic area: steppe – Skelya Culture, Stog Culture, Lower Mikhailovka Culture, Konstantinovsk Culture, Usatovo Culture; forest-steppe – Dereivka Culture, Pivikha Culture; steppe and forest-steppe – Kvityana Culture, Repin Culture etc. (Rassamakin 1999: 73-97). The economic strategies of these cultures were different, but they had a complex character as they combined various forms of economic activities - agriculture, cattle breeding, hunting, fishing and gathering. The balance of these forms of activity varied with the economy of each population. The dynamics and level of development of these societies depended on influences from the agricultural societies, primarily, the Cucuteni-Tripolye Culture, and also the cultures of the Northern Caucasus (Movsha 1981; 1993; Rassamakin 1999: 97-127; 2000). Therefore, the most advanced among them represent such Late Eneolithic cultures as Konstantinovsk Cultures on the Lower Don and Usatovo in the Dniester-Danube region. They show also much more developed forms of animal husbandry (Zbenovich 1974: 113; Patokova et al. 1989; Kiyashko 1994).

The steppe (in part forest-steppe) population in the Eneolithic has created the economic preconditions for the formation in the last quarter of the 4th - the beginning of 3rd millennium B.C. such a cultural and economic unified phenomenon of the Early Bronze Age as the Yamnaya cultural - historical unity (first - second third of the 3rd millennium B.C.)[3].

---

[3] There are some problems about the absolute chronology of the Eneolithic and Early Bronze Age. They are connected with a new series of

1.1.3. EARLY BRONZE AGE

That pastoralism as basic form of economy of the Yamnaya cultural - historical unity is unquestionable for scholars. In works of many of them the Yamnaya Culture or cultural - historical unity is presented as a culture of semi-nomads or nomads (Danilenko 1974; Merpert 1974; Gimbutas 1994: 20)[4]. But in general the Yamnaya cultural - historical unity represents local populations with similar funeral ceremonies and material culture. These groups occupied various ecological niches in the steppe and forest-steppe regions. The main problem in studying this huge system consists of finding - out the economic strategy of each of these local groups. Therefore, the most productive perspectives are those, which study the Yamnaya cultural - historical unity economy through a prism of the local natural distinctions and the distribution area of this phenomenon.

The other original culture of the Early Bronze Age of the Black Sea area was the Kemi-Oba Culture (Shchepinsky 1985a) though some researchers doubt its existence. In my opinion, this culture undoubtedly existed, but it is necessary to study it as a phenomenon of foothill, mountain and, probably, seacoast of the Crimea, which researchers assumed was the first characteristic of this culture (Shchepinsky 1963: 38; 1966: 11-12; Leskov, 1965: 140-146). The economic strategy of the Kemi-Oba Culture still is obscure. Some researchers assume the existence of foothill and mountain cattle breeding of the distant pasturing type (Leskov 1974: 10). Researchers also connect to this culture the shell accumulations with ceramics and animal bones on the southern seacoast of the Crimea. In A.A.Shchepinsky's opinion, these shell accumulations reflect seasonal economic activities of the "Kemi-Oba" population connected to a coastal sea gathering (Shchepinsky 1977: 37)[5].

1.1.4. METHODOLOGICAL PROBLEMS

The fact is that questions about the hydrostrategy of the steppe region in the Eneolithic and Early Bronze Age have not been a subject of special researches. There are isolated data on this problem among which the characteristic of fishing prevails, for example, for Sredny Stog culture (according to D.Ya.Telegin), illustrated by the Dereivka settlement, partly Sredny Stog II and Stril'cha Skelya (Telegin 1973: 141; 1986: 87); for Usatovo culture, illustrated by the settlements of Mayaki and Usatovo (Zbenovich 1974: 116-117) or for the Yamnaya culture, illustrated by the Mikhailovka settlement (Lagodovska, Shaposhnikova and Makarevich 1962).

---

radiocarbon dates for Eneolithic and Yamnaya culture monuments. These dates extend the beginning of the steppe Eneolithic to the first quarter of the 5th millennium B.C. and have defined more exactly the transition period between the Late Eneolithic and Early Bronze Age from the end of the 4th millennium B.C. to the first quarter of the 3rd millennium B.C. This problem needs subsequent investigation, because there are some contradictions with the relative chronology of monuments (see Burdo and Videiko 1998; Rassamakin 1999: 127-129; Kośko 1999).

[4] See more detailed: Shilov 1975a; 1975b; 1985; Rassamakin 1994; 1999: 129-132, 151-154; Kuzmina 2000; Shishlina and Bulatov 2000.

[5] What the Eneolithic memorials in the Crimea are is not clear, though A.A. Shchepinsky attributed the Eneolithic settlemens which were earlier as Kemi-Oba culture (Shchepinsky 1985b).

Undoubtedly, the hydrostrategy of Eneolithic and Early Bronze Age societies was different from the one in the Neolithic. It is connected to the change of the general economic strategy of the population and the appearance of essentially new forms of economic activities connected first of all with cattle breeding. It is natural that hydrostrategy was directed to the maintenance of the cattle breeding economy. On the other hand, hydrostrategy of each group of the steppe and forest-steppe population differed among themselves due to distinctions of the local ecological zones and especially hydroresources, and features of local economic systems.

It is necessary to note that we do not have enough artifact data to get a complete picture of the hydrostrategy of the population in the Eneolithic and Early Bronze Age. For this purpose now it is necessary to resort not only to a simple search of the little archaeological data from the various literatures, but also to develop new excavations with the use of modern technologies. I intend to study the hydrostrategy in a context of complex researches of the separate ecological zones where different times and archaeological monuments (settlements, cemeteries, kurgans) are well presented. It seems that such approach and perspective is more important, but its realization demands a search of well-preserved ecological niches for research. Such ecological niches could be, for example, areas around already known settlements (Fig. 1):

a) in the forest-steppe: the multi-layered settlements of Dereivka[6] and Molyukhov Bugor[7] in the Dnieper area, and the Alexandriya settlement[8] with layers from Neolithic to the Bronze Age on river Oskol, in the Severski Donets area (Danilenko 1959; Telegin 1959; 1973:15-16, 28-30; 1986: 5-8);

b) in the steppe: the multi-layered settlements in the part of the Dnieper – Stril'cha Skelya rapids, Sredny Stog and also the settlements on the Dnieper islands with layers from the Neolithic to Bronze Age (Dobrovolsky 1929; Danilenko 1974: 40-59; Telegin and Konstantinesku 1992);

c) the multilayered Mikhailovka settlement with three layers from the Eneolithic to Middle Bronze Age (Lagodovs'ka, Shaposhnikova and Makarevich 1962);

d) the Usatovo and Mayaki settlements and their cemeteries located in zones of lakes, estuaries and small rivers running into these estuaries between Dniester and Danube (Zbenovich 1974: 11-14; Patokova 1979; Patokova et al. 1989).

Undoubtedly, each of these settlements was a part of the specific local economic system. It would be necessary also in the context of such systems to examine the hydrostrategy of the societies appropriate to them. These data would become the basis for the comparative study of the dynamics of hydrostrategy development in the Eneolithic and Early Bronze Age. Unfortunately, we had no such opportunity earlier and now we can develop only long-term plans for the future[9].

2. RIVER VALLEYS AND SEACOAST AS A COMMUNICATION NETWORK

2.1. CULTURAL CONTACTS AND EXCHANGE AS A FACTOR OF DEVELOPMENT OF THE COMMUNICATION NETWORK

The communication strategy of the steppe population was predetermined by presence of a long line of coast of the Black and Azov seas and the developed hydrosystem in the Pontic steppe area. Powerful rivers such as the Danube, Dniester, Southern Bug, Dnieper and Don with their numerous large and small tributaries as the Prut, Ingul, Ingulets, Bazavluk, Konka, Samara, Orel', Seversky Donets, Manych, Sal and others determined this hydrosystem (Fig. 1). In the Azov steppe region the smaller river systems of Molochnaya, Obitochnaya, Kal'mius, Mius and other small rivers played an important role for this region. In general, the steppe and forest-steppe hydrosystem of the Black Sea area represented a convenient natural communication network. It exempted the local ancient societies from the necessity of extended, difficult and dangerous overland movements through open steppe spaces. It is possible even to assume that at early stages of pastoralism development these movements were impossible in general. Paraphrasing N.Ya. Merpert's well-known expression, it is possible to say that open steppes in the given situation still acted as a disjoining instead of uniting factor.

In the Eneolithic the river valleys and obviously the watersheds zones adjoining them connected the steppe area and the Dnieper's left-bank forest-steppe with its local societies of hunters and fishers (Samara, Orel', Seversky Donets) to the Dnieper right-bank forest-steppes with local early agricultural societies of the Cucuteni-Tripolye Culture (Tyas'min, Ingulets and the tributaries of the Southern Bug and Dniester). Similar communication existed, on the one hand, with the Pre Caucasus area through tributaries of the Don (Sal, Manych and a network of the smaller rivers), and on the other hand, with the Carpathian region and the Balkans through the river networks of the Dniester and especially the Danube. The directions of the riverbeds are important factor. They have a prevailing South orientation in the steppe zone and a latitudinal one at the boundary between steppe and forest-steppe zone (Fig. 1). It determined the character of the movement of the population and the basic directions of contacts and transfers of cultural influences between different cultural and economic societies.

Therefore, the Black Sea and Azov Sea steppe was a special territory considerably more actively connected in the Eneolithic and Early Bronze Age with regions, which were

---

[6] Settlements, Neolithic, Eneolithic and Early Bronze Age cemeteries.

[7] There are here settlements from Neolithic to Bronze Age which have different topographic localizations in the valley of river Tyasmin.

[8] Alexandriya is one of different settlements on the river Oskol and other tributarys of the Severskiy Donets.

[9] I can note in this context the perspective of the investigation in the Kalmyk steppe under direction of N. Shishlina (Shishlina 1999; 2000a; Shishlina and Tsutskin 1999).

situated around the Black Sea than with the Volga region. In this case the most important role was not so much the general or close cultural standards and influences which are well known among archaeological materials, but was one played by the landscape and ecological conditions, and primarily, the presence of an advanced and convenient hydro system and a common sea coast. It favored the formation of stable cultural connections around the Black Sea for a long time, the way to the Volga region developed through the Don and its tributaries (Fig. 1).

Already in the Early Eneolithic (the first quarter - the end of the 4th millennium B.C.) we can identify a system of wide cultural connections from the Northern Caucasus (settlements of group Svobodnoe – Zamok – Meshoko of the Pre Maykop time) through Black Sea steppe (Skelya culture) to the area of the Cucuteni-Tripolye culture (stage B/1) and further over the Danube and its tributarys to the Carpathians (Tisapolgar culture) and to the western coast of the Black Sea (Varna Culture according to H. Todorova)[10]. It follows the distribution of the ceramic imports (Tripolye type vessels and ceramics from Svobodnoe – Zamok - Meshoko settlements type in the steppe area and steppe Skelya type ceramics in the Cucuteni-Tripolye settlements and settlements of the Svobodnoe type), and finished prestige objects made from copper, gold, high-quality flint, obsidian, serpentine, and at last, stone scepters. That is, a primary factor of the development of a communication network was long distance prestige exchange. If we consider the distribution of the elite burials of the Skelya culture in the steppe area at this time then we can see a clear picture of use by intermediary groups who planned optimum ways of connecting various regions of the Northern Caucasus to the Balkan-Danubian area (Rassamakin1999: 97-112).

The ways along the river valleys around the steppe region, and along the forest-steppe boundary represent the most practical ones. Specifically, it is the route from the Don along the Seversky Donets, Samara and Orel' to the Dnieper and further from the Dnieper along the Bazavluk, Ingulets, tributaries of the Southern Bug and the Dniester to the border with an area of the Cucuteni-Tripolye culture (Rassamakin 1999: Fig. 3.1). In the given context the question is, undoubtedly, about an establishment of a certain communication network between the different cultural worlds.

The most regular and intensive contacts existed in the Eneolithic due to the developed river network between the steppe population and their nearest forest-steppe neighbors - the population of the Tripolye culture. Undoubtedly, borders between these two cultural areas were determined by the river network of the Dniester and Southern Bug on the boundary of steppe and forest-steppe.

T.G. Movsha, considering the contacts between steppe and Tripolye culture population during the blossoming of the Tripolye culture (period B/2-C/1 and C/1, the first half of the 4th millennium B.C.), assumes that in the formation of these connections the important role was played by river fords on the Southern Bug, its tributaries and on the tributary of Dnieper Ingulets. She sees the significance of these fords also in the settling of the Tripolye groups to the steppe area (Movsha, 1993, 42). In particular, T.G. Movsha considers that the main ways of movement of the Tomashovka local group (or culture in Movsha's opinion[11]) in a southern direction passed along the Southern Bug and its left tributaries – Gorny Tikich, Yatran', Sinyukha and Ingul and that river fords were an important factor in this movement. In her opinion, the settlements of the Tomashovka group which were situated near fords on the Southern Bug and its tributaries are evidence for this. These fords are known to us from Medieval chronicles and geographical descriptions of the 17th – 19th centuries. T.G. Movsha mentions nine fords on the Southern Bug: Vitovtov, Sokolansky or the Sinyukha in the area of Sinyukha river mouth; Migiysky, Pischany, Gardov and Kremenetsk in the area around Gard and also Bezimyanny, Chartaysky and Ovechy. On the Ingulets river, most known are the Davydov and Bekensky or Bely fords according to D.I. Yavornitsky, who has also described twenty two fords on the Dnieper and seven on its left tributary Samara (Yavornitsky 1990: 65-69; Movsha 1993: 42)[12].

Overland trading roads which existed still in the 17th–18th centuries are connected to fords also. T.G. Movsha does not exclude the importance of similar roads already during the movement of the Tripolye population to the south. She mentions the well known overland roads which could connect the Tripolye groups and the steppe population and near to which the monuments with Tripolye C/1 and C/2 materials are located (Movsha 1993: 42):

"Cherny road[13]" - along the modern town of Uman, on the Torgovitsa river the through Sinyukha river to the Vysoka Vys' river;

"Gardov road" – from Podoliya to the Crimea;

"Big Dnieper salt road" - from the modern city of Kiev, along a line of modern towns on the Dnieper Tripillya - Kaniv - Cherkassy - Zaporizhzhya and further to the Crimea;

"Muravsky road" - through the Orel' river towards the modern town of Zaporizhzhya;

"Izyum road" - through the riverhead of Orel' where it crossed the "Muravsky road" to the Seversky Donets river and from there to the Don River.

Obviously, we can assume that the hydrosystem of the Black Sea steppe with the convenient river fords and seasonal opportunities of their use promoted the formation of a specific

---

[10] H. Todorova assumes the presence of the coasting trade along Black Sea west coast (Todorova 1993).

[11] The Tomashovka local group is presented by huge settlements situated on the middle Sothern Bug and its left-bank tributarys: Dobrovody, Sushkovka, Maydanetskoe, Tal'yanki etc. (Movsha 1985: 228-232; Videiko 1995).

[12] The fords are presented on other rivers too: on the Danube, near modern town Reni and Orlovka village. In this region the settlements of the local Gumelnita culture (Subbotin 1983) and Eneolithic and Bronze Age kurgans are known.

[13] In Ukrainian: road is "shlyakh" – "Gardov shlyakh".

system of overland and river communications already in the Early and Middle Eneolithic. The functioning of such a system proves to be true also in the Late and Final Eneolithic (the second half of the 4th - the beginning of the 3rd millennium B.C.). At this time the ways of population migration routes with Zhivotilovka-Volchansk type burials are significant. These burials were accompanied by the Latest Tripolye ceramics of the forest-steppe Gordineshty local group and by ceramics of the Maykop-Novosvobodnaya unity from the Northern Caucasus, i.e. two completely polar regions relative to the Pontic steppes. These routes were connected by the Kuban', Don, Severski Donets, Samara - Orel', Dnieper, Middle Southern Bug, Dniester, Prut and the Lower Danube rivers (Rassamakin 1996; 1999: 92-97, Fig.3.3; 2000).

On the other hand, in this period, obviously, there was a way along the Kuban' river through the Kerch strait to the Crimea, and along its foothills and the western coast to the Pontic steppe. This way was more obvious in the Early Bronze Age as exemplified by the distribution of the Kemi-Oba culture (Telegin 1971: 17). A.M. Leskov considers this culture as a direct migration of the population of the Dolmen culture from the Northwest Caucasus along the Laba, Belaya and Kuban' rivers, through the Taman' peninsula and the Kerch strait to the Crimea (Leskov 1974: 10)[14]. The burial in a dolmen type cist near Vilino village recently discovered in the Crimea confirms this connection (Fig. 2) (Khrapunov 1992).

In the Early Bronze Age, in the period of the Yamnaya culture, undoubtedly, there was a constant network of overland communications. It has predetermined the formation of so-called local variants of the Yamnaya cultural - historical unity, or in other words, separate cultural - economic groups of the population of this time. N.Ya. Merpert has allocated nine local variants for all areas of distribution of the Yamnaya cultural - historical unity. Within of some of them, in particular the Lower Dnieper variant, separate local groups were also established (Merpert 1968). Later, for the territory of the Ukrainian steppe and forest-steppe, O.G. Shaposhnikova has offered 5 large variants: Donetsk, Middle Dnieper, Lower Dnieper, Azov-Crimea and Southern Bug (Shaposhnikova 1985: 348). At the present time it is possible to identify many more such local groups because new excavations have allowed the study of Yamnaya culture materials within more limited local zones, for example, between the Orel'and Samara rivers, in the Northwest and Northeast Azov steppe area, on the left and right banks of the Dnieper, on the Southern Bug and Ingul, Dniester and Danube etc. (Fig. 3)

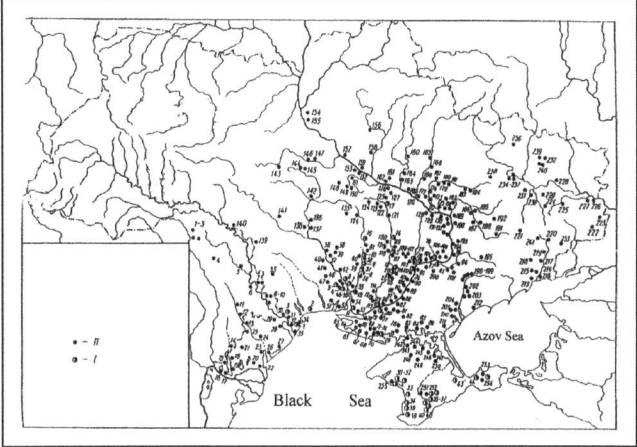

Fig. 3

The borders of these regions are mainly limited by river networks and, obviously, they can seem to have the status of separate ecological zones. But also within these zones it is possible to identify separate ecological niches as well. (Photos 1-4) Therefore, the Yamnaya culture or cultural - historical unity can be considered as a mosaic of local societies, features of whose economic strategy depend on local environment and particularly on the degree of development of local hydroresources. This connection was more significant than in the Eneolithic because in the Early Bronze Age a drier climate is established. It has predetermined also a more mobile way of life of the Yamnaya population without numerous

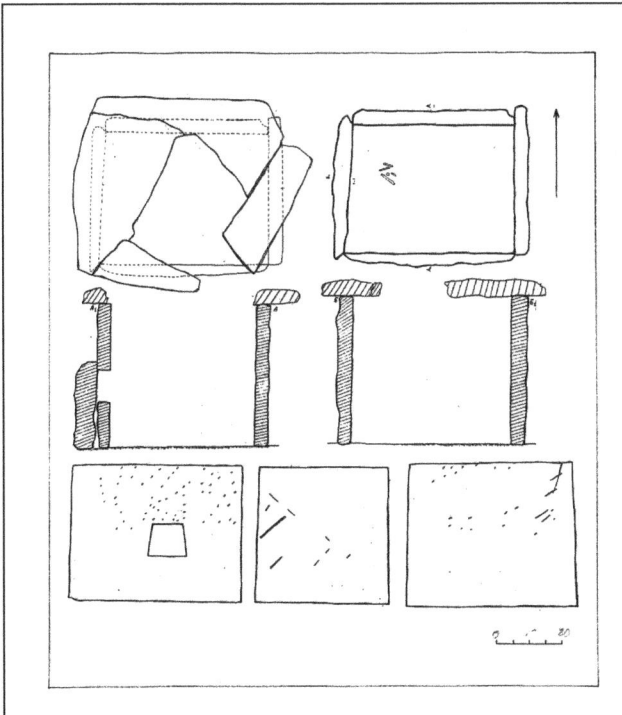

Fig. 2

Photo 1: Dnieper

---

[14] We can only assume the presence of overland and river roads in Eneolithic. We know really about trade road network from Schytian time (Boltrik 1990) and later according to medieval chronicles (Yavornitsky 1990; Kudryashov 1949).

Photos 2-4: Molocnaya

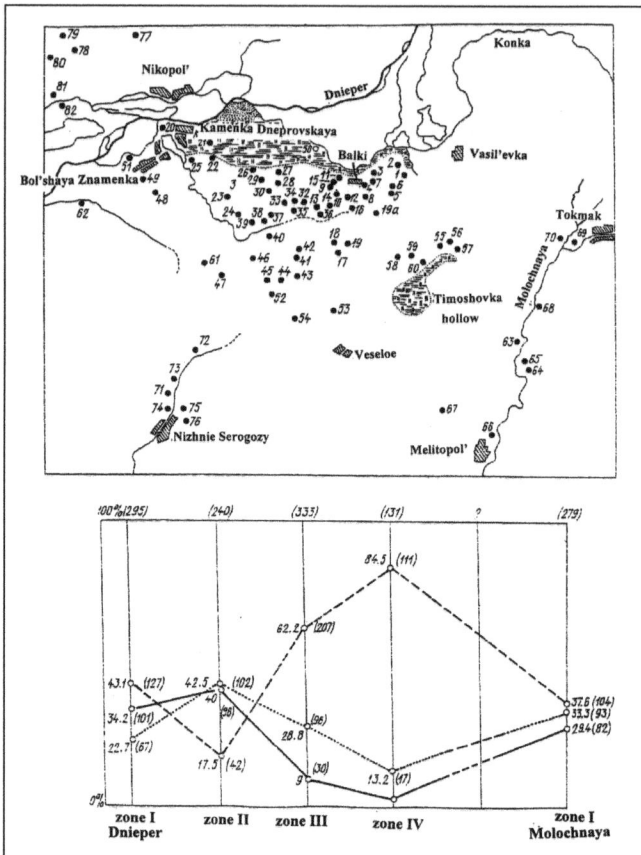

Fig. 4

long-term settlements[15]. In this situation the borders between the separate societies of the Yamnaya unity and their neighbours including distribution of pastures and water resources (with a presumably high population density) were extremely determined by river systems.

The distribution of kurgans with burials from the Eneolithic to Early Iron Age and Middle Ages show the significance of river systems and their resources in the life of the local group in the Pontic steppe. The northern part of an extensive zone between the Dnieper and Molochnaya River may be most demonstrative of this. First, this part of steppe is one of the driest and waterless (Marynych 1982). Second, in this zone numerous kurgans different time periods were investigated.

Originally, V.V. Otroshchenko and Yu.V. Boltrik presented 1987 burials from 430 kurgans, among them 1278 burials of the Bronze Age. The extent of the territory selected for the analysis from west to east was 135 km, and from south to north - 60 km (Otroshchenko and Boltrik 1982: 38-39) (Fig. 4/1).

The researchers then divided this territory into four zones. The criterion of this division was the extent of remoteness of each zone from the rivers Dnieper, Molochnaya, Konka and Belozerka (Otroshchenko and Boltrik 1982: 38-39) (Table 3).

The diagram of the distribution of Kurgan burials of different cultures of the Bronze Age (1278 burials) has allowed researchers to determine the dynamics of occupation of these four zones in the various periods of the Bronze Age (Fig. 4/2). The first two zones were settled continuously and provided the necessary requirements due to the rich resources of the river valleys and also adjoining areas of the steppe. In the third and fourth zones the burials of the Yamnaya Culture represent a very small number[16]. The authors of the article leave open the question of the settling of the steppe spaces. They assume gradual moving onto the steppe of the pastoral-agricultural population and their use the poor water resources of boggy hollows and gullies supplied with water where the remains of short-term Late Bronze Age settlements were found (Otroshchenko and Boltrik 1982: 39). Obviously, most attractive were the hollows, which were in open steppe between the Dnieper and Molochnaya. In the northern part of this territory the most known is the Timashovka hollow centrally situated between the Dnieper and Molochnaya

---

[15] This is not exactly correct. There are ceramics of the Yamnaya culture in the many settlements on the Dnieper, Azov area, Lower Don. But these materials are not numerous and poorly, investigated, because they were found in the mixed layers.

[16] Eneolithic burials are absent.

Table 3. Ecological zones and distribution of the Bronze Age burials in these zones (according to Otroshchenko and Boltrik 1982):

Zones	Characteristic	Number and % of burials[17]
Zone I	River valleys with plentiful meadows and water sources. A special place had the Dnieper's flood plain known on chronicles of the 17-19th centuries as "the Great Meadow".	YaC –279 (35, 8%) CC –252 (28, 9%) CMC & SC – 273 (35, 3%)
Zone II	Parts of the steppe which adjoin to river valleys and occupy a belt along banks of the rivers in width up to 3 km. The most part of kurgans is located in this zone.	
Zone III	The flat steppe removed from the rivers on distance more as 3 km. Occupation of this zone depends on economic development of societies and presence vehicles.	YaC –33 CC – 113 CMC & SC – 318 (73, 4%)
Zone IV	The most waterless flat steppe removed from the rivers on distance more as 10 km. Numerous kurgan cemeteries and height kurgans are not presented here. This zone is most accessible in the spring - the beginning of summer.	

(Molodykh 1982: 5-6, Fig. 17) (Fig. 4/1)[18]. The kurgans with a predominance of the Late Bronze Age burials (Srubnaya culture) have been investigated there. There are an insignificant number of the Middle Bronze Age burials (Catacomb culture) there, but the Early Bronze burials of the Yamnaya culture are entirely absent[19].

The authors of the article connected the settling of the deep steppe zones to the dynamics of increasing or reducing of the population in different periods (Otroshchenko and Boltrik 1982: 41). But it is clear that this process was much more complex and was not limited to this parameter. Climatic changes played a doubtless role, and besides, one should speak not about constant settling, but about the seasonal using of resources of the open steppe in the favorable periods of the year. New excavations of 1980-1990 on the Dnieper, Belozerka, Konka and, especially, Molochnaya have considerably increased the number of archaeological sources and have completely confirmed the conclusions of the researchers (Otroshchenko 1987; Rassamakin and Kolosov 1992). The kurgans of the Late Bronze Age in zone IV not only significantly predominated, but also formed difficult cult complexes from long and round mounds with complicated constructions (Otroshchenko 1976; 1977: 10-12; Rassamakin 1992: 131-133; Rassamakin and Kolosov 1992).

The special investigations have shown that a favorable climatic changes played important role in the exploitation of the open steppe zones in the Late Bronze Age. The structure of kurgans of the Srubnaya culture clearly shows a significant presence of moisture during their building. It corresponds to the conclusions of the researchers about the significant humidifying of the climate during the Late Bronze Age (Gerasimenko and Gershkovich 1998: 70; Gerasimenko 1998: 54-55; Gershkovich 1998: 81, 89; Gershkovich 1999: 88-89). Obviously, it was a basic factor because hollows remained in the open steppe for a long period with water and preserved their bio-resources.

The distribution of the kurgans planned for the region between the Dnieper and Molochnaya was typical for all of the different zones of the Pontic steppe areas. Some of their distinctions were connected to local environment and landscape features. The situation is similar in other regions as well, particularly, in the East Azov area (Gey 2000: 25), in Kalmyk steppe (Shilov 1982; Shishlina and Bulatov 2000: 46-47, 51; Shishlina 2000b: 60-64) and the Volga region (Turetsky 1999) (Fig. 5). A.N. Gey, for example, writes about "the Eastern Azov kurgan country" separated from the neighboring zones by natural borders or, in other words steppe waterless spaces (Gey 2000: 25-26). In truth, we can occasionally observe the population of the Yamnaya culture moving into the open steppe, but it demands the search for special explanations.

There is a question whether we can consider the distribution of kurgans as a reflection of the economic strategy of the pastoral societies, and whether it includes such important aspects as a presence of constant overland communications and seasonal use of the resources of river valleys and open steppe. N.I. Shishlina and V.E. Bulatov address the second aspect in the affirmative. They are studying the separate kurgan groups of the Yamnaya culture in the Kalmyk steppe as indicators of local seasonal pastures of small groups of the population. These kurgan groups, in the opinion of the researchers, reflect seasonal movement guided by a principle of "the river valley - the watershed (steppe)". One of the main conditions of these movements was the presence of water sources near to pastures. These conclusions are especially evident in the comparison of the distribution of the Yamnaya culture with the later Catacomb culture (Shishlina and Bulatov 2000: 46-5; Shishlina 2000b).

For the Pontic steppe it is difficult to find the answer to a question about roads and "pastures" in the Eneolithic and

---

[17] YaC – Yamnaya Culture, CC – Catacomb Culture, C?C – Cultura Mnogovalikovoi Ceramics, SC – Srubnaya Culture. Yamnaya Culture includs here the Eneolithic burials.

[18] There are between the Dnieper and Molochnaya other big hollows: Chernaya Dolina, Agaymanskiy, Askaniyskiy, Petro-pavlovskiy, Domuzlinskiy, etc (Molodykh 1982: 5-6, Fig. 17).

[19] Otroshchenko and Boltrik give data from 18 excavated kurgans in 1975 near the northern border of Timashovka hollow: burials of the Yamnaya culture are absent, Catacomb culture – 4 burials, Mnogovalikovaya culture – 11 burials, Srubnaya culture 37 burials, Scythian burials – 5, Sarmat burial – 1 and medieval burials – 7 (Otroshchenko and Boltrik 1983: 41).

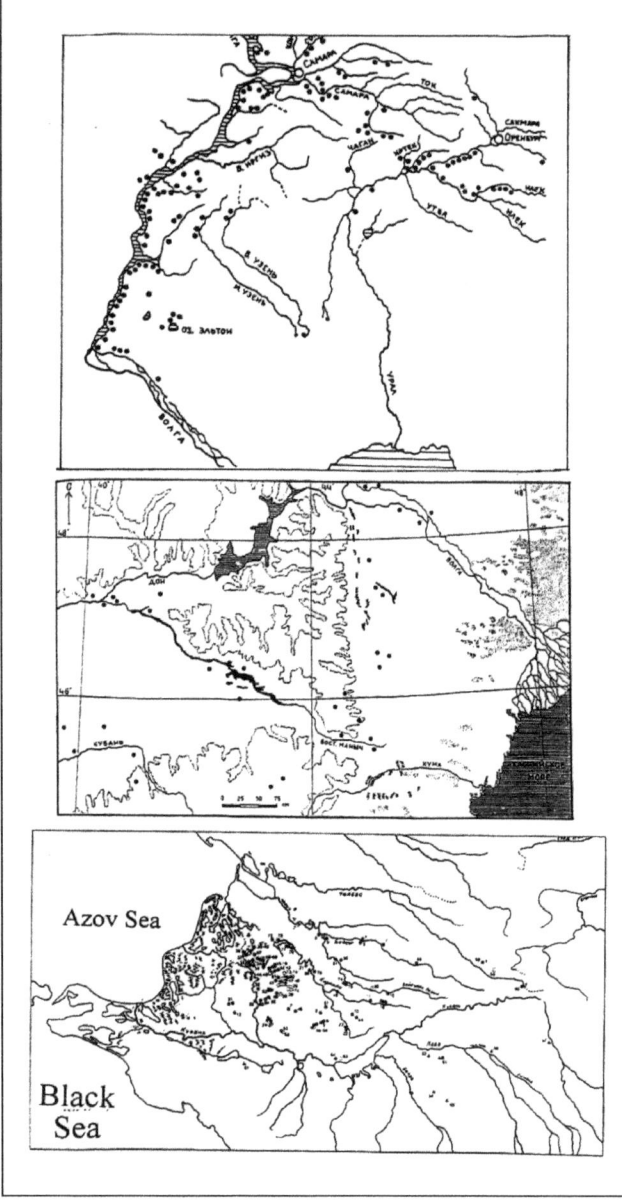

Fig. 5

through the Budzhak steppe to the Lower Dniester and further along to the estuaries of the Southern Bug and Ingul and there from to the Dnieper (Subbotin, Chernyakov 1982: 20-21). This way was later connected to the fords on the Dnieper and continued from the Dnieper south to Perekop and to the east along the coast of the Azov Sea to the Don (Berezanskaya et al. 1986: 147).

Could this have been the way in the Eneolithic or Early Bronze Age? The distribution of monuments of the Early and Late Eneolithic does not contradict such an assumption under the one condition that there were water sources along these ways. The way through the open steppe spaces must be excluded. Formation of the steppe communication networks needs a brief discussion about the means of transportation.

2.2. MEANS OF TRANSPORTATION.

2.2.1. VEHICLES AND OTHER OVERLAND MEANS OF TRANSPORTATION

The first wheeled transport in the Pontic steppe is fixed in the Final Eneolithic. The first finds of wheels are known in burials of the Zhivotilovka-Volchansk type on the Lower Don – Koldyri, kurgan 14, burial 7 (Izbitser 1993: 12; Rassamakin 2000) and in a burial of the Maykop-Novosvobodnaya type on the Kuban – Starokorsunskaya, kurgan 2, burial 18 (Rezepkin and Kondrashov 1988). The vehicles are present as regular finds in the Yamnaya culture burials and later in those of the Catacomb culture (Izbitser 1993). According to E.V. Izbitser, by the beginning of the 90s about 100 Yamnaya culture burials with vehicles were know in the Pontic steppe (Izbitser 1993). It is possible to assume that these data confirm the presence of transport communications in the Early Bronze Age. But the topography of kurgans with the Yamnaya culture burials shows in contrast to the Late Bronze Age (Srubnaya culture) and, partly, Middle Bronze Age (Catacomb culture) that this transport network could be developed in zones I and II (according to V.V. Otroshchenko and Yu.V. Boltrik), that is only along river valleys. It seems that the population of the Yamnaya culture used the vehicles within limited local economic systems instead of long-distance movements. Indirect arguments to this, for example, can be the conclusions of scholars about the presence of the local seasonal movement of the "river valley - a watershed" type in the population of the Yamnya culture in the Kalmyk steppe. This type of movement is the least mobile system (Shishlina and Bulatov 2000: 50). Concentration of a significant number of vehicles in the burials of the so-called Novotitorovka culture, occupying limited territory of the East Azov area between the Kuban' and Beysug rivers, confirms this also (Fig. 5,3). 110 vehicles or their wooden parts in the 877 burials of this culture were found here according to A.N. Gey before 1990 (Gey 2000: 17,128). (Fig. 6)

For the Early and Middle Eneolithic the data about wheeled transport are not available. We can assume the use of other overland means of transportation. Indirectly, this is confirmed by finds on the Tripolye culture settlements of clay figurines

Early Bronze Age. We do not have the results of special research of local ecological niches. Indirectly, connected to this problem are two unique cases of investigations under kurgans of the Late Bronze Age (Srubnaya Culture) into the road remains as a track from the movement of vehicles (Balki village, Vasil'evka district, and Vysokoe village, Mikhailovka district of the Zaporizhzhya province between the Dnieper and Molochnaya) (Otroshchenko, Savovsky and Tomashevsky 1977: 57, Fig. 26, 1; Rassamakin 1992: 131-133[20]). It proves the development in the Late Bronze Age of the transport communications crossing all four zones identified by V.V. Otroshchenko and Yu.V. Boltrik. In the first case, the kurgan was situated in zone II, adjoining to the so-called "Dnieper's Big Meadow" and in the second case - in open steppe of zone IV[21]. Besides, for the Late Bronze Age, due to finds of hoards with bronze subjects, the trade road was reconstructed from the fords on the Lower Danube

---

[20] Excavation by the author. All materials are unpublished (Rassamakin 1992: 131-133).

[21] Maybe, these roads were temporary for the period of building of kurgans.

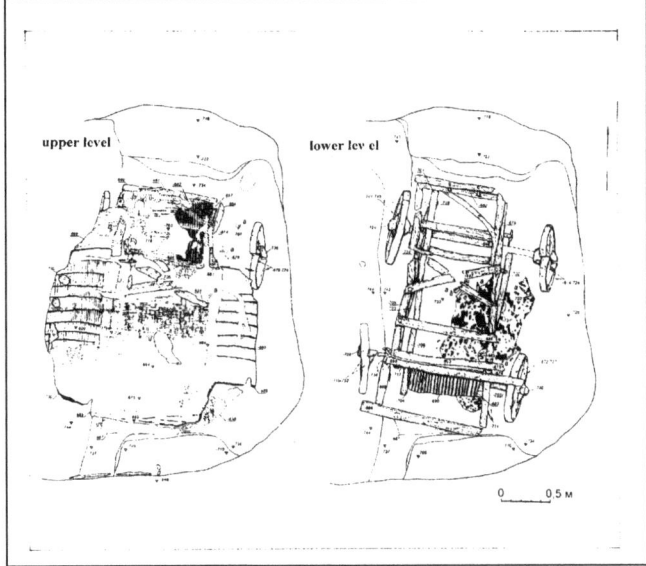

Fig.6

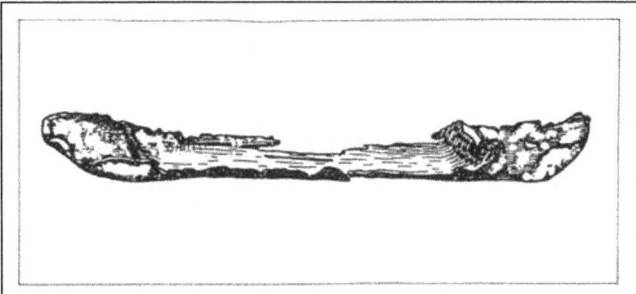

Fig. 7

of pack bulls and also clay models of sledges with one or a pair of bulls (Ryzhov 1988). These models are earlier than the well-known pictograms of the Late Uruk period because they date to the period Tropolye C/1 (about the 1st half of the 4th millennium B.C.) (Rassamakin 1999: 137-142, 147-149, Fig. 3.51). The sledge was well known to the population of the above-mentioned Tomashevka local group. It was a time when contacts and influences of the Tripolye cultures on the steppe were intensive and moved in one direction. Therefore it is possible to assume that there was the opportunity of using sledge and pack animals in the local steppe and forest-steppe zones in the Eneolithic. Obviously, these means of transportation were made more possible, before constant transport communications, in particular, by moving through spaces with plentiful herbage and also in the winter. Reliable archaeological evidence of horse riding has not been found (Levine 1990; 1999; Benecke 1998; Kuzmina 2000: 189). Besides, this means of transport was a least effective for exchange trade if we do not assume the existence of horse caravans.

2.2.2. WATER TRANSPORT

We can assume the existence of water transport in the Eneolithic and Early Bronze Age only. D.Y. Telegin mentions the use of boats and rafts by the Neolithic population of the Dnieper-Donetsk culture. As evidence he describes the wooden boat found at the depth of 10 m in the leers of the bank precipice of the Oskol river - the left forest–steppe tributary of the Seversky Donets (Telegin 1968: 205, Fig. 61) (Fig. 7)[22]. These data only indirectly can specify the use of this type of water transport by the settled population in the Eneolithic. V.G. Zbenovich does not doubt that the boats were used in the Usatovo culture (Zbenovich 1974: 116).

As far as boats were distributed among the more mobile population of the Yamnaya culture remains a mystery. It is possible to assume that during changes of the general

economic strategy of the steppe population, with the development of pastoralism and the use of vehicles, water transport lost its importance. Besides, fishing in the Eneolithic and Early Bronze Age could be without the use of boats and rafts.

3. WATER AS THE FIRST VITAL NECESSITY

When considering questions about hydrostrategy, it is necessary to touch upon a problem of maintenance of the steppe populations potable water and also use of water in daily life, for various economic purposes and, naturally, for maintenance of a herd. Certainly the main sources were the fresh-water rivers and springs. Access to such sources was open and simple. Data on the use of man-made wells are not available.

The analysis of topography of the Eneolithic settlements shows that they always were situated on the sections of riverbank, which were comfortable for the use of river resources. It is not necessary to describe the rocky and island settlements in the rapids part of the Dnieper: Sredny Stog, Stril'cha Skelya, the islands of Vinogradny and Pokhily, and the peninsula of Igren' etc. The location of the forest-steppe settlements of Molyukhov Bugor, Dereivka and Alexandriya is expressive enough. The steppe settlements of Mayaki and Usatovo in the zones of estuaries of the Dniester area are a little singular, but are illustrative also. The Azov steppe settlements are not less significant: Kamennaya Mogila (Danilenko 1974: 41; 1986), Semenovka (Kotova and Tuboltsev 1996) on the Molochnaya river; Razdol'noe (Shaposhnikova 1970) on the Kal'mius river and Razdorskaya I, Konstantinovsk (Kiyashko 1994), Liventsovka I (Bratchenko 1969), Samsonovskoe (Gey 1979) on the Lower Don.

The example of the well-known settlement of Mikhailovka is very significant (Lagodovs'ka, Shaposhnikova and Ìàkarevich 1962). The settlement was situated at the small river of Pidpil'na running into the Dnieper. The Pidpil'na River provided the basic resources for inhabitants of the settlement. There was a convenient approach to the river that simplified the use of its resources. The place for a settlement at the early stage (the Eneolithic lower layer) was chosen for these reasons. This place was the most convenient for the

---

[22] This boat has no date.

local landscape conditions. From the point of view of safety, most likely we should speak about safety from the elements - from sewage and mud streams, from bank slopes after rains, from strong winds etc. An important factor was also the protection against wild animals. The choice of a place for settlement was so successful that its exploitation continued a long time after the first settlers in the Eneolithic, namely until the Early and Middle Bronze Age. In the period of Yamnaya culture the settlement was considerably extended, having occupied the neighboring hills. The settlement of Îikhailovka is not an exception. Many sites where were the Neolithic and Eneolithic settlements, also were populated in other epochs.

In general, the practice of settling on the banks of small rivers or gullies running into larger rivers in the Eneolithic and Early Bronze Age was typical. It simplified the exploitation of river resources, including springs in nearby gullies, and the maintenance of the population with drinking and technical water.

In truth, despite the presence of water in the immediate proximity of settlements, two questions exist:

a) Whether there was and in what way a system of water storage on settlements;

b) How necessary was water transportation during development of pastoralism?

3.1. STORAGE OF WATER

Let's assume that despite the availability of water sources it is certain that a supply was always kept on settlements. It is possible to explain it only for household needs. Partly, the question of the storage of water could be investigated by the presence of the well-developed and detailed classification of Eneolithic and Early Bronze Age ceramics by capacity and use. As research on ceramics of the Late Bronze Age show, the calculations of the capacity of pottery in combination with its typological variety and allocation of functional groups can give a positive result and prospect for the reconstruction of the life of the steppe population (Gershkovich 2001).

Here it is necessary to note that for the Eneolithic steppe cultures the wide variability of forms and types of the pottery, technological features of its manufacturing is absolutely not characteristic. We notice it in the Neolithic. It is also typical for the Eneolithic. As examples it is possible to present the ceramics of the Skelya culture, Stog culture, Kvityana culture and Repin culture (Fig. 8). The import vessels only brought a variety in the ceramic assemblages of these cultures, in particular, the Tpipolye culture vessels, which had prestigious and ritual significance. Thus, the ceramics of the separate Eneolithic steppe cultures is extremely monotonous and rather primitive. Vessels differ only in their sizes which vary from 5-7 cm to 50-60 cm in height. Obviously, these parameters also were the main criterion of their use.

New forms and types of ceramics appear in the steppe and forest-steppe cultures, which had long contacts to agricultural

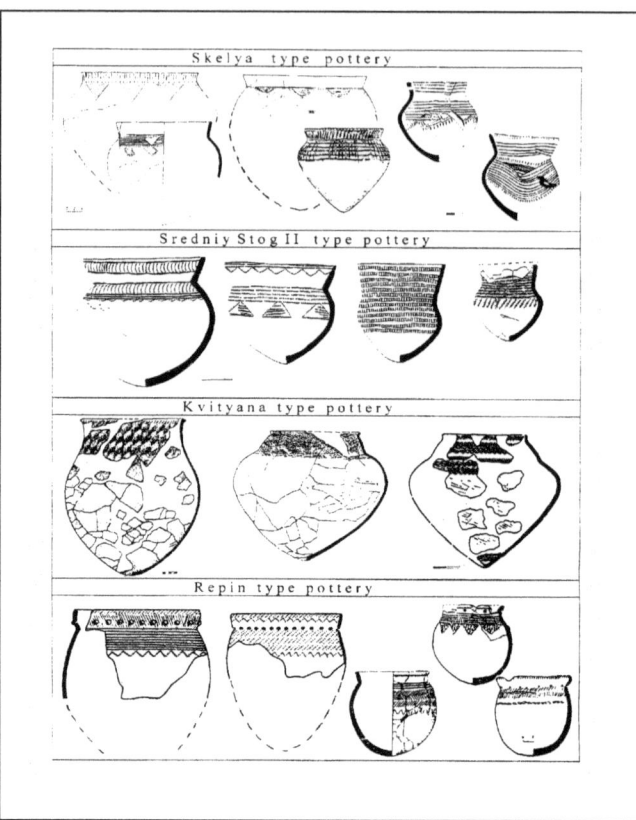

Fig. 8

cultures or at least took part in their formation. We notice this process in the forest-steppe Dereivka culture, particularly, at the settlements of Dereivka and Molyukhov Bugor. Side by side with typical and basic monotonous ceramics of the Dereivka type, there are flat-bottomed vessels and bowls whose forms recall Tripolye pottery (Fig. 9).

Most clearly this process developed further in the Late and Final Eneolithic. We notice strong Maykop-Novosvobodnaya influences in the Konstantinovsk culture on the Lower Don (at the settlement of Konstantinovsk) where various types and forms of ceramics and various manufacturing techniques have been identified. The author of the excavation notes that the variability of forms and types of pottery is directly connected to the economic level of the development of a society (Kiyashko 1994). The Usatovo culture also represents one of most vivid examples of a variety of forms and types of ceramics by virtue of its Tripolye culture background. Besides in the Usatovo and Konstantinovsk cultures the basic classification of ceramics into table-wares and kitchen-wares is presented (Kiyashko 1994; Zbenovich 1974: 79-103; Patokova 1979; Patokova et al. 1989). The wide variability of vessels specifies a high level of development in the household culture of the population. Clearly, it is more convenient to pour out a water and other fluids with a cup, beaker or mug with a handle or to drink from them; to eat from table-pottery and to cook in kitchen pottery is more pleasant; to transfer water, milk etc. it is convenient to use special vessels with handles or suspended with cords through special eyes on the pottery. On the other hand, the typological variability of ceramics specifies its functional distinctions and consequently the flexibility of the general economic strategy of the population.

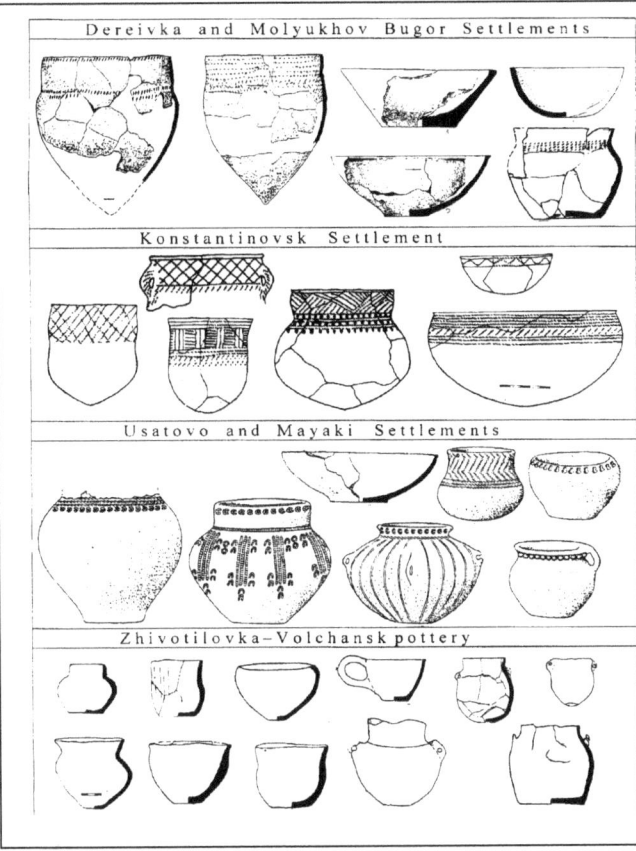

Fig. 9

Shaposhnikova and Makarevich 1962). Clearly, these ceramics represent forms transformed under steppe conditions and made in local technological traditions (Fig. 10). Occurrence of a typological variety of ceramics in the Yamnaya culture specifies, obviously, the stability of functions, for example, in the sphere of manufacture and storage of milk and other products on the settlements and during seasonal movement of the local groups of the population.

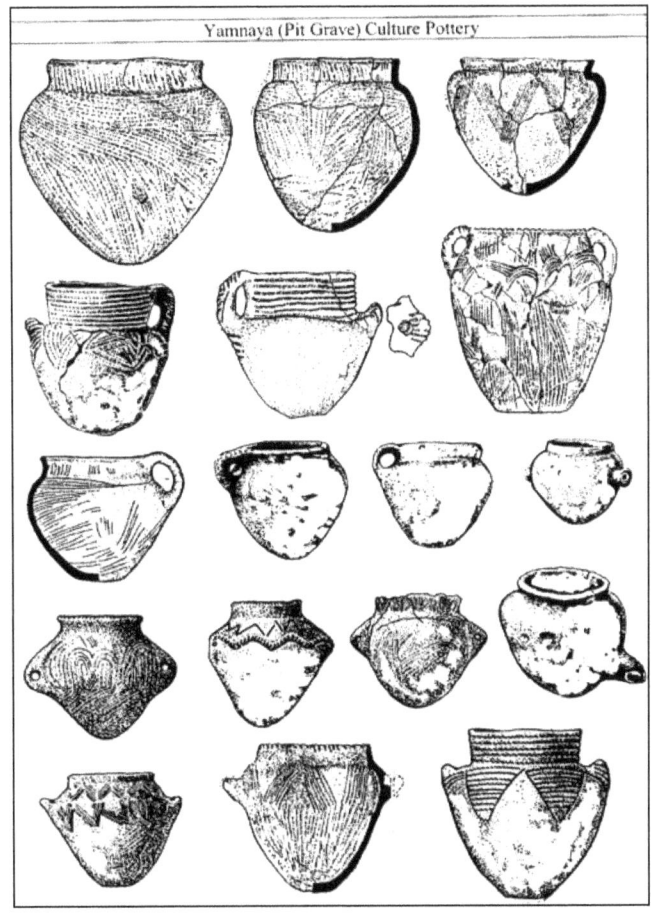

Fig. 10

The Usatovo and Konstantinovsk cultures occupied zones at the ends of the Northern Black Sea area: the first between the Danube and Dniester; the second - on the Lower Don. In the centre of the Pontic steppe zone such new forms as bowls, beakers, "amphora" and cups with handles and eyes appear for the first time in the burials of the Zhivotilovka-Volchansk type which in materials and ritual suggest connections to the Tripolye and Maykop-Novosvobodnaya worlds (Rassamakin 1996) (Fig. 9). These ceramics were made in nontraditional technology for the steppe cultures. Thus, towards the end of Eneolithic in addition to the traditional steppe pottery types there comes a new assortment of ceramics.

Despite this, we cannot assert that there were a special vessels for the storage of water. It is possible to assume that for this purpose on settlements, the large vessels were used. For example, at the settlement of Dereivka the rests of the large vessels were driven in the ground (Telegin 1973: 36). They were obviously intended for the long storage of various products. It is possible that they also kept water in them. The same large vessels are known in the Kvityana and Skelya cultures (Figs. 8- 9).

In the Early Bronze Age, the ceramics of the Yamnaya culture of the Black Sea steppe region include not only traditional bottom vessels, but also those new types of ceramics which have appeared in the end of Eneolithic - bowls, beakers, "amphora" and cups with various handles and eyes (Nikolova and Mamchych 1997). For example, at the settlement of Mikhailovka a fine collection of fragments of pottery with various handles and eyes is represented (Lagodovs'ka,

In any case, we should recognize that in the process of the formation of pastoral way of life during the Eneolithic and Early Bronze Age there was a certain system of storage of water and its multi-purpose use was considerably facilitated by the appearance of special types of pottery beginning from the Late Eneolithic. There is a special significance to the appearance of the "mugs" and "suspended" vessels. This pottery is more practical for transportation of fluids over short, rather then long distances. From the aesthetic point of view, such ceramics have considerably changed the interior of dwellings.

3.2. USING OF WATER FOR ECONOMIC NEEDS AND ITS TRANSPORTATION

Many tasks such as grinding and drilling of stone tools, preparation of building raw material with use of water, manufacture of clay for manufacturing ceramics, processing of animal skins etc. could be carried out on the riverside near to a settlement. But it is impossible to exclude that many of these could be undertaken directly on settlements. The products of manufacture and remains of workshops on settlements confirm it. D.Ya. Telegin, for example, identifies such sites at the settlement of Dereivka ("a place of the potter", "a place of the grinder"), on one of which the sharp bottom of a vessel driven in the ground was found. The author of the excavation assumes that in this vessel there was water for grinding works (Telegin 1973: 36; 1987: 29).

In the period of the Yamnaya culture the sets of tools, waste products of manufacture and semi finished items in burials represent the presence of craftsmen. These sets indicate the manufacture of flint and bone objects, bows and arrows, and metalworking. It is impossible to forget about pottery manufacture. Productions demanded a certain system of water delivery and consequently the container for the transportation and storage of water in the immediate zone of production. The building needs demanded water also, particularly, at the construction of dwellings walls from wattles and clay plastering as, for example, at the Mikhailovka settlement (Lagodovs'ka, Shaposhnikova and Makarevich 1962).

The transportation of water, in particular, over long distances during the development of pastoralism is one of the basic moments of life-support in a society. It doubtless existed in the Eneolithic and Early Bronze Age.

For carrying water over close distances, particularly, for daily technical and household needs, most convenient could be the "suspended" vessels of the medium sizes with handles and eyes. Such vessels appear in the steppe only in the Late Eneolithic and reflect, probably, the process of the active development of pastoralism. For example, in a burial of the Yamnaya culture was found a vessel whose neck had been tied by a thin cord in three lines through eyes (kurgan 24, burial. 14, Vinogradnoe village, Tokmak district, Zaporizhzhya province on the Molochnaya river) (Fig. 11)[23]. Obviously, such "suspended" vessels of the medium and small sizes were used for more long distance moving because they were convenient not only to carry, but also to fasten on vehicles.

For transportation of a large quantity of water, the most convenient may was, probably, by the "soft" containers from leather. Impressions of leather in the Yamnaya culture burials of the Azov steppe area confirm the existence of such containers. These impressions preserved the form of small bags in which was stored ochre and pitch in a fluid condition.

4. RIVER RESOURCES: DIET AND ECONOMY

4.1. RIVER RESOURCES AND A DIET

We do not know the diet system of the Pontic steppe population in the Eneolithic and Early Bronze Age. Partly, it is possible to be guided by the interesting results from Kalmykia, but only as an example for a local ecological niche (Shishlina *et al. in press*). Naturally, water was an important and most accessible natural element of a daily diet, but we do not know the balance between drinking water and other drinks, such as, milk.

The products with which the river valleys provided the steppe population were not less important, first of all, due to the fishing and the hunting of water animals. The researcher of a Sredny Stog settlement, A. Dobrovol'sky, even wrote that the territorial location of this settlement corresponds more to the activity of fishers and hunters than shepherds (Dobrovol'sky 1929). This conclusion can be related to many settlements, especially in rapids parts of the Dnieper. It confirms the shell lever and numerous bone harpoons found on the settlement of Stril'cha Skelya. These harpoons even have received the term "harpoons of Stril'cha Skelya type" (Danilenko 1974, 48)

4.2. FISH AND OTHER RIVER ANIMALS

A special isotopic analysis defining fish in the diet of the prehistoric steppe population recently was conducted by researchers from Cambridge. They investigated the animal and human bones from some Neolithic, Eneolithic and Early Bronze Age memorials: animal bones from the Neolithic-Eneolithic settlements of Semenovka on the Molochnaya river (steppe), Molyukhov Bugor on the Tyasmin river (forest-steppe); the Early Bronze Age settlement of Desyatiny which

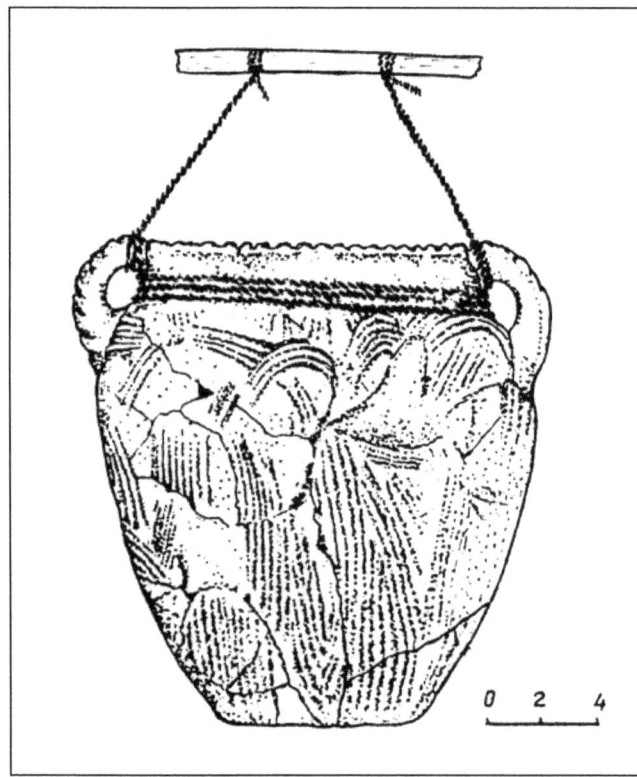

Fig. 11

[23] Excavation by the author in 1984.

Table 4. Discription of fish on the settlement Mayaki (according to Zbenovich 1974: Òàbl. 4).

Description	Correlation of sort of fishes (%)	Dimension (sm) (min.–max.)	Average dimension (sm)
Sterlet	4, 4	55 - 70	60, 8
Sturgeon	6, 0	50 – 55	71, 3
Stellate sturgeon	0, 4	-	-
Pike	0, 2	-	-
Roach	1, 3	20 - 45	34, 9
Pearl roach	4, 6	-	-
Chub	0, 4	-	-
Sazan	3, 1	50 - 80	61, 8
Catfish	65, 7	40 - 270	108, 1
Pike-perch	13, 9	40 - 85	57, 1
Amphibious:	*bones*	*individuals*	
Tortoise	85	23	

is not far from Molyukhov Bugor, and human bones from the Early Eneolithic burials in Krivoi Rog on the Ingulets river (steppe) (O'Connel et al. 2000). The conclusion of the researchers about the great significance of fish protein in the diet of the steppe population during all these eras is very important (O'Connel et al. 2000: 305-306). This conclusion has confirmation among archaeological materials, but, obviously, the significance of fish in the diet for each period not was identical.

Unfortunately, the information about the number and specific definition of fishes is not presented for all of Eneolithic settlements. It considerably complicates an estimation of the densities of fish in the diet of the population. It was possible to assemble some data together (Tab. 4). These data undoubtedly reflect the importance of fishing in an economy of the Eneolithic and Early Bronze Age population. They are really an objective parameter. D.Ya. Telegin considers even that in the Sredny Stog culture fishing had more important role than hunting, but he does not explain why this was. The researcher has devoted some lines to the characteristics of this kind of activity. The presence of big concentrations of fish scales and fish bones in kitchen waste at the settlement of Dereivka is, in Telegin's opinion, better evidence for fishing (Telegin 1973: 141; 1987: 87).

The data from the Usatovo culture settlement of Mayaki on the Dniester are rather significant. It is difficult to talk about the densities of fish in the general diet of the population at this steppe settlement, but V.G. Zbenovich writes about a huge number of fish bones and gives data about specific definition and the sizes of fishes (Zbenovich 1974: 116, table 4) (Table 5). First of all, V.G. Zbenovich notes the significance of catfish, pike, perch and sturgeon which were fished both on the Dniester and in a nearby estuary[24]. The researcher does not doubt that fishing had a subsidiary role in the pastoral-agricultural economy of the inhabitants of the settlement (Zbenovich 1973: 116). Nevertheless, taking into account the strongly pronounced steppe structure of wild fauna at the settlement making only 15, 2 % or 97 individuals in comparison with 84, 8% or 540 domestic individuals (Zbenovich 1974: 115, table. 2; 3), it is possible to note the highest significance of the fish in a diet of the population at the settlement of Mayaki.

Concerning Yamnaya culture we have only the data from the Mikhailovka settlements (Bibikova and Shevchenko 1962: Table 1) (Table 4). Besides, only rare cases of finds of fish bones in the burials of this culture are known[25]. One of such burials was investigated by the author in 1984 in kurgan 24, burial 31 near Vinogradnoe village, Tokmak district, Zaporizhzhya province, on the high right bank of the Molochnaya river. A small fish (carp) in length up to 15-20 cm laid under the head of the dead[26] (Fig. 12/6). The presence of fish in a burial, which is situated not in river valley, but at very high plateau border, is interesting. It is possible to assume a variety of interpretation regarding this fact:

a) fish was a fresh product: from the point of view of the seasonal change of pastures in a "valley - steppe" pattern in the given area, such a pattern was not seasonal, but the usual practice in the course of the year with a regular return to the river valley. In other words, it was breeding within the limits of zone II (according to Otroshchenko and Boltrik 1982);

b) fish was dried fish: on one hand, it is possible to assume the seasonal pasture of the herd, and on the other, the existence of a system for the preparation of products for storage over the long term, and the use of these products during seasonal pasture. It, in particular, confirms the necessity of the transportation of water.

I am inclined to accept the first variant for the ecological niche of the Molochnaya river proceeds from an immediate

---

[24] D.Ya. Telegin notes the special significance of catfish at settlement Dereivka (Telegin 1973: 141).

[25] V.P. Shylov noted the absent of fish bones in 263 burials of the Yamnaya culture on the Volga, but they there are in burials of the Poltavkinskaya culture (Shilov 1975a: 66, tabl. 2; 1975b: 14, Table 3 and 4). The situation is similar in Kalmyk steppe, where N. Shishlina mentioned the rare fish bones in the burials. She also writes about the insignificant role of fishing in this ecological niche.

[26] Definition by Daniel Makoviecki (Poznan, Poland).

Tabl. 5 (according to: Telegin 1986: pp. 84 and 88).

Settlement	Description	Number of bones	Number of individuals	Period
Foreststeppe				
Dereivka	Silurus (Silurus granis)	94	21	ME-LE
	Perch (Lucioperca Lucioperca)	20	5	
	Roach (Rutilus rutilus)	11	5	
	Red-eye (Scardinius erhythrophtalmus)	2	1	
	Carp (Cyprinus carpio)	3	2	
	Carp (Aspius aspius)	1	1	
	Pike (Esox lucius)	5	2	
	Fish total:	136	37	
	Tortoise (Emys onbicularis)	177	32	
	Beaver	50	15	
	Otter (Lutra lutra)	2	2	
Molyukhov Bugor*	Fish	?	?	ME-LE
	Tortoise (Emys onbicularis)	156	22	
	Otter (Lutra lutra)	1	1	
Aleksandriya	Fish	?	?	EA-LE
	Tortoise (Emys onbicularis)	1	1	
	Beaver	13	3	
Steppe				
Sredniy Stog II	Beaver	10	2	ME
	Otter (Lutra lutra)	1	1	
Konstantinovsk	Fish	44	8	LE
	Tortoise (Emys onbicularis)	38	7	
	Beaver	6	3	
	Otter (Lutra lutra)	1	1	
Mikhailovka I	Beaver	3	2	
Mikhailovka II and III	Fish	236	120	EBA
	Tortoise (Emys onbicularis)	20	13	
	Beaver	7	6	
	Otter (Lutra lutra)	13	10	
	Water-rat (Arvicola amphibius)	2	2	

- The numerous tortoises and fish bones are presented at this settlement after new excavation (according to information by O.P. Zhuravlev).
- EA – Early Eneolithic; ME – Middle Eneolithic; LE – Late Eneolithic; EBA – Early Bronze Age.

proximity of flood-lands and steppe watershed sites and there is a complete absence of the Eneolithic and Yamnaya Culture kurgans in depth of zone II (according to Otroshchenko 1987). Obviously, the main questions are:

a) did there exist the seasonal pasture of herds within a "north - south" system in the Eneolithic or Early Bronze Age along rivers, flood-lands and its nearest steppe zone?

b) What extent was occupied by pasture areas in the use of this system? In this case was the problem not the presence of water, but a problem of herd maintenance with forage reserves or natural meadowlands.

Tortoises have an important place in a river strategy of the prehistoric population. They were widespread food for the steppe and forest-steppe population, obviously, due to the simple way they could be caught and their nutritious characteristics. The tortoises appear at all the settlements of the Eneolithic and Early Bronze Age (Table. 4).

Beavers and otters had a smaller significance, but, for example, bones of a beaver regularly appear in the settlements of the Eneolithic and Early Bronze Age in the forest-steppe (Dereivka, Molyukhov Bugor) and steppe areas (Konstantinovsk, Mayaki, Mikhailovka) (Table 4).

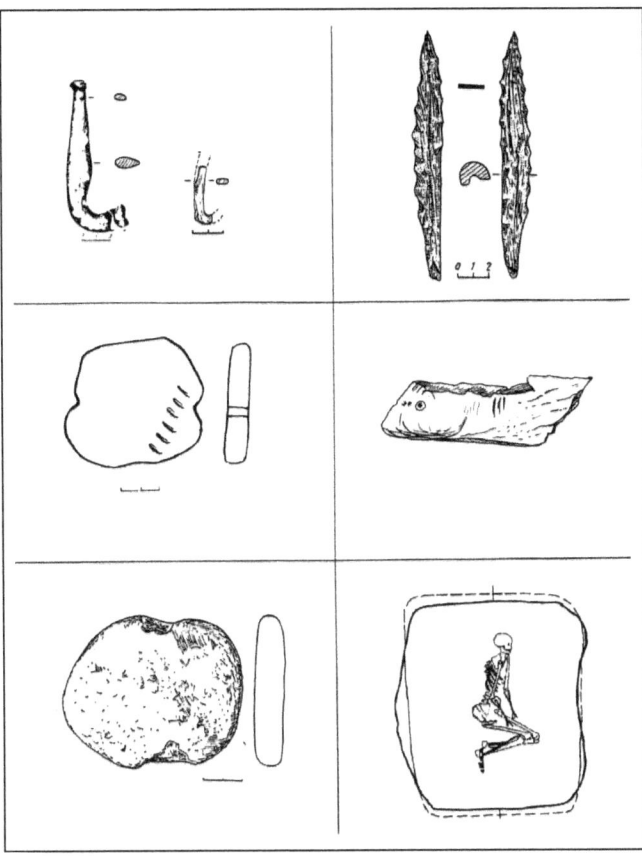

Fig.12

4.3. GATHERING

The layers, accumulations and separate shells of river mollusks on the settlements are direct evidence for river gathering. The most indicative is the settlement of Dereivka in the forest-steppe zone (Telegin 1973: 28-29; 1987: 8) and Stril'chya Skelya in steppe zone (Danilenko 1974: 47-48; Telegin and Konstantinesku 1992). D.Ya. Telegin writes about the gathering of the mollusks *Unio* and *Poludino* in Dereivka (Telegin 1973: 141). The same sorts of mollusks appear in Stril'cha Skelya. Gathering of the mollusks *Unio* and *Drissena polymorpha* in rivers, the mollusk *Monodacna colorata* in estuaries, and also the mollusks *Cardium edule*, *Mytilus galloprovincialis* in the sea are mentioned by V.G. Zbenovich at the settlement of Mayaki. Here their numerous fragments were found (Zbenovich 1974: 116).

On the southern coast of the Crimea the seasonal sits of, probably, Kemi-Oba culture with accumulations of sea mollusks are enumerated by A.A. Shchepinsky (Shchepinsky 1977).

It is clear that mollusks were a part of the human daily or seasonal food ration. Besides mollusk shells were used in the economic needs, for example:

a) as an admixture in clay by manufacturing of ceramics that is especially typical for the Eneolithic[27];

b) as tools, in particular, as a stamp for the ornamentation of vessels[28]; as a part of handicraft sets of tools in the burials etc.

4.4. FISHING EQUIPMENT

Fishing rods were, in the opinion of many researchers, the basic means of individual catching in the Eneolithic. As evidence the researchers mention the bone hooks found at the settlements of Dereivka, Sredny Stog II, Stril'cha Skelya, Mayaki and others (Telegin 1973: 141, Fig. 66; Zbenovich 1974: 116; Neprina 1988) (Fig. 12/1).

Other tools of individual river hunting were harpoons. The best evidence for of harpoons is found at Stril'cha Skelya (Danilenko 1974: 48, Fig. 22; Neprina 1988; Telegin and Konstantinescu 1992).

One of the harpoons was found by the author in the Yamnaya culture burial (Vinogradnoe, kurgan 18, burial 6) (Fig. 12/2).

Nets were, naturally, a broader and more intensive way of fishing. Rounded fragments of vessels from 4 up to 10 cm in diameter were found in a great quantity at the settlement of Dereivka (Fig. 12/3). In Telegin's opinion they were used as weights for fishing nets (Telegin 1974: 141, Fig. 24, 2-5; 1987: 87; Fig. 19, 4-7). Stone weights for fishing nets are found in Usatovo (Zbenovich: 1974, 61, 116, Fig. 24,18) (Fig. 12/4). On the basis of the accumulation of ceramic weights for fishing nets, numerous fish bones and scales, and the find of a bone hook, D.Ya. Telegin even assumes the existence of a special place for the repair of fishing nets and working of fishing products at the settlement of Dereivka (Telegin 1974: 42; 1987: 15).

Bone "shuttles" confirm the manufacture of nets as well, but their determination from other bone tools is not always possible without special microscopic analysis. One such "shuttle" from an animal rib was found by the author in the Eneolithic burial on the Molochnaya river (Vinogradnoe village, kurgan 2, burial 3) (Rassamakin 1987)[29]. I do not rule out that some of the bone tools from the settlements, including some of the so-called "cheek-pieces" in Dereivka, could serve this purpose (Rassamakin 1999: 147, Fig. 3.55, 1-5).

4.5. RIVER RESOURCES AND ECONOMY

Fluvial plains under Pontic steppe conditions provided the basic resources for the economic needs of the pastoral societies. The adjoining steppe zones were used as a seasonal forage reserve for herds and also for hunting steppe animals (wild donkey, saiga, horse etc.), though these also could be killed near watering places. First of all, river valleys with inundated meadows were irreplaceable pastures for cattle.

---

[27] At the settlement of Dereivka shells were in vessels on "the place of potter", in other vessel was clay (Telegin 1973: 36).

[28] See: Dobrovol'sky 1925: 127-128, Fig. 25.

[29] Determination by G.F. Korobkova.

Small cattle were seasonally pastured in the same place as well. Natural water sources were intensively used during the pasturing of herds.

In the Eneolithic and Early Bronze Age the river valleys provided building materials (clay, sand, reed and rush, wood etc.), which were used for the building of dwellings (for example at the settlement of Mikhailovka). The widest use was for wicker mats, bags, baskets and subjects from wood. The steppe was a special place for the making of vehicles.

The funeral practice using a plenty of rush mats and wooden constructions, particularly, massive logs 20-30 cm in diameter in burial design, confirms the intensive exploitation of the flood-lands resources. The most widespread were objects plaited of a reed or other flood-lands plants - mats, bags etc. Special investigations have allowed the study of the structure and character of the manufacturing of mats in the Kalmyk ecological niche (Shishlina 1999; Gol'eva 1999). They are very close to the results of researches of a series of textile products from the Yamnaya and Early Catacomb burials on the Molochnaya River[30]. Popularity of mats as one of the basic and universal objects in life is visible from the examples of Early Bronze Age burials with vehicles (Rassamakin 1991; Gey 2000:171) (Fig. 6).

Obviously, in the economy of the steppe population an important role was played also by the secondary processing of products of a river craft (the fur and skin of beavers and otters, their fat, bone, tooth etc.).

5. RITUAL

In summary it is necessary to examine a ritual practice. In the Eneolithic the tortoises are more representative in funeral ritual. I know three burials of different Eneolithic cultures in which the shells of tortoises are found: on the left bank of the Dnieper (Balki, "Vysoka Mogila", burial 7); on the left bank of Ingulets (Velikaya Aleksandrovka, kurgan 1, burial 7[31]) and at Samara, on the left tributary of the Dnieper (Sokolovo IV, kurgan 2, burial 22) (Rassamakin 1999: Fig. 3.25, 3; Shilov 1988: 8; Kovaleva 1979: 63-64). It is possible that the shells of tortoises are represented as ritual vessels in the burials. I don't know if they are in the later burials of the Yamnaya culture.

The one case of the presence of fish in the Yamnaya culture burial is described above. This case is one exception of the usual practice, but for this reason requires special attention and explanation in the future.

The situation with use of water in funeral practice is not clear. There are the definitions of water in vessels for the Yamnaya culture burials in the Kalmyk ecological niche. It is no doubt, that water in vessels was a usual ritual present in the Pontic steppe and had a symbolical significance.

From fish vertebrae were made various necklaces and ritual pendants. The author knows a necklace from large fish vertebrae found in an Early Catacomb burial on the Molochnaya river (Vinogradnoe village, kurgan 1, burial 6)[32].

At the settlements, a unique find is the stone figurine of a fish found at Dereivka (Telegin 1973: 37, Fig. 22, 12; 1987: Fig. 22,12). Whether this figurine had ritual significance or is a result of art talent of local fishermen remain unclear (Fig. 12/5).

CONCLUSIONS

Appraising the hydrostrategy of the Eneolithic and Early Bronze Age as a part of the general economic strategy of the steppe and forest-steppe population during the development of pastoralism, I can assume that in comparison with the Neolithic its significance has considerably increased. If even we were to assume that such a sphere of hydrostrategy as fishing could play only a supporting role in the different forms of cattle breeding economy (see O'Connell et al. 2000), general exploitation of the flood-lands and hydroresources is considerably more intensive. The Eneolithic was an epoch when river valleys started to recieve their most serious anthropogenic pressure.

The special complex program on studying the dynamics of use of hydroresources in the Neolithic, Eneolithic and Bronze Age is necessary to confirm this conclusion. Here I have presented a preliminary review of this theme, which is far from a full reflection of the problems.

Acknowledgements

I would like to thank Dragos Gheorghiu for the interesting perspective and idea and for the invitation to take part in the project about studying hydrostrategy of the ancient populations. My thanks to Yakov Gershkovich for his constant help during the preparation of this article and for useful comments on the text. I am also grateful to Natalia Shishlina and Elena Izbitser for the information help. My special thanks to Alexander Bauer for his discussion about paper and for his corrections of this text.

This paper was written by support of the Fulbright Program in the Department of Anthropology of the Museum of Archaeology and Anthropology of University of Pennsylvania. The author is especial grateful to Fredrik Hiebert for friendly help and constant support.

Bibliography

ANTHONY, D.W., 1994, On Subsistend Change at the Mesolithic-Neolithic Transition. *Current Anthropology* 35,1, 49-52.

BENECKE, N., 1998, Die Wildpferde aus der spätmesolithischen Station Mirnoe in der Südwest-Ukraine. *Man and The Animal*

---

[30] Results are unpublished.

[31] This burial is published as a burial of Kemi-Oba culture.

[32] Unpublished excavation by author in 1982.

World (Studies in Archaeozoology, Archaeology, Anthropology and Palaeolinguistics, eds. P. Anreiter, L. Bartosiewicz, E. Jerem and W.Meid. Budapest, *Archaeolingua Alapítvány*, 87-107.

BEREZANSKAYA,S.S., 1986, Otroshchenko V.V., Cherednichenko N.N., Sharafutdinova B.Y. *Kul'tury epokhi bronzy na territorii Ukrainy*. Kiev: Naukova dumka.

BIBIKOVA,V.I., SHEVCHENKO A.I., 1962, Fauna Mykhailivs'kogo poselennya. *Lagodovs'ka, O.F., Shaposhnikova, O.G., Makarevich, 1962. Mykhailivs'ke poselennya.* Kyiv: vydavnytstvo Akademii Nauk.

BOLTRIK,YU. V., 1990, Cukhoputnye kommunikatsii Skifii (po materialam novostroechnykh issledovanii ot Priazov'ya do Dnepra. *Sovetskaya arkheologiya* 4, 30-44.

BRATCHENKO,S. N., 1969, Bagatosharove poselennya Liventsivka I na Donu. *Archeologiya* XXII, 210-231

BUNYATYAN, K.P., 1994, Klasyfikatsiya ta typologiya skotarstva. *Teoriya ta praktyka archeologichnykh doslidzhen* (V.F. Gening, K.P. Bunyatyan, eds.). Kiev: Naukova dumka.

BUNYATYAN, K., 1997, Skotarstvo yak sposib zhyttya. *Arkheologiya* 3, 32-39.

BURDO, N.B. and VIDEIKO, M.Yu., 1998, Osnovy khronologii Trypillya-Kukuteni. *Arkheologiya* 2, 17-29.

DANILENKO, V.N., 1959, Arkheologicheskie issledovaniya 1956 goda v Chigirinskom rayone. *Kratkie soobshcheniya Instituta arkheologii AN USSR* 8, 13-21.

DANILENKO, V.N., 1969, *Neolit Ukrainy*. Kiev: Naukova dumka.

DANILENKO, V.N., 1974, *Eneolith Ukrainy*. Kiev: Naukova dumka.

DANILENKO, V.N., 1986, *Kamennaya Mogila*. Kiev: Naukova dumka.

DOBROVOLSKY, A., 1929, Zwit za arkheologichni daslidzhennya na terytorii Dniprel'stanu. *Zbirnyk Dnipropetrovs'kogo istoryko-arkheologichnogo muzeyu* 1 (D.I. Yavornytsky, ed.). Dnipropetrovs'k, 61-156.

GERASIMENKO, N.P., 1998, Prirodnaya sreda obitaniya cheloveka na vostoke Ukrainy v pozdneledernikov'e i golotsene (po materialam paleogeogravicheskogo izucheniya pamyatnikov). *Arheologicheskiy al'manakh* 6 (A. Kolesnik, ed.). Donetsk.

GERASIMENKO, N.P., and GERSHKOVICH, Ya.P., 1998, K paleoekologii basseyna Severskogo Dontsa i Severo-Vostochnogo Priazov'ya v epokhu pozdney bronzy. *Dono-Donetskii region v sisteme drevnostey Vostochnoevropeyskoi stepi i lesostepi* 2. Voronezh.

GERŠKOVIČ, J. P., 1999, *Zur Studien der spätbronzezeitlichen Sabatinovka- Kultur am unteren Dnepr und an der Westküste des Azovschen Meeres*. Archäologie in Eurasien, Band 7. Berlin.

GERSHKOVICH, Ya. P., 2001, Etnokul'turnye svyazi v epokhu pozdnei bronzy v svete khronologicheskogo sootnosheniya pamyatnikov (Nizhnee Podneprov'e - Severo-Vostochnoe Priazov'e - Podoncov'e). *Arheologicheskii al'manakh* 7 (A. Kolesnik, ed.). Donetsk.

GEY, A.N., 1979, Samsonovskoe mnogosloinoe poselenie. *Sovetskaya arkheologiya* 3, 119-131.

GEY, A.N., 2000, *Novotitorovskaya kul'tura*. Moskow: TOO "Stary sad".

GIMBUTAS, M., 1994, *Das Ende Alteuropas. Das Einfall von Steppennomaden aus Südrussland und die Indogermanisierung Mitteleuropas*. Archaeolingua Alapítváni (E. Jerem, W.Maid, eds.). Budapest: Archaeolingua Alapítváni, 13-135.

GOL'EVA, A.A., 1999, Rastitel'nye podstilki epokhi bronzy Kalmykii. *Tekstil epokhi bronzy Evrasiiskikh stepei* (N.I. Shishlina, ed.). Trudy Gosudarstvennogo Istoricheskogo museya 109. Moskow, 185-203.

IZBITSER, E.V., 1993, *Pogrebeniya s povozkami stepnoi polosy Vostochnoi Evropy i Severnogo Kavkaza III – II tys. do n.e.* Unpublished Ph.D. dissertation.

KHRAPUNOV, I.N., 1992, Kemi-obinskii kurgan u s. Vilino. *Problemy istorii "peshchernykh gorodov" v Krymu*. Simferopol': Tavriya, 215-221.

KIYASHKO, V.Ya., 1994, Mezhdu kamnem i bronzoi (Nizhnee Podon'ye v V – III tys. do n.e.). *Donskie drevnosti* 3, 8-83.

KOŚKO, A. (ed.), 1999, *The Foundations of Radiocarbon Chronology of Cultures Between the Vistula and Dnieper: 3150-1850 BC*. Baltic-Pontic Studies 7, Poznan.

KOTOVA, N.S., 1994, *Mariupol'skaya kul'turno-istoricheskaya oblast' (Dnepro-Donskoe mezhdurech'ye)*. Kovel': Vezha.

KOTOVA, N.S., Tuboltsev, O.V., 1996, New Settlements of the Neolithic-Eneolithic Period at Melitopol. *Eurasia-Antiqua. Zeitschrift für Archäologie Eurasiens* 2, 29-58.

KOVALEVA, I.F., 1979, Vytyanutye pogrebeniya Dneprovskogo areala Volgo-Dneprovskoi kul'turno-istoricheskoi obshchnosti epokhi eneolita. *Kurgannye drevnosti Stepnogo Podneprov'ya III-I tys. do n.e.* (I.F. Kovaleva, ed.). Dnepropetrovsk, DGU, 60-70.

KUDRYASHOV, K.V., 1949, *Polovetskaya step'*. Moskow.

KUZMINA, E.E., 2000, Proiskhozhdenie pastushestva v stepyakh Evrasii. *Late Prehistoric Exploitation of the Eurasian Steppe*. Papers presented for the Symposium to be held 12-16 January 2000, vol. II. McDonald Institute for Archaeological Research, Cambridge, 178-202.

LAGODOVSKA, O.F., SHAPOSHNIKOVA, O.G., and MAKAREVICH, V.I., 1962, *Mykhailivs'ke poselennya*. Kiew: Vydavnytstvo Akademii Nauk.

LEVINE, M., 1990, Dereivka and the problem of horse domestication. *Antiquity* 64, 727-740.

LEVINE, M., 1999, Botai and the Origins of the Horse Domestication. *Journal of Anthropological Archaeology* 18, 29-78.

LESKOV, A.M., 1965, *Gorny Krym v I tysyacheletii do n.e*. Kiev: Naukova dumka.

LESKOV, A.M., 1974, Die Skytischen Kurgane. Die Erforschung der Hügelgräber Südrusslands. *Antike Welt* 5 (Sondernummer).

MALLORY, J., 1987, Editor's introduction. *Telegin, D.Ya., Potekhina, I.D., 1987. Neolithic Cemeteries and Populations in the Dnieper Basin*. British Archaeological Reports, International series 383. Oxford: BAR, v-ix.

MARYNYCH, V.I., 1982, *Fizychna geografiya Ukrainy*. Kiew: Naukova dumka.

MERPERT, N.Ya., 1968, *Drevneishaya istoriya naseleniya stepnoi polosy Vostochnoi Evropy (III – nachalo II tys. do n.e.)*. Moskow: Unpublished dissertation.

MERPERT, N.Ya., 1974, *Drevneishye skotovody Volzhsko-Ural'skogo mezhdurech'ya*. Moskow: Nauka.

MOLODYKH I.N., 1982, *Grunty podov i stepnykh blyudets subaeral'nogo pokrova Ukrainy*. Kiev: Naukova dumka.

MOVSHA, T.G., 1981, Problemy svyazei Tripol'ye-Kukuteni s plemenami kul'tur stepnogo areala. *Studia Praehistorica* 5-6, 61-72.

MOVSHA, T.G., 1985, Pozdnii etap tripol'skoi kul'tury. *Arkheologiya Ukrainskoi SSR* 1 (D.Ya. Telegin, ed.). Kiev : Naukova dumka, 223-253.

MOVSHA, T.G., 1993, Vzaemovidnosyny stepovykh i zemlerobs'kukh kul'tur v epokhu eneolitu-rann'obronzovogo viku. *Arkheologiya* 3, 36-51.

NEPRINA, V.I., 1988, Vynyknennya ta rozvytok rybal'stva na terutorii Ukrainy. *Arkheologiya* 64, 28-33.

NIKOLOVA, A.V. and MAMCHYCH, T.I., 1997, Do metodyky klasufikatsii posudu yamnoi kul'tury. *Arkheologiya* 3, 101-114.

O'CONNEL, T.C., LEVINE, M.A., HEDGES, R.E.M., 2000, The Importance of Fish in the Diet of Central Eurasian Peoples from the Mesolithic to the Early Iron Age. pp. 303-312 *Late Prehistoric Exploitation of the Eurasian Steppe*. Papers presented for the Symposium to be held 12-16 January 2000, vol. II. McDonald Institute for Archaeological Research, Cambridge.

OTROSHCHENKO, V.V., 1976, Konstruktivnye osobennosti dlinnykh kurganov Nizhnego Podneprov'ya. *Otkrytiya molodykh arkheologov Ukrainy 1*. Kiev, 16-18.

OTROSHCHENKO, V.V., 1977, Katakombnye i srubnye kurgany v okrestnostyakh s. Balki. *Kurgannye mogil'niki Ryasnue Mogilu i Nosaki* (V.V. Otroshchenko, ed.). Kiev: Naukova dumka.

OTROSHCHENKO, V.V., 1987, Ohrannye raskopki v basseine reki Molochnoi (osobennosti topografii kurganov). *Problemy okhrany i issledovaniya pamyatnikov arkheologii v Donbasse* (tesisy konferentsii). Donetsk, 104-106.

OTROSHCHENKO, V.V., and BOLTRIK, Yu.V., 1982, Kul'turno-khronologicheskoe i territorial'noe raspredelenie mogil'nikov Dnepro-Molochanskoi stepnoi oblasti. *Iaterialy po khronologii arkheologicheskikh pamyatnikov Ukrainy*. Kiev: Naukova dumka, 38-46.

OTROSHCHENKO, V.V., SAVOVSKY, I.P., TOMASHEVSKY, V.A., 1977, Kurgannye mogil'niki Ryasnye Mogily u sela Balki. *Kurgannye mogil'niki Ryasnue Mogilu i Nosaki* (V.V. Otroshchenko, ed.). Kiev: Naukova dumka.

PATOKOVA, E.F., 1979, *Usatovskoe poselenie i mogil'niki*. Kiev: Naukova dumka.

PATOKOVA, E.F., PETRENKO, V.G., BURDO, N.B., POLISHCHUK, L.Y., 1989, *Pamyatniki Tripol'skoi kul'tury v Severo-Zapadnom Prichernomor'ye*. Kiev: Naukova dumka.

POTEKHINA, I.D., TELEGIN, D.Ya., 1997, Deyaki spirni pytannya z istorii naselennya pivdennogo Podniprov'ya. *Arkheologoya* 2, 117-123.

RASSAMAKIN, Yu.Ya., 1987, Eneoliticheskie pogrebeniya basseina reki Molochnoi. *Drevneishye skotovody stepei yuga Ukrainy* (O.G. Shaposhnikova, ed.). Kiev: Naukova dumka, 31-47.

RASSAMAKIN, Yu.Ya., 1991, Î pogrebeniyakh predkatakombnogo vremeni v Severo-Zapadnom Priazov'ye. *Êatakombnye kul'tury Severnogo Prichernomor'ya* (Î.G.Shaposhnikova, ed.). Kiev, 42-56.

RASSAMAKIN, Yu.Ya., 1992, Do problemy vyvchennya kurgannykh sporud. *Arkheologiya* 4, 121-137.

RASSAMAKIN, Yu.Ya., 1994, The Main Directions of the Development of Early Pastoral Societies of Northern Pontic Zone: 4500-2450 B.C. (Pre-Yamnaya Cultures and Yamnaya Culture). *Nomadism and Pastoralism in the Circle of Baltic-Pontic Early Agrarian Cultures: 5000-1650. Baltic-Pontic Studies* 2 (A. Koœko, ed.). Poznan: Adam Mickiewicz University, Eastern Institute, Institute of Prehistory, 29-70.

RASSAMAKIN, Yu.Ya., 1996, On the Early Elementes of the Globular Amphora Culture and Other Central European Cultures in the Late Eneolithic of Northern Black Sea Region. *Eastern Exodus of the Globular Amphora Reople: 2950-2350 BC. Baltic-Pontic Studies* 4 (A. Kośko, ed.). Poznan: Adam Mickewicz University, Eastern Institute, Institute of Prehistory, 112-132.

RASSAMAKIN, Yu.Ya., 1999, The Eneolithic of the Black Sea Steppe: Dynamics of Cultural and Economic Development 4500-2300 BC. *Levine M., Rassamakin Yu., Kislenko A. and Tatarintseva N. (with an introduction by C.Renfrew), 1999. Late Prehistoric Exploitation of the Eurasian Steppe*. McDonald Institute Monographs, University of Cambridge, 59-182.

RASSAMAKIN, Yu.Ya., 2000, Some Aspects of the Pontic Steppe Development (4550-3000 BC) in the Light of the New Cultural-Chronological Model. *Late Prehistoric Exploitation of the Eurasian Steppe*. Papers presented for the Symposium to be held 12-16 January 2000, vol. II. McDonald Institute for Archaeological Research, Cambridge, 336-347.

RASSAMAKIN Yu.Ya., and KOLOSOV Yu.G., 1992, *Kurgannaya gruppa u pgt. Prishyb*. Kiev.

REZEPKIN, A.D., and KONDRASHOV, A.V., 1988, Novosvobodnenskoe pogrebenie s povozkoy. *Kratkie soobshcheniya Instituta arkheologii AN SSSR (KSIA)* 193, 91-7.

RYZHOV, S.M., 1988, Modeli sanei z pizn'yotrypil's'kykh pam'yatok Bugo-Dnistrovs'kogo mezhyrichya. *Materialy VI Winnyts'koi istoriko-kraeznavchoi konferentsii* (tezy dopovidei). Winnytsya, 45.

SHAPOSHNIKOVA, O.G., 1970, Bagatosharove poselennya poblyzu s. Razdol'ne na r. Kal'mius. *Arkheologiya* XXIII, 142-151.

SHAPOSHNIKOVA, O.G., 1985, Yamnaya kul'turno-istoricheskaya obshchnost'. *Arkheologiya Ukrainskoi SSR* 1 (D.Ya. Telegin, ed.). Kiev : Naukova dumka, 336-352.

SHCHEPINSKY, A.A., 1963, Pamyatniki iskusstva epokhi rannego metalla v Krymu. *Sovetskaya arkheologiya* 3, 38-47.

SHCHEPINSKY, A.A., 1966, Kul'tury eneolita i bronzy v Krymu. *Sovetskaya arkheologiya* 2, 10-23.

SHCHEPINSKY, A.A., 1977, Rakovinnye kuchi na eneoliticheskikh stoyankakh Kryma. *Sovetskaya Arkheologiya* 1, 27-38.

SHCHEPINSKY, A.A., 1985a, Kemi-Obinskaya kul'tura. *Arkheologiya Ukrainskoy SSR* 1 (D.Ya. Telegin, ed.). Kiev: Naukova dumka, 331-336.

SHCHEPINSKY, A.A., 1985b, Rannii eneolit Kryma. *Arkheologiya Ukrainskoy SSR* 1 (D.Ya. Telegin, ed.). Kiev: Naukova dumka, 320-324.

SHILOV, V.P., 1975a, *Ocherki po istorii drevnikh plemen Nizhnego Povolzh'ya*. Moskow: Nauka.

SHILOV, V.P., 1975b, Modeli skotovodcheskikh khozyaistv stepnukh oblastei Evrazii v epokhu eneolita i rannego bronzovogo veka. *Sovetskaya arkheologiya* 1, 5-16.

SHILOV, V.P., 1982, Problema osvoeniya otkrytykh stepei Kalmykii ot epokhi bronzy do srednevekov'ya. *Pamyatniki Kalmykii kamennogo i bronzovogo vekov*. Elista.

SHILOV, V.P., 1985, Problemy proiskhozhdeniya kochevogo skotovodstva v Vostochnoi Evrope. *Drevnosti Kalmykii*. Elista.

SHILOV, V.P., 1988, "Grot byka" po materialam drevneishykh kurganov. *Novye pamyatniki yamnoi kul'tury na yuge Ukrainy* (O.G. Shaposhnikova, ed.). Kiev: Naukova dumka, 3-13.

SHISHLINA, N.I. (ed.), 1999, Tekstil epokhi bronzy evrasiiskikh stepei. *Trudy Gosudarstvennogo Istoricheskogo muzeya* 109. Moskow.

SHISHLINA, N.I. (ed.), 2000a, Sezonnyi ekonomicheskii tsykl naseleniya Severo-Zapadnogo Prikaspiya v bronzovom veke. *Trudy Gosudarstvennogo Istoricheskogo muzeya* 120. Moskow.

SHISHLINA, N.I. (ed.), 2000b, Potentsial'nyi sezonno-khozyaistvennyi tsykl nositelei katakombnoi kul'tury Severo-Zapadnogo Prikaspiya: problema rekonstruktsii. *Sezonnyi ekonomicheskii tsykl naseleniya Severo-Zapadnogo Prikaspiya v bronzovom veke (N.I. Shishlina, ed.). Trudy Gosudarstvennogo Istoricheskogo muzeya* 120. Moskow, 54-71.

SHISHLINA, N.I., and TSUTSKIN, E.V. (eds.), 1999, *Mogil'nik Mandzhykiny-1 – pamyatnik epokhi bronzy-rannego zheleznogo veka Kalmykii (opyt kompleksnogo issledovaniya)*. Moskow-Elista.

SHISHLINA, N.I., and TSUTSKIN, E.V. (eds.), 2001, *Mogil'nik Mu-Sharet v Kalmykii: kompleksnoe issledovanie*. Moskow-Elista.

SHISHLINA, N.I., DEMKIN, V.A., and BOBROV, A.A., 2002, Izuchenie sistemy pitaniya stepnykh zhyteley Severo-Zapadnogo Prikaspiya v epokhu bronzy i rannego zheleznogo veka (in press).

SHPET, G.I., 1956, Zuby z Vovnyz'kogo livoberezhnogo mogyl'nyka. *Arkheologichni pem'yatky URSR* VI, 160.

SUBBOTIN, L.V., and CHERNYAKOV, I.T., 1982, Nowotroyanivs'kyi skarb ta pytannya obminu metalom za doby pizn'yoi bronzy. *Arkheologiya* 39, 15-23.

SUBBOTIN, L.V., 1983, *Pamyatniki kul'tury Gumel'nitsa Yugo-Zapada Ukrainy*. Kiev: Naukova dumka.

TELEGIN, D.Ya., 1959, Eneoliticheskoe poselenie i mogil'nik u khutora Aleksandriya. *Kratkie soobshcheniya Instituta Arkheologii AN USSR* 9, 10-20.

TELEGIN, D.Ya., 1968, *Dnipro-Donets'ka kul'tura*. Kyiv: Naukova dumka.

TELEGIN, D.Ya., 1971, Eneolitychni stely i pam'yatky nyzhn'yo-mykhailivs'kogo typu. *Arkheologiya* 4, 3-17.

TELEGIN, D.Ya., 1985, Dnepro-Donetskaya kul'tura. *Arkheologiya Ukrainskoi SSR* 1 (D.Ya. Telegin, ed.). Kiev: Naukova dumka, 156-172.

TELEGIN, D.Ya., 1986, *Dereivka: a Settlement and Semetery of Copper Age Horse Keepers on the Middle Dnieper*. British Archaeological Reports, International Series 287. Oxford: BAR.

TELEGIN, D.YA., and POTEKHINA, I.D., 1987, *Neolithic Cemeteries and Populations in the Dnieper Basin* (J.P. Mallory, ed.). British Archaeological Reports, International Series 383. Oxford: BAR.

TELEGIN, D.YA., and KONSTANTINESKU, L.F., 1992, Mnogosloinoe poselenie na Stril'chei Skele epokhi neolita-eneolita v Dneprovskom Nadporozh'ye. *Sovetskaya arkheologiya* 1, 13-25.

TODOROVA, H., 1993, Nairannite trgovski kontakty na Severozapadnoto Prichernomorie. *Dobrudzha*, 10, 10-20.

TURETSKY, M.A., 1999, Problemy slozheniya srednevolzhsko-priural'skogo varianta yamnoi kul'tury. *Arkheologicheskie pamyatniki Orenburzh'ya* (N.L. Morgunova, ed.). Orenburg: Dimur.

VIDEIKO, M.Ju., 1995, Großsiedlungen der Tripol'e-Kultur in der Ukraine. *Eurasia-Antiqua. Zeitschrift für Archäologie Eurasiens* 1, 45-80.

ZBENOVICH, V.G., 1974, *Pozdnetripol'skie plemena Severo-Zapadnogo Prichernomor'ya*. Kiev: Naukova dumka.

ZHURAVLEV O.P., and KOTOVA, N.S., 1996, Twarynnytstwo neolitychnogo naselennya Ukrainy. *Arkheologiya* 2, 3-17.

YAVORNYTSKY, D.I., 1990, *Istoriya zaporiz"kykh kozakiv* I. Kyiv: Naukova dumka.

HYDROSTRATEGIES IN SOUTHERN LUXEMBOURG

Ralph M. ROWLETT

Abstract : The Neolithic persisted for a long time in northern Gaul. The renowned Seine-Oise-Marne Cultural tradition persisted, with a low level of metal usage, until the earlier Bronze Age. In southern Luxembourg, the similar Rollange Group shows a riparian adaptation, depending on major waterways as its main routes of communication, in the relatively dry Sub-Boreal climate. Some houses of this culture were atop the 400 m. high "Titelberg" in southwestern Luxembourg. Access to the Titelberg would have been routine, since the Chiers River, a tributary of the Meuse, flows right at the foot of the Titelberg. A hydrostrategic problem for the group on the Titelberg was drinking water. The Iron Age and Gallo-Roman occupants relied upon wells, but no wells have yet been found in excavations. The folk must have made use of the spring, which spouts out on the east slope of the butte. The ceramic inventory of the Rollange Group does not exhibit water jugs, so water transport must have been in organic containers. A bizarre local folktale may describe the hydrostrategy of the inhabitants.

Resumé : Le Néolithique a persisté longtemps au nord de la Gaulle. La tradition culturelle Seine-Oise-Marne a persisté, avec un niveau minimal d'utilisation du metal, jus-qu'à l'Âge du Bronze. Au sud du Luxembourg, le Groupe Rollange démontre une adaptation côtiere, en dependant des voies riveraines en tant que voies de communication dans le climat sec Sous-Boreal. Quelques maisons appartenant à cette culture ont e été baties sur la colline "Titelberg", haute de 400 m, situeé au sud-ouest du Luxemburg. L'accès facile au Titelberg était du à la rivière Chiers qui coulait au pied de la colline. Un problème hydrostratégique du groupe Titelberg a été l'eau potable. On sait que les occupants de l' Âge du Fer et les Gallo-Romains utilisait des puits, mais aucun puits n'a pas été trouvé dans les excavations, donc on suppose que les habitants ont utilisé la source qui éxiste sur le versant est de la colline. L'inventaire céramique du Groupe Rollange ne contient pas des cruches pour le transport de l'eau, donc l'eau pouvait être transporté dans des récipients en matière organique. Une étrange légende locale paraît décrire les hydrostrategies des habitants.

The Titelberg, in the southwestern corner of Luxembourg, near where the Grand Duchy, Belgium and France all come together, is most famous for its La Tene Iron Age and Gallo-Roman remains, having been continuously inhabited from early La Tene (Metzler 1995; Rowlett 1992) until the fall of the Roman Empire about AD 400, when Mosel Franks with a drastically different settlement system took over the area (Metzler 1995; Metzler and Weiller 1977; Thill 1965; Thomas, Rowlett, and Sander-Jorgensen 1976; Rowlett, Thomas and Sander-Jorgensen 1982; Rowlett 1995). However, in earlier times the 400 m. high butte of the Titelberg was intermittently occupied in the stone ages. Apparently non-continuous middle Neolithic components are well known (Sander-Jorgensen, Thomas, and Rowlett 1980; Heuretz 1969; Theis 1993) and there is sparse but firm evidence of Mesolithic occupation (Fig. 1). Surface finds have produced many examples of flint tools with an Aurignacian typology, although as yet no Aurignacian component has been encountered in situ. A Levallois-Mousterian point actually came from a Gallo-Roman well of the third century.

The most extensive excavated remains were published in Sander-Jorgensen, Thomas, and Rowlett and Thomas 1980, where my colleagues elected to call it "Upper Neolithic," from its stratigraphic position, but as the late Norbert Theis insisted to me, it is really the earliest Bronze Age or Chalcolihtic of this and neighboring districts. The tip end of a copper or bronze probe, awl or pin was actually encountered in excavation near the high center of the site in the project concentrated primarily on the mint foundry complex dating from the the Iron Age and early Gallo-Roman (GR1 and GR2: Metzler 1995: 552-554). The Chalcolithic in the Ardennes and the neighboring zones of northern France came rather late and persisted through the Bell Beaker episodes into the early Bronze Age, primarily as the S.O.M. Variant of the late Western "Neolithic" Areal Culture (Thomas and Rowlett 1992). The Titelberg component, defined as a cultural type and not an cultural-historical period, yields produces TL dates in the late third millennium, ranging from 2,305 to 2,508 B.C. with plus or minus readings at 5% of the calculated age (Thomas, Rowlett, and Sander-Jorgensen 1976: 38-40).

The component at the central, highest point of the butte Titelberg was affected more by erosion resulting from the

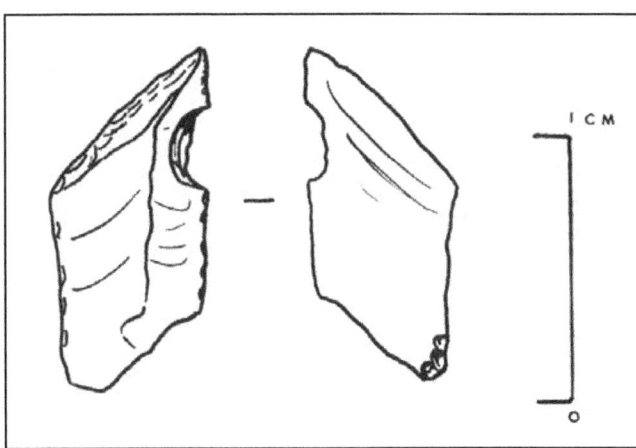

Fig 1. Mesolithic microlith excavated near the center of the Titelberg.

increased rainfall of the Sub-Atlantic Climatic period than the more protected, underlying middle Neolithic, but enough can be seen of features of this culture. The Titelberg occupation shows some structures in the form of ditches, brownish and gray plain pottery, including both vases and a flat ceramic disk similar to those used in the Chasseean and Michelberg Western Neolithic variants. Stone tools include stemmed points, drills and endscrapers, some of the latter made on quartz (Fig. 2). Recovered axes are of flint, flaked and subsequently polished to have a lenticular cross section, contrasting with the more circular cross sections of the Western Neolithic axes and the rectangular ones farther north. Burnt wheat and barley grains are small, as is the bovine metatarsal bone recovered (Sander-Jorgensen, Thomas, and Rowlett 1980: 23-24). A noteworthy aspect of the culture is the polished stone horse-head pendants and other trapezoidal pendants of stone. Similar finds have been made in the neighboring regions of southern Luxembourg in what can be called the Rollange Group, from one of the name variants of a village near the Titelberg (Rowlett 1992). The members of this group who dwelt on the Titelberg were faced with some fundamental hydrostrategic adaptive problems, centering primarily upon climate, communication, and water supplies.

experienced greater rainfall than other villagers of their particular group, the Rollange Group. What adjustments they made as compared to those of other Group sites for protection from the weather is unknown at this moment, but they must have had somewhat more substantial houses, or they endured being wetter, than the folk at other, lower villages. If the 48 cm. wide ditch, now badly mangled by later Iron Age and Gallo-Roman pits, posts and works, was a sleeper beam trench as part of a housing structure, it was certainly more substantial in than the earlier Neolithic house found nearby (Fig. 3).

Fig. 3 Chalcolithic activities near the canter of the Titleberg.

RIVERINE ADAPTATION

The entire Rollange Group, including the Titelbergers, were strongly oriented toward use of the rivers, the Meuse/Maas and its tributary, the Chiers/Korn (derived from the Celtic word for cherry tree) River, which takes its source at Oberkorn in southern Luxembourg and flows around roughly one-half the Titelberg butte. Dutch and Belgian archaeologists have long noted that the non-Corded Ware cultures of western Netherlands have their closest cultural affinities along the valley of the Meuse (Regeertan Altena et al 1962; Louwe Koojiman 1974, 1983, and 1987; Prummel 1987; Cauwe, vander Linden and Vanmontfort 2001: 81-83; Leotard and Cauwe 1997; Toussaint et al 1997; Toussaint and Jadin 1997), now seen as extending as far south as Luxembourg (Rowlett 1992; Bellaire, Moulin and Cahen-Delhaye 2001: 90-101), and perhaps even farther. This culture in the Netherlands is called the Vlaardingen Culture. The stone points, axe type, and pottery of the Rollange Group, best known from the Titelberg, most closely resembles that of the Vlaardingen and related sites in eastern Belgium along the Meuse valley (Rowlett 1992) (Fig. 4).

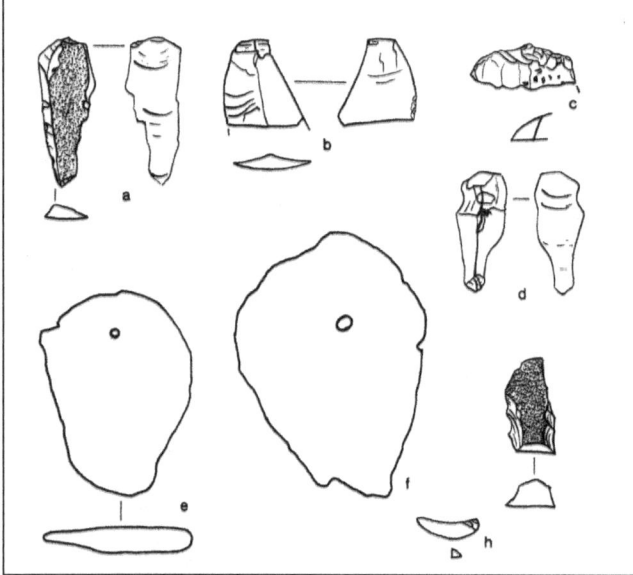

Fig. 2 Stone artifacts, including quartz scraper (c) and horse head pendants (e, f). After Sander-Jorgensen, Thomas, and Rowlett 1980.

INCREASED RAINFALL

As the first of a series of buttes that arise in Lorraine in eastern Gaul, the Titelberg intercepts the wet westerly winds from the Atlantic sweeping over relatively flat northern France, with the result that the Titelberg itself has an a rainfall budget a few centimeters greater than its environs, at the present time receiving over a meter of rain per annum. Although in mid-Sub-Boreal times during the occupation the absolute rainfall was probably less, but since the topography was essentially the same, the Neolithic Titelbergers would have

West of the Meuse valley proper it blends in with the S.O.M. Culture. These cultures are noteworthy for their relative indifferences to, and resistance of, the Corded Ware and Bell Beaker groups that neighbored them in central Champagne, eastern Netherlands, and western Germany. The cultural similarities along the Meuse suggest that this river was used

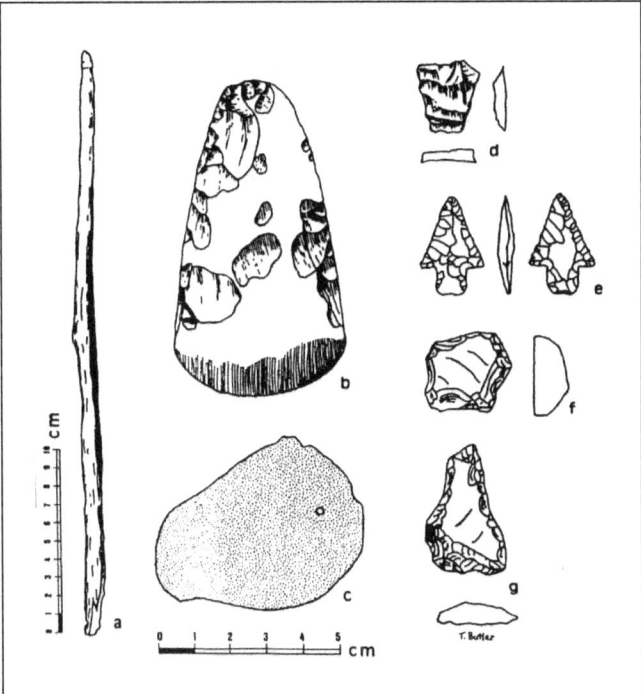

Fig. 4 Rollange and Vlaardingen cultural resemblances. Wooden bow from Hekelingen, Netherlands (a); Southern-Type polished axe, Hekelingen (b), projectile points (d-e), Hekelingen. After Prummel 1987. Endscraper(f) and borer (g) on Grand Pressigny flint, sandstone pendant of a horse head (c). After Rowlett 1992.

as the major waterway, thoroughfare, and connecting link for these people (Fig. 5), perhaps similar to the way some tribes in, like the Iban, in 19th and 20th century Borneo, used the rivers as their foci of settlement and communication (Sandin 1968; Wadley 2000).

Note however, that while the Chiers provides direct access to the Meuse for the Titelbergers, the site is actually closer to the Mosel, but which would have to be reached by overland travel. This region is heavily forested today and in the Iron Age, but pollen from the Titelberg shows that the environs of the site were appreciably less forested during times (Vehik 1980), so overland passage might have been relatively easy, thus making the Mosel a secondary outlet to the north while the Chiers constituted the major access route for the central thoroughfare, the Meuse. The Mosel valley was occupied by culturally different Corded Ware folk, so passage along it may not have been as easy along Meuse. The Chiers in France eventually attains riverine scale, but where it passes near the foot of the Titelberg, it is still quite small, of creek size, scarcely attaining more than 5 meters in width. Thus the canoes, presumably log dugouts, used for transportation from the Titelberg to the Meuse, were probably made from relatively small trees, need not be more than 2-2.5 m. in width. A log boat 14C dated to this time is known from the Vlaardingen components at Hazendonk, Netherlands. The absence of oak in the pollen from the Titelberg, which consists primarily of maple and ash at this time (Vehik 1980), is not a problem, for many of the early log boats were made of pine, linden and alder, with oak not being established as the preferred wood until later. Fig. 6 shows a hypothetical, predictive model of what such a canoe may have looked like. Future archaeology will confirm or disprove this hypothesis.

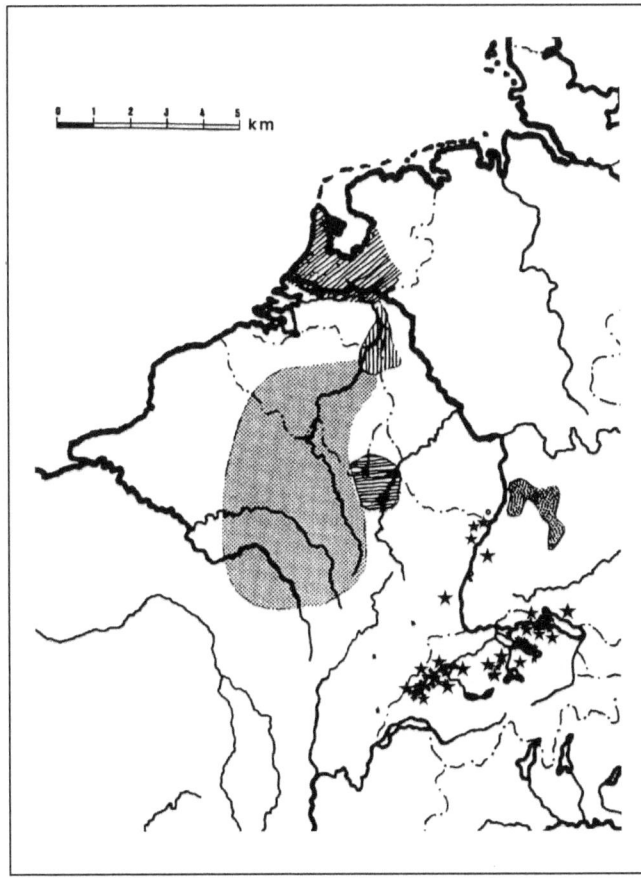

Fig. 5 Map of cultural distributions in the Meuse River valley. Star = Corded.

Fig. 6 Predictive model of a Chalcolithic log boat suitable for the Chiers/Korn River.

The Meuse River formed a binder to hold together the Vlaardingen and related groups. Just exactly what motivated these communications along the Meuse is presently poorly understood. No doubt mates were obtainable by these contacts. Luxembourg itself is relatively poor in flint sources (Theis 1993), so that might have been a desirable commodity.

The polished stone adze, similar to the Vlaardingen axe/adze is made of brownish flint of the region of Aubel-Fourons, Belgium. The quartz endscraper suggests that difficult to flake local materials were utilized. The high quality Cretaceous and Paleocene flint from Champagne in France, not more than 75 km. away, must have been desirable, but the brown flint axe was not of this material although some of the flint points were. Taking the Chiers to the confluence of the Meuse would have put the Titelbergers in close proximity to the flint sources of Champagne. The focus of communications along the Meuse, and secondarily toward Champagne, did not lead these people in the direction of ready sources of copper or tin, so what little metal they had must have been obtained by other strategies than the hydroscopic one.

The heavy use of the rivers for cultural interaction, of course, put the Titelbergers and other members of their group into close proximity to fish, which must have been exploited for food and perhaps for skin. Fish such as trout, pike, bass, and perch can be obtained today, and perhaps in earlier times the "Rhine salmon" came up the Meuse to spawn. The absence of shellfish remains upon the Titelberg indicates that either the nutritious but low calorie shellfish were not part of the hydrostrategy of the Rollange Group, or else they were eaten along the rivers and creeks and not carried up the 100 m. to the butte habitation.

Despite the relative indifference of the Vlaardingen and related cultures to the ceramic, military, and other styles of the Corded Ware and Bell Beaker complexes, the horse, associated first with those cultures in these districts, was emphasized symbolically in form of the pendants (Fig. 4). Perhaps the Titelbergs even imagined the horse as the totem for a sib or moitie, with the trapezoidal pendant representing another such social unit. If horses they had, this would have given them a secondary, not hydroscopic basis of communication. The significance of the horse for this purpose, however, is not as obvious as their riverine adaptation. Perhaps the other kind of stone pendant, trapezoidal in shape, represented an oar?

CONSUMABLE WATER

The butte Titelberg consists of Jurassic and Triassic limestones capped by an unconsolidated early Tertiary subsoil overlain, of course, by Quaternary weathered loess and soil. At present these bedrocks are very water permeable, a situation aggravated by the numerous iron ore mines that perforate the mountain so that in modern it resembles stoney Immenthal cheese. Thus the top of the Titelberg in principle is over 100 meters higher than the water in the Chiers River. Even in Gallo-Roman times and the Iron Age, household and industrial water was obtained by the means of wells and cisterns (Metzler 1995: vol. I). There is no evidence of wells and cisterns from the and earlier times either in Luxembourg or the low countries farther north in a Vlaardingen context, even if wells are known from the Corded Ware PF Group of the eastern Netherlands (Zuurdeeg et al 1989). The surviving pottery, all broken, seems to have consisted of various jar, bowl, and disk forms, none of which seem conducive to catching and storing any large quantity of water. Certainly in full Sub-Boreal times, the retention of rain water for drinking would have been a notable concern, but there should have been an adequate amount of rainfall for farming atop the butte's plateau.

Although the ceramics seem not to have significantly figured in the hydrostrategies of the Titelbergers, obviously they must have had some way to get water to their habitations for drinking, since humans are such notoriously thirsty mammals, cooking and whatever immediate washing and cleaning that they did. By implication they must have used containers of organic materials for hauling water. They would not have had to go all the way down 100 meters, however, for two springs east of the Titelberg would have been accessible. One of them, now called the "Wagenwasch", spouts out cold water on the northeast side of the Titelberg at ca. 875 km east of the center of the site (Fig. 7) by a traversable route. A second, the "Erzwasch", is another natural spring to the east. While this second spring is a full kilometer away, it lies on an easier route at the height of the plateau, at an elevation only a few meters lower than the Titelberg. Both of these springs were conducive for obtaining water, especially if animal skin containers were hauled on the backs of oxen or horses or in carts pulled by these animals.

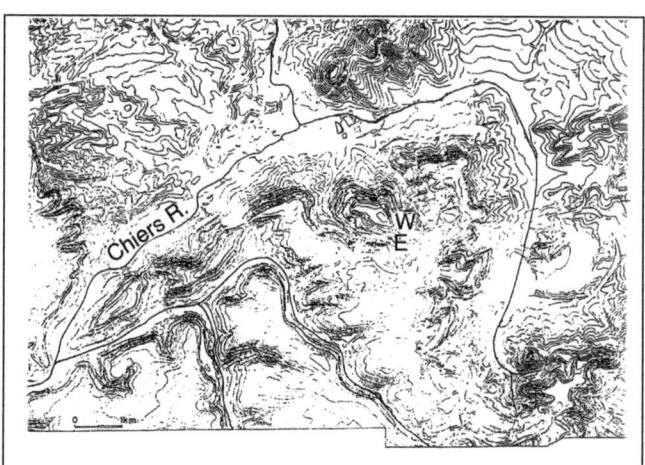

Fig. 7 Map of the Titelberg and its environs. The locus of the excavation that produced remains is indicated by the gray area. W = location of the closest spring, the Wagenwasch, while E = location of the second spring, the Erzwasch, accessible from the Titelberg.

The possible use of these springs at an earlier time finds some support in non-archaeological evidence. The Titelberg has given rise to a vast amount of folklore (Gredt 1883; Colette 1979 and 1993). Some of this clearly goes back to the time of the Migration Period, Gallo-Roman times and the Iron Age. For example, folklore collected in the 19th century maintained that "gnomes" manufactured coins on the Titelberg by tossing silver into bonfires; folklore localized this activity at the middle of the Titelberg (Gredt 1883: 309; Colette 1979), where in the 1970's and 80's archaeological research recovered a series of mint foundries (Rowlett 1989), only a few dozen meters south of the locus indicated by the folklore. One bizarre folktale about the Titelberg is not so easily relateable to events of the past 3,000 years. This folktale concerns Spring #2, the easternmost spring, referred to above. According to folklore (Gredt 1883: 253) the spring is haunted by a headless red cow, that comes to the spring to drink rapaciously in a vain attempt to quench its insatiable thirst. Is this folk tale a long-lived memory of the time that animals skins (headless, of course, if they were water containers) were brought upon oxen repeatedly to the spring for refilling to slake the demands for water by human inhabitants of the Titelberg (Fig. 8). The folktale, also asserting that sometimes a bushel basket (Kornwanne) floats on the water when the headless cow is present, implies perhaps that baskets, made watertight by beeswax, grease, or pitch were occasionally used for the transport of water as well.

Fig. 8 Collecting water of the Erzwash spring with an calf-skin containes and a water proof basket (kornwanner).

CONCLUSIONS

The hydrostrategies of the Titelbergers would have been greatly concerned with protection from the elements and obtaining water for their high, windswept eyrie, the Titelberg. Beyond these necessities, the Titelbergers and other members of the Rollange Group would have depended on the rivers like the Chiers, the Meuse, and to a lesser extent the Mosel-Rhine, to keep them in contact with their cultural relatives in extreme northeastern Gaul. The emphasis on the Korn(Chiers)/Meuse corridor seems reflected in the material cultural inventory, creating some points of contrast with the less riverine related S.O.M. Culture not very far to the west. The hydrostrategies of the Rollange Group facilitated their external contacts with other communities and sources of supply instead of providing much of a basis for internal control and organization. Any organizational impetus provided by the hydrostrategy of this group would have revolved around travel and expeditionary arrangements rather than directly affecting internal structure.

(Drawings are made by the author).

Bibliography

BELLAIRE, C., MOULIN, J. and CAHEN-DELHAYE A., 2001, Guide des sites prehistorique et protohistorique de Wallonie. *La Vie Archeologique* Numero special: 1-152

CAUWE, N., VANDER LINDEN, M. and VANMONTFORT, B., 2001, The Middle and Late Neolitic. pp. 77-90. In: Nicolas Cauwe, Anne Hauzeur and Paul-Louis van Berg, (eds.) *Prehistory in Belgium-Prehistoire en Belgique*, Brussels: Belgian Royal Society of Anthropology and Prehistory:

COLETTE, J., 1979, Histories, Traditions, Contes et Fantasises du Titelberg. *Arbechter Ennerstetzungs Verien Rodange Anniversaire.* 88: 99-134

COLETTE, J., 1993, A Folk Practice at the Titelberg Archaeological Site, Grand Duchy of Luxembourg. pp. 19-28. In: Rowlett R. M. (ed.) *Horizons and Styles, Studies in Mediterranean Archaeology* vol. CI, Jonsered: Paul Astroms Forlag.

GREDT, N., 1883, *Sagenchatz des Luxemburger Landes*. Druckerie Kremer-Muller Cie.

HEURETZ, M., 1969, *Documents Prehistoriques du Territoire luxembourgeois.* Musees de l'Etat: Luxembourg Lanting, J.N.

LEOTARD, L. and CAUWE, F. N., 1997, Une sepulture neolithique dans la "Grotte Bibiche". pp. 191-193. In: Corbiau, M.-H. (ed.) *Le Patrimonie Archeologique deWallonie*.

LEOTARD, L. and CAUWE, F. N., 1998, Namur: DGATLP

LOUWE, K. L., 1974, The Rhine/Meuse Delta. *Analecta Prehistorian Leidensia* 7.

LOUWE, K. L., 1983, Tussen SOM en TRB, enige gedacthen over het laatneolithicumin Nederland en Belgie. *Bulletin des Musees Royaux d'Art et d' Historie* 54, 1: 55-57

LOUWE, K. L., 1987, Neolithic Settlements and Subsistence in the wetland of the Netherlands pp. 227-251. In: Coles, J.M. and Lawson, A.J. (eds.) *European Wetlands in Prehistory*, Oxford: Clarendon Press.

METZLER, J., 1995, *Das treverische Oppidum auf dem Titelberg (G.H. Luxembourg)*, 2 vols. Luxembourg: Musee national d'histoire et d'art.

METZLER, J. and WEILLER, R., 1977, *Beitrage zur Archaeoloie und Numismatik des Titelberges*. Luxembourg: Musees de l'Etat.

PRUMMEL, W., 1987, The Faunal Remains from the Neolithic Site of Hekelingen III. *Helinium* 27: 190-257

REGEERTAN ALTENA, J.F. VAN, BAKKER, J.A., CLASON, A. T., GLASBERGEN, W., GROENMAN VAN WATTERINGE W. and PONS, I. J., 1962, The Vlaardingen Cutlure. *Helinium* 2: 3-36, 97-103, 215-243.

ROWLETT, R. M., 1989, Titelberg. *Expedition* 30: 31-40

ROWLETT, R. M., 1992, Western "Old European" Response to Early Indo-European Chiefdoms. *Journal of Indo-European Studies* 20: 93-122

ROWLETT, R. M., 1995, North Gaulish and North Balkanic Forms on the Gundestrup Cauldron. *Proceedings of the Harvard Celtic Colloquium* 13: 166-182

ROWLETT, R. M., THOMAS, H. L. and SANDER-JORGENSEN, E. R., 1982, Stratified Iron Age House Floors on the Titelberg, Luxembourg. *Journal of Field Archaeology* 9: 301-312.

SANDER-JORGENSEN, E. R., THOMAS, H. L. and ROWLETT, R. M., 1980, Neolithic Levels on the Titelberg. *Museum Brief* 18, 2nd Revised Edition, Columbia, Missouri: Museum of Anthropology, University of Missouri.

SANDIN, B., 1968, *The Sea Dayaks of Borneo before Rajah Rule*. East Lansing: Michigan State University Press.

THEIS, N., 1993, Notice preliminaire sur la presence de silex et de chaille au Grand-Duche de Luxembourg. pp. 229-236 In: Rowlett, R. M. (ed.). *Horizons and Styles, Studies in Mediterranean Archaeology* vol. CI, Jonsered: Paul Astroms Forlag.

THILL, G., 1965, *Tetelbierg*. Luxembourg: Musees de l'Etat.

THOMAS, H. L. and ROWLETT, R. M., 1992, The Archaeological Chronology of Western Europe. pp. 323-344. In: Ehrich, R. W., (ed.). *Chronologies in Old World Archaeology*, 2nd ed., Chicago: University of Chicago Press.

THOMAS, H. L., ROWLETT, R. M. and SANDER-JORGENSEN, E. R., 1976, Excavations on the Titelberg, Luxembourg. *Journal of Field Archaeology* 3: 241-259.

TOUSSAINT, M.,. BECKER, A., FREBUTTE C. and HUBERT, F., 1997, Durbuy, Weris: L'ensemble megalithique. pp. 194-196. In: Corbiau, M.-H. (ed.). *Le Patrimonie Archeologique de Wallonie*, Namur: DGATLP.

TOUSSAINT, M. and JADIN I., 1997, Rochefort, Jemelle: L'allee couverte de Lamsoul. pp. 197-199. In: Corbiau, M.-H. (ed.). *Le Patrimonie Archeologique de Wallonie*, Namur: DGATLP.

VEHIK, S., 1980, Neolithic Pollen on the Titelberg, Luxembourg. pp. 49-52. In: SANDER-JORGENSEN, E. R., THOMAS, H. L., and ROWLETT, R. M., (eds.). Neolithic Levels on he Titelberg, *Museum Brief* 18, 2nd Revised Edition, Columbia, Missouri: Museum of Anthropology, University of Missouri.

WADLEY, R., 2000, Warfare, Pacification, and Environment: Population Dynamics in the West Borneo Borderlands (1823-1934). *Social Research on Southeast Asia* 1:41-66

ZUURDEEG, B.W., Y.M.A. COENEGRACHT, J. VAN DE WAL and J.J. REYNDERS, 1989, Geochemical Investigation of the Late Neolithic Well of Kolhorn (Province of Noord-Holland). *Palaeohistoria* 31: 189

www.ingramcontent.com/pod-product-compliance
Lightning Source LLC
Chambersburg PA
CBHW061546010526
44113CB00023B/2813